OUTCOME-BASED EDUCATION

Outcome-Based Education

Developing Programs Through Strategic Planning

FLOYD BOSCHEE, Ed.D.

Associate Professor, Division of Educational Administration
School of Education, University of South Dakota
Vermillion, South Dakota

MARK A. BARON, Ph.D.

Assistant Professor, Division of Educational Administration
School of Education, University of South Dakota
Vermillion, South Dakota

TECHNOMIC
PUBLISHING CO., INC.

LANCASTER · BASEL

Outcome-Based Education
a **TECHNOMIC**® publication

Published in the Western Hemisphere by
Technomic Publishing Company, Inc.
851 New Holland Avenue, Box 3535
Lancaster, Pennsylvania 17604 U.S.A.

Distributed in the Rest of the World by
Technomic Publishing AG
Missionsstrasse 44
CH-4055 Basel, Switzerland

Printed in the United States of America
10 9 8 7 6 5 4 3 2 1

Main entry under title:
    Outcome-Based Education: Developing Programs Through Strategic Planning

A Technomic Publishing Company book
Bibliography: p.
Includes index p. 139

Library of Congress Catalog Card No. 93-61024
ISBN No. 1-56676-083-6

8. CONSIDERING ALTERNATIVE APPROACHES FOR RESTRUCTURING THE SCHOOL ORGANIZATION   125

FOR the past six years, I have been involved with a broad base of educators and citizens in the reshaping of our school district's programs in an effort to become outcome-based. We have been through the struggles of where to begin, who to involve, how to sort through commitment and accountability issues, how to align teaching practice with new beliefs, and how to assess the progress and results of our program and students. Through all of this, I wished I'd had something concrete in my hands to provide the perspective and guidance needed to move forward with a change process larger in magnitude than I ever imagined.

Fortunately, Floyd Boschee and Mark A. Baron have taken the time to provide reflection on the significant issues associated with outcome-based education and have developed a series of suggested steps which practitioners can use in their efforts to change from an education system based on seat time to one that has a success philosophy and is results-oriented. Their book goes well beyond the basic foundations of outcome-based education and provides the reader with a well thought out comprehensive model for change. It presents the change model in a carefully integrated manner so that change is viewed as a system rather than just another piecemeal, patchwork effort. The book will make you think about the complexities of the change process and the challenges of revamping the paradigm of teaching and learning.

This book is an excellent practical guide for practitioners who are responsible for, or who are participating in, the change process leading to an outcome-based system. It is a book that should be on the "must read" list for every educator across the country! I believe that parents and citizens involved in moving to an outcome-based program at the district level can also benefit from the foundational information and the implementation strategies presented by the authors.

Niccolò Machiavelli wrote in *The Prince* that "there is nothing more difficult to take in hand, more perilous to conduct, or more uncertain in its success than to take the lead in the introduction of a new order of things." Such is the case when educators begin to undertake the dramatic changes necessary to become outcome-based. This book provides vital information which will assist the practitioner in avoiding serious peril and pitfalls in the implementation of a system-wide change process.

Vernon Johnson, Ed.D
Superintendent
Rochester Public Schools
Rochester, Minnesota

EDUCATION is America's most important enterprise. The future of our competitive culture and economy, as well as our social cohesion, depends on the success of progressive educational change in the form of outcome-based education. In this context, educational change is not about reinventing seat time, nor about sorting children like vegetables. It is about equipping children better to succeed in an expanding economy, about shared values, and about building sound moral behavior that will knit communities together.

The overriding aim of outcome-based education is to improve the opportunity for *all* children of whatever background in our public schools, so that by the end of this century the borders between school and the independent sectors will be blurred. Excellence in our schools must be available to all students.

Educators need to look for other ways to achieve excellence in our schools. Like other professionals, educators must understand that changes in society require them not only to improve their performance, but to substantially redefine education's mission as well. For example, the health-care profession is changing because it must modify existing in-patient facilities to accommodate out-patient needs, and a patient-treatment philosophy that must be converted to one of wellness or preventive care. Like health-care professionals, educators cannot continue to use their equivalent of the Model-T Ford. They require the delivery capacity of the supersonic jet, a post-industrial information-age model, if they are to educate youth for the workplace and for social cohesion in the twenty-first century.

The education reform movements of recent years, stimulated by the report *A Nation at Risk,* * cannot be seen in isolation. They are part of a

*National Commission on Excellence in Education. 1983. *A Nation at Risk: The Imperative for Educational Reform.* Washington, D.C.: U.S. Government Printing Office.

tightly knit package that is redrawing the educational landscape. The reforms, ranging from public schooling of four-year-olds to federal funding of private schools, were designed to generate excellence in education. The excellence movement is foundering and, at best, it has brought on devastating consequences of apathy and alienation that pervade the nation's public schools. As *Time*** magazine wrote in a 1980 cover story, "Like some vast jury gradually and reluctantly arriving at a verdict, politicians, educators, and especially millions of parents have come to believe that the U.S. public schools are in parlous trouble." Consequently, public schools must adopt an educational process that will keep them from collapsing.

Outcome-based education can be the supersonic jet model for the next generation of schoolchildren who will grow up in a world where nearly all of them will be brain workers, not manual workers. As Rosa Parks,† at age eighty, so eloquently states: "The young people are our future, and we must be more concerned about giving them inspiration and training and motivation."

This book is about the process of developing an outcome-based education program for inspiring, training, and motivating America's future. The process to accomplish the task is presented in step-by-step order.

Floyd Boschee
Mark A. Baron

**Time*. June 16, 1980. "Help! Teacher Can't Teach!" 115(24), p. 54.

†Parks, R. 1993. "Rosa Parks, at Age 80, Says Educating Youth Is America's New Battle," *Argus Leader* (February 7):1C.

WE would like to express our sincere appreciation to Marlene J. Lang, English instructor at the University of South Dakota, Vermillion, for editing and for her promptness and guidance. Gratitude is extended to our wives, Marlys Ann Boschee and Jackeline Carmen Baron, for their many helpful comments, suggestions, and understanding.

We dedicate this book to all educators who recognize how thoughtful change in education can affect the lives of young people and who labor to ensure that education is as positive as possible. Educational change must never mask the fact that we in education are dealing first with human beings, not regulations.

CHAPTER 1

Initiating Outcome-Based Education

AS outcome-based education is considered, planned, and/or implemented in schools throughout America, educators and interested citizens are likely to ask a number of questions about what outcome-based education is and how it might work in their communities.[1] This book will assist those who are considering, continuing, and/or advancing the outcome-based education dialogue. The key questions are as follows.

1. What is outcome-based education?
2. What are the underlying beliefs of outcome-based education?
3. What are the characteristics of outcome-based education?
4. Why change to outcome-based education?
5. What needs can outcome-based education fulfill?
6. How does outcome-based education begin?

The answers to these questions, in prescription form and outlined in the pages that follow, emerge from observations of practice, research, and theory. Applying them will require thoughtful and constant review and attention, and lofty doses of practical wisdom by those who daily confront the infinite variations in all the circumstances of schooling.

WHAT IS OUTCOME-BASED EDUCATION?

Outcome-based education is a student-centered, results-oriented design premised on the belief that all individuals can learn.
Outcome-based education is:

- a commitment to the success of every learner
- a philosophy which focuses educational choices on the needs of each learner
- a process for continuous improvement

1

The strategy for outcome-based education implies the following.

- What a student is to learn is clearly identified.
- Each student's progress is based on demonstrated achievement.
- Each student's needs are accommodated through multiple instructional strategies and assessment tools.
- Each student is provided time and assistance to realize his or her potential.

WHAT ARE THE UNDERLYING BELIEFS OF OUTCOME-BASED EDUCATION?

Essential to outcome-based education is a commitment to the following beliefs.

- *All individuals can learn successfully.* Without a commitment to the high expectations for successful learning for all students, regardless of background, age, learning style, previous achievement, or other factors, education is not outcome-based.
- *Success results in further success.* Without a common vision that every success experienced by a learner builds self-esteem and the willingness to strive for further successes, education is not outcome-based.
- *Schools create and control the conditions under which learners succeed.* Without a belief that schools are responsible for learner success by the way they set priorities and provide for their learners, education is not outcome-based.
- *The community, educators, learners, and parents share in the responsibility for learning.* Without partnerships which treat all stakeholders as significant resources for every learner's success, education is not outcome-based.

WHAT ARE THE CHARACTERISTICS OF OUTCOME-BASED EDUCATION?

Outcome-based education is based on the premise that learners can and must be successful. There is no limit to human potential, individual or collective, if all stakeholders develop partnerships to ensure genuine success for all students. The following characteristics (regardless of formats, styles, procedures, or systems) provide a flexible process for meeting the needs of all learners.

1. What a student is to learn is clearly identified.
   - Outcomes are
     - future-oriented
     - publicly defined
     - learner-centered
     - focused on life skills and context
     - characterized by high expectations of and for all learners
     - sources from which all other educational decisions flow
   - Learning is
     - facilitated carefully toward achievement of the outcomes
     - characterized by its appropriateness to each learner's needs, interests, and developmental level
     - active and experienced-based for maximum application of the knowledge, skills, and orientations necessary to learner success in the present and future

2. Each student's progress is based on his or her demonstrated achievement.
   - Emphasis is on achievement of outcomes and application of learning, rather than ''covering'' material.
   - Assessment of learning is appropriate to the learning, its life context, and the learner.
   - Advancement is based on achievement of outcomes, rather than on seat time or comparative data.
   - Progress is demonstrated and recorded based on criterion-referenced, rather than norm-referenced assessment.
   - Learners advance because they demonstrate accomplishment of significant skills for independence and future success.

3. Each student's needs are accommodated through multiple instructional strategies and assessment tools.
   - Instructional decisions are based on each learner's needs, desires, and readiness for achieving outcomes.
   - Instructional design for each learner is an ongoing process of reflection and analysis that is focused on meeting the learner's needs.
   - Teachers facilitate the learning process and coach learners based on the best theory, research, and analysis.

- Assessments are effectively used to practice and substantiate learning and to provide data for further learning decisions.
- Learners become progressively more able to design their own learning options and assessments.

4. Each student is provided time and assistance to realize his or her potential.
   - All learners work to become more
     − responsible for their own learning
     − able to make appropriate learning decisions
     − independent in their learning and thinking
     − self-assessing
     − successful
   - Time is
     − viewed and applied as a variable, while learning is a constant
     − managed wisely by the learner and the school to achieve ever-increasing levels of accomplishment
   - Assistance is
     − sought from every available resource for providing significant learning opportunities
     − ensured to maximize each learner's success
     − not limited to traditional definitions of school, learning, or teaching
     − provided to meet the needs of the whole learner

WHY CHANGE TO OUTCOME-BASED EDUCATION?

Increasing World Complexity

In this post-industrial information age, technology, societal change, and a global focus characterize our complex world. By the time today's kindergartners enter the world of work, half of today's jobs will no longer exist and new jobs will have taken their place. And, as John Naisbitt and Patricia Aburdene predict in *Megatrends 2000*,[2] the overarching trends influencing our lives going into the twenty-first century will be:

- the booming global economy
- a renaissance in the arts
- the emergence of free-market socialism

- the privatization of the welfare state
- the rise of the Pacific Rim
- the decade of women in leadership
- the age of biology
- the religious revival of the new millennium
- the triumph of the individual

To meet the complex needs required of learners for the twenty-first century, a structure for learning designed for simpler times will no longer suffice.

Educational Research

The way learners are viewed has changed as a result of research. The following sources give evidence to the shift in preparing learners for tomorrow's society.

- Benjamin S. Bloom, in *Human Characteristics and School Learning,*[3] brings widespread attention to the concept that all children could be expected to learn and that they would learn given sufficient time and proper assistance.
- John B. Carroll, in an eleven-page article in the *Teachers College Record* titled "A Model of School Learning,"[4] sets forth and defends the concept that differences in student scores on aptitude and intelligence tests are measures of time that is required for different students to learn the same material – not, as previously believed, measures of students' innate capabilities to learn.
- The results of the Educational Research Service's series of reports on effective schools, compiled by Robinson,[5,6] support the tenet that all students *can* learn and that they *will* learn given sufficient time and proper assistance.

Beliefs about Learning

A widely held presumption is that human learning potential is measurable or demonstrable on a bell-shaped curve. The assumption for outcome-based education is that all students can learn and variables in schools ought to be time, amount of instruction, and opportunities for achieving and demonstrating competence. Success of learners should be measured according to their own individual accomplishments, rather than comparisons with accomplishments of other learners.

Public Expectations

The mission of a school district, its system for lifelong learning, should be to ensure individual academic achievement, an informed citizenry, and a highly productive work force. Such a system:

- focuses on the learner
- promotes and values diversity
- provides participatory decision making
- ensures accountability
- models democratic principles
- creates and sustains a climate for change
- provides personalized learning environments
- encourages learners to reach their maximum potential
- integrates and coordinates human services for learners

As society calls for higher and more rigorous standards in education, greater concern is emerging that schools need to re-examine their requirements and that graduation from high school be based on demonstration of skills which prepare students to perform in the future.

WHAT NEEDS CAN OUTCOME-BASED EDUCATION FULFILL?

Because outcome-based education is learner-centered, results-oriented, and designed to meet the needs of *all* individual learners in achieving outcomes of life significance, the process of outcome-based education is offered as a means of fulfilling the demands placed on education today.

1. Outcome-based education is
   - a process congruent with the public's current and future demands of high expectations for all learners
   - a process for partnership among all parties who need and expect productive learning
   - a belief system which reflects America's cultural value of the individual and each individual's self-esteem, citizenship, and potential for local and global leadership

- a means of fulfilling the promise of public education to build the future by preparing every learner today
2. Schools which have begun outcome-based processes
   - report success for their learners and their systems
   - report that, though implementation is a slow process, outcome-based education is a belief, an environment, and a way of doing business which has built support for schools, learners, and learning
   - report higher learner, educator, and public satisfaction with schools

HOW DOES OUTCOME-BASED EDUCATION BEGIN?

School districts or schools interested in becoming outcome-based must make a commitment to educational improvement which is learner-centered and results-oriented. The process begins by identifying a common set of educational beliefs held by educators, learners, parents, and the community. These beliefs will drive the process to a definition of what outcomes learners should accomplish in their preparation for the future and what processes need to be in place to ensure achievement of those outcomes by *all* learners.

Clearly, there is no template of behaviors which can be placed on an educational system to make it outcome-based. The public dialogue which the outcome-based education process will create has the potential to energize and empower whole communities of learners as they design—for themselves, their children, and the future—a vision and a reality of education that is truly successful.

REVIEW ACTIVITIES

(1) Think of a student who surprised you with his or her success. (Perhaps you had a student who did poorly in school and became very accomplished as an adult or a student who one time performed unexpectedly well in the classroom.) What influenced that student's success? Review the seven characteristics which describe outcome-based education and apply the specific questions that enabled that student's achievement.

(2) Recall a lesson you taught or a student you have had that disappointed you. Review the four underlying beliefs of outcome-based education and complete the following statement: ''If only I could have _____.''

(3) Consider the four reasons given for changing to outcome-based education. Compare your school days with those of your students. What differences do you find in what the world looked like to you and what the world looks like to your students? What beliefs did your teachers exhibit that you do not? What attitudes did society hold toward your school that today's society does not?

(4) Select a criticism of education that you hear or read such as, ''Why don't those kids today learn how to read/write/do math?'' Examine the seven needs that outcome-based education can fulfill and explain how an outcome-based education approach will rectify the source of public criticism.

NOTES

1 The questions and most answers are from ''Success for Every Learner,'' a document produced by the Minnesota Department of Education, St. Paul, MN, 1991.

2 Naisbitt, J. and P. Aburdene. 1990. *Megatrends 2000: Ten New Directions for the 1990's.* New York, NY: Avon Books, p. xix.

3 Bloom, B. S. 1976. *Human Characteristics and School Learning.* New York, NY: McGraw-Hill.

4 Carroll, J. B. 1963. ''A Model of School Learning,'' *Teachers College Record,* 64(8):723 – 733.

5 Robinson, G. E. 1985. ''Effective Schools Research: A Guide to School Improvement,'' *ERS Concerns in Education.* Washington, D.C.: Educational Research Service, Inc.

6 Robinson, G. E. 1986. ''Learning Expectancy: A Force Changing Education,'' *ERS Concerns in Education.* Washington, D.C.: Educational Research Service, Inc.

CHAPTER 2

Initiating the Strategic Planning Process

WHAT IS STRATEGIC PLANNING?

WITHIN an educational context, strategic planning constitutes a process of identifying desired learner outcomes based upon shared visions of an ideal future. It becomes a dynamic process for involving all educational stakeholders who identify and create a preferred future for the school district or an individual school. Educational stakeholders include students, teachers, parents, and community members — all the individuals and groups within the district affected in any way by the educational process.

Based on the premise that we can create the future of our choice, strategic planning provides a proactive approach that enables us to take the initiative in shaping the future to prepare learners for the challenges and opportunities that await them. Strategic planning, a future-oriented process, defines the knowledge, skills, and attitudes that will enable *all* students to succeed in a world undergoing rapidly changing social, political, economic, environmental, and cultural conditions.

A well-designed strategic plan provides the framework for transforming current instructional practices into an outcome-based educational system. The strategic plan must embrace the philosophies, premises, and principles of outcome-based education and should consist of:

- a district philosophy (a set of collective beliefs)
- a district vision
- a district mission
- a set of learner exit outcomes

WHY PLAN AT THE DISTRICT LEVEL?

Advantages of District-Wide Planning

Among the first important decisions to make involves determining the level at which strategic planning will occur. Although strategic planning may be a powerful tool for focusing the efforts of individual schools, we recommend giving primary consideration to planning at the district level. In contrast to individual school planning, district-wide planning offers the following advantages.

- Controlling the smooth instructional transition from kindergarten through twelfth grade assures continuity throughout the educational program.
- When all of the schools throughout the district have developed and implemented the same strategic plan, students easily transfer from one school to another within the district.
- The entire district can contribute a much broader knowledge base and set of educational philosophies than those associated with only one school within the district.
- Individual schools within the district avoid duplication of effort and gain more efficient use of human and material resources through coordination of planning at the district level.
- Individuals develop throughout the district who will eventually implement the district plan and provide leadership to every school.

Site-Based Planning

Site-based planning refers to the activities taking place at each school throughout the district necessary to implement the district's strategic plan. This process allows each school in the district to use its own talents and resources to achieve the district's mission while simultaneously realizing its own unique goals.

While the strategic plan developed at the district level provides direction and support for site-based planning, each school remains responsible for making decisions that will result in maximum achievement for its own learners. Site-based planning and decision making offer the following benefits.

- Educators and community members most familiar with the individual school and its students realize increased participation and ownership.
- Schools more effectively distribute and manage resources allocated by the district.
- Each school has more accountability for increased achievement by its own students.

The final product will be a site-based strategic plan consisting of a school philosophy (set of collective beliefs), vision, and mission that are consistent with those of the district. While all schools adopt the district's learner exit outcomes, each individual school determines the specific techniques employed to achieve those outcomes.

Strategic Planning for Independent Schools

Due to the unique characteristics and needs of schools and their neighboring communities, planning exclusively at the individual school level may be necessary or desirable. This situation might occur in public school districts consisting entirely of one $K-8$ or $K-12$ school, or independent private, parochial, or special-needs schools (such as vocational-technical schools or schools for exceptional children) that are responsible for their own planning and instructional programs.

Strategic planning still provides an extremely effective mechanism for involving all of the school's stakeholders in the creation of an outcome-based education program that will meet the particular needs of its students. The process will be identical to that described for planning at the district level, with the exception that the vision, mission statement, and learner exit outcomes will focus on the individual school rather than the district as a whole.

WHO SHOULD COMPRISE DISTRICT AND SITE PLANNING TEAMS?

Shared decision making is the cornerstone of the strategic planning process. It involves collaborative planning and problem solving designed to improve the quality of decisions and increase the community's satisfaction with the planning process and educational program.

District Planning Team

It is essential that the district planning team be comprised of individuals representing all of the diverse interests and perspectives of the school district and community. Planning team members should be articulate people of goodwill who are committed to positive change through the development of an outcome-based education program for the district. They should have well-developed human relations skills enabling them to work effectively with other members of the planning team, as well as members of the groups they represent. The district planning team should include members representing:

- the board of education
- the superintendent
- central office personnel
- building-level administrators
- elementary, middle/junior high, and high school teachers
- noncertified personnel/classified employees
- local universities or colleges
- local educational cooperatives/agencies
- parents (PTA members and/or other parents)
- members of the business community/community leaders
- recent graduates living in the community
- students

Although planning team members must represent all the district's educational stakeholders, the actual size of the team will vary from district to district. Various factors that should determine the number of district planning team members include:

- the district's size and enrollment
- the number of school buildings within the district
- the amount of time and resources available for the strategic planning process
- the number and diversity of special educational programs offered throughout the district
- the number and diversity of neighborhoods and communities served by the district

Site Planning Teams

A planning team should be selected in each school building to translate the district's strategic plan into a site-based plan. Site planning team members will make decisions regarding how best to use locally available resources to maximize student achievement in their own building while working within the framework of the district's plan.

The site planning team should include representatives of stakeholder groups in the school and local community. At least one member of the site planning team should also be a member of the district planning team or serve as a liaison between the district and site planning teams. Members of the site planning team should include:

- the principal and/or assistant principal
- teachers representing each grade level/subject area
- noncertified/classified school personnel
- students
- parents
- local community/business leaders

HOW TO BUILD SUPPORT FOR STRATEGIC PLANNING

As is true of any major educational reform effort, the successful development and implementation of a strategic plan depends upon widespread understanding of the process and commitment to seeing it through. Laying the groundwork for strategic planning consists of informing district educators, parents, and community members how the process works; providing a rationale and general timeline for the planning process; and specifying what outcomes and results can be expected. The following steps provide a framework for building support and commitment to strategic planning.

1. Provide comprehensive training and orientation for all members of the district planning team.
   - Employ outside consultants or trained team members as facilitators for training all planning team members.
   - Assure that all planning team members are familiar with relevant future trends and all aspects of the strategic planning process.
   - Develop strategies to enable all planning team members to share their knowledge and enthusiasm with other stakeholder groups throughout the district.
2. District planning team members provide a rationale and share information regarding relevant future trends and strategic planning with all stakeholder groups in order to enlist their support.
   - Hold small group meetings with individual stakeholder groups throughout the district.
   - Record and discuss feedback and suggestions from stakeholder groups with the district planning team.

- Include stakeholder groups that represent school administrators, teachers, and other school personnel, as well as parent and other community interest groups.
- Target school board members to build support and commitment for strategic planning throughout the district.

3. The district planning team should communicate regularly with all stakeholder groups throughout the district and continually solicit their feedback.
   - Regularly apprise individuals and groups within the district of progress throughout the planning process.
   - In addition to occasional face-to-face meetings, use publications such as newsletters and bulletins to keep the public informed of progress.
   - Continually seek and incorporate positive feedback from the community into the planning process whenever possible.

The importance of open two-way communications between the planning team and the community cannot be overemphasized. The success of the strategic planning and shared decision-making process is contingent upon generating ownership and support from all the district's clients in the educational process.

WHAT IS "PLANNING-TO-PLAN"?

Once the public has been informed about strategic planning and support for the process has been established, the district planning team must focus its attention on creating the strategic plan. The first step is identifying what needs to be decided or produced, who should be involved, and by what dates these decisions and products should be completed. This planning-to-plan process will provide the framework for creating the district philosophy, vision, mission, and learner exit outcomes that constitute the remainder of the strategic plan.

A planning chart similar to the sample displayed in Figure 2.1 may provide a useful tool for each work group to organize their work and record their progress. A separate chart should be completed for planning to create the district philosophy, vision, mission, and learner exit outcomes.

The following steps provide a useful guideline for completing the planning-to-plan process.

DISTRICT PHILOSOPHY			
1. What needs to be decided or produced?	2. Who needs to be involved in the decision?	3. How will people be involved and what tools will be used?	4. What are the timelines and responsibilities?
• A set of collective belief statements regarding learners, staff, parents, and administrators for developing the district philosophy	• All members of the district planning team • Representatives of all educational stakeholders in the school and community	• Small groups of the district planning team will meet with various stakeholder groups and solicit their beliefs • Planning team members will meet to adopt/amend beliefs collected from stakeholder groups throughout the district	• Oct. 1: Community meetings – all planning team members • Oct. 15: Community meetings – all planning team members • Nov. 1: District planning team meeting – all members
• A district philosophy to serve as a decision screen for developing the district vision, mission, and learner exit outcomes	• A selected group of members from the planning team to draft a district philosophy	• Collective beliefs adopted by the district planning team will be consolidated into a district philosophy • District philosophy will be shared with stakeholder groups in the schools and community	• Nov. 15: Selected planning team members develop district philosophy • Dec. 1: All members of the district planning meet with district stakeholder groups to share the district philosophy

FIGURE 2.1 A sample planning-to-plan chart for developing a district philosophy.[1]

Step 1

- Divide the district planning team into work groups of four to eight members so that each work group contains representatives of diverse stakeholder groups.
- Each work group selects a facilitator to keep the group on task and a recorder to take notes of the group's decisions.

Step 2

- Each work group completes all columns of its planning charts for the district philosophy, vision, mission, and learner exit outcomes. (The completed planning charts serve as a first draft of each group's work to be shared with members of all the other work groups.)

Step 3

- Each work group selects one member to represent them in a consensus group whose task will be to formulate a collective plan to create a district philosophy.
- Each work group selects three additional members to represent them in three other consensus groups with the following tasks: to formulate a collective plan to create a district vision; to formulate a collective plan to create a district mission; and to formulate a collective plan to create a set of learner exit outcomes.

Step 4

- Each newly formed consensus group reviews all of the planning-to-plan documents related to their topic (district philosophy, vision, mission, or learner exit outcomes).
- Each consensus group discusses and revises their topic until they have developed a collective plan that is acceptable to the entire consensus group.

Step 5

- Members of the consensus groups return to their original work groups to present and discuss revised plans for creating a district philosophy, vision, mission, and learner exit outcomes.

- Each work group either accepts revisions made by the consensus groups or makes additional changes and modifications to the revised plans.

Step 6

- If necessary, consensus groups reconvene to develop new collective plans that incorporate work groups' changes and modifications.
- The process continues until plans for creating a district philosophy, vision, mission, and set of learner exit outcomes are acceptable to all members of the district planning team.

A concise summary of the planning-to-plan process is illustrated in Figure 2.2. Although the diagram depicts formation of the district philosophy consensus group only, the same procedure is also followed for formation of groups to reach agreement on plans to create a district vision, mission, and learner exit outcomes.

Upon completion of the planning-to-plan process, the district planning team will have outlined the procedures, responsibilities, and timelines for creating the strategic plan. The results and final planning-to-plan documents should be discussed with community members and groups to keep them apprised of the planning team's progress, collect feedback regarding possible improvements or refinements in the plan, and prepare them for future participation in the planning process. If necessary, the district planning team may meet once more to incorporate helpful suggestions offered by community members or groups.

HOW TO IDENTIFY SIGNIFICANT FUTURE TRENDS

The strategic planning process presumes that the world of tomorrow in which today's students will live and work will be significantly different from the world of today. Future global trends and conditions will determine the knowledge, skills, and attitudes learners will need to successfully face the challenges and opportunities of the twenty-first century. Therefore, everyone involved in the planning process must be well grounded in the shifts and trends that are shaping the United States and the world.

District and site planning teams should conclude the initiation phase of their strategic planning process with a discussion of future trends and the implications these global changes have for their own instructional

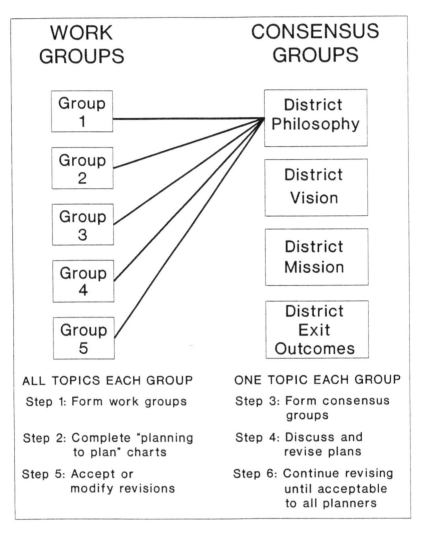

FIGURE 2.2 Steps in the planning-to-plan process.

programs. Creating a common understanding of tomorrow's world among all planning partners provides:

- a rationale and support for the decision to adopt a future-oriented outcome-based education program
- a frame of reference for developing a district or site-based philosophy, vision, and mission
- a basis for identifying learner exit outcomes

Gathering Information

The first step in identifying significant future trends involves collecting information regarding changes that are taking place in our country and the world. Being aware of such changes is particularly important for those who will facilitate training of district and site planning team members, and for those who will present information and provide orientation for other educators and community members throughout the district.

A number of excellent books that critically examine the subject of future trends and their implications are available. Among these are:

- *Future Edge* by Joel Barker[2]
- *Megatrends 2000* by John Naisbitt and Patricia Aburdene[3]
- *Powershift* by Alvin Toffler[4]
- *Schools for the 21st Century* by Phillip Schlechty[5]
- *Schools of the Future* by Marvin Cetron[6]
- *Trend Tracking* by Gerald Celente and Tom Milton[7]
- *Workplace 2000* by Joseph Boyett and Henry Conn[8]

Although each of these books focuses on future trends related to a particular setting or theme, a number of common trends emerge. Some of the commonly mentioned trends that have implications for education are presented in Figure 2.3.

Identifying Future Trends

When all available information regarding future trends has been collected, planning teams and stakeholder groups must decide which trends appear most significant for the district's students and educational process. This may be accomplished in the following manner.

- **Globalization.** The world continues to get smaller and countries are becoming more closely tied politically, economically, and socially.

- **Technology.** The increased use of computers, robotics, and other technological innovations is changing how we live and work.

- **Communication.** Instant worldwide communication is making news and information available to everyone almost as soon as it happens.

- **Knowledge Explosion.** The rate of knowledge and information acquisition continues to increase more rapidly every day.

- **Cultural Diversity.** Increased immigration and high birth rates will soon make minorities the majority of the population in the United States and other industrialized countries.

- **Environmental Conditions.** There is increasing concern about the negative consequences of our failure to preserve our planet.

- **Family Structure.** Single parent and two working parent families are quickly replacing the traditional nuclear family.

- **Distribution of Wealth.** While the rich get richer and the poor get poorer, the middle class is becoming an increasingly endangered species.

- **Quality Revolution.** Consumers are increasingly expecting higher quality products and services at more reasonable prices.

- **New World Order.** The demise of communism and realignment of Eastern Europe has created a new world order in which there exists a greatly reduced military threat.

- **Aging Population.** Declining birth rates and longevity are increasing the median age of the population in the United States and many other industrialized countries.

- **National Debt.** The growing national debt in the United States and other industrialized countries is having a profound impact on many economic and political decisions and policies.

- **Service-Oriented Economy.** The economies of many industrialized countries are shifting from industrial-oriented to service-oriented economies.

- **Cooperation.** Many organizations are replacing competition with cooperation to increase productivity and worker satisfaction.

- **Rate of Change.** Change is occurring at an increasingly rapid rate in nearly all aspects of our lives.

FIGURE 2.3 Some commonly mentioned future trends.

Step 1

- Provide participants with a list or outline of the future trends that appear most frequently in the literature. (The above listing of future trends could be employed as a starter list for this purpose.)
- Discuss these trends and their potential implications with the entire group.
- Encourage participants to modify items or add additional items to the list of future trends.

Step 2

- Divide participants into groups of four to eight members so that each group contains representatives of various stakeholder or interest groups.
- Each group selects a facilitator to keep the group on task and a recorder to take notes of the group's decisions.

Step 3

- Each group ranks all the future trends on the list in order of importance.
- Rankings for each trend should take into consideration
  - the likelihood that the trend will actually occur
  - how significantly the trend would (or should) affect education in the district or school if it did occur

Step 4

- Each group shares its results with the entire participant group.
- Summarize results on large sheets of paper with markers and hang these sheets around the room to permit all participants to examine the results from each individual group. (Alternately, photocopy individual group results and distribute photocopies to the entire participant group.)

Step 5

- Identify five to ten future trends considered most important by the entire participant group (as indicated by the collective rankings of all individual groups).

Step 6

- Discuss the implications of these five to ten future trends by projecting future conditions that will likely be created by each trend. (Advancing technology, for example, suggests that today's students will be living in a world that will require more technological knowledge and more specialized skills, if they are to live and work successfully, than is necessary today.) More than one future condition should be listed for each trend, and many future conditions may be listed for some.
- Record the most important future trends and projections for resulting future conditions.
- Provide a copy of this information for all participants. (This information provides a useful reference for subsequent development of a district/school philosophy, vision, mission, and learner exit outcomes.)

The essential steps to initiate the strategic planning process at the school district level are outlined in Figure 2.4. The next phase of the strategic planning process, developing the district philosophy, vision, mission, and learner exit outcomes, will be described in Chapter 3.

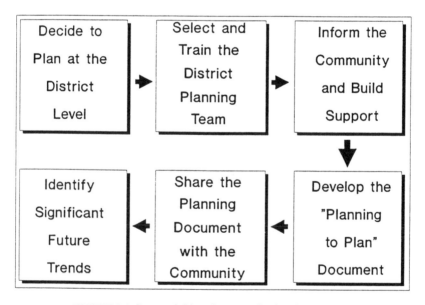

FIGURE 2.4 Steps to initiate the strategic planning process.

REVIEW ACTIVITIES

(1) Examine the long-range planning process that your own school district or school uses and compare it to the strategic planning process described in Chapter 2.

- What are some of the apparent advantages and disadvantages of strategic planning compared to the present planning process in your district or school?
- What tactics would you use in trying to convince your school board or building administrator to consider switching to a strategic planning approach?

(2) As a member of the district planning team, you have been asked to arrange meetings to inform each of the district's stakeholder groups about strategic planning and how beneficial it could be for students in your schools.

- Develop a schedule of meetings that includes which groups would be invited to attend each meeting, where each meeting would be held, and what resources you would need to conduct the meetings.
- How would you advertise your planned meetings to produce the greatest possible attendance at each?

(3) You have just been selected by your school board to put together a district strategic planning team.

- What specific stakeholder groups from your school district would you select to be represented on the district planning team? Provide a brief rationale for selecting each of these stakeholder groups.
- Are there any stakeholder groups within your district that you would intentionally *not* select for the district planning team? Why?

(4) As one of the veteran members of your faculty, the principal has asked you to put together a site planning team for your school.

- Who from among your school staff would you invite to participate as a member of the site planning team?
- How much representation would you offer students in your school and how would you select them?
- What local community stakeholder groups would you invite to place a representative on the site planning team?

- How would you assure that members of your site planning team become well informed about the district planning team's progress?

(5) Your superintendent has assigned various strategic planning tasks to different teachers throughout the district and you have been asked to coordinate the creation of a planning-to-plan document.

- Would you involve the entire district planning team in the planning-to-plan process? Why or why not?
- How would you share the results of the planning-to-plan process with all of the stakeholder groups throughout your district?

(6) You have been asked to gather information regarding future trends and lead the district planning team in identifying those trends that appear to have significant implications for education within the district.

- Aside from books that focus on future trends and their implications, what other forms of media might provide valuable insights into the world of tomorrow? List several specific examples for each form of media you identify and describe how each would be useful.
- Aside from those outlined in Figure 2.3, what other future trends can you think of that appear likely to affect the way education is conducted?
- Which of the future trends outlined in Figure 2.3 are already beginning to influence society in the United States and the world?

NOTES

1 The sample planning-to-plan chart is adapted from the *Strategic Planning Planner* by Charles Schwahn, 1991.
2 Barker, J. 1992. *Future Edge*. New York, NY: Morrow Publishing Co.
3 Naisbitt, J. and P. Aburdene. 1990. *Megatrends 2000: Ten New Directions for the 1990's*. New York, NY: Avon Books.
4 Toffler, A. 1990. *Powershift: Knowledge, Wealth, and Violence at the Edge of the 21st Century*. New York, NY: Bantam Books.
5 Schlechty, P. 1990. *Schools for the 21st Century*. San Francisco, CA: Jossey-Bass Publishers.

6 Cetron, M. 1985. *Schools of the Future*. Arlington, VA: American Association of School Administrators.

7 Celente, G. and T. Milton. 1991. *Trend Tracking: The System to Profit from Today's Trends*. New York, NY: Warner Books.

8 Boyett, J. and H. Conn. 1991. *Workplace 2000: The Revolution Shaping American Business*. Bergenfield, NJ: NAL-Dutton Publishing Co.

CHAPTER 3

Developing the Strategic Plan

HAVING completed the planning-to-plan document and identified significant future trends, the district planning team now proceeds to collectively develop the strategic plan itself. This phase of the strategic planning process involves developing a district philosophy, vision, mission, and set of learner exit outcomes.

HOW TO DEVELOP A DISTRICT PHILOSOPHY

The district philosophy consists of the stakeholders' collective beliefs regarding the educational process. Beliefs concerning the roles and responsibilities of learners, school staff, parents, and the school community greatly influence how teaching and learning occur in schools and classrooms throughout the district. In essence, beliefs define the local educational culture by determining "how things get done" in the school or district. An example of a school district philosophy that includes beliefs about learners, school staff, parents, and the community is presented in Figure 3.1.[1]

Identifying Beliefs

Since belief statements comprising the district philosophy provide the framework for developing an outcome-based education program, all of the district's stakeholders should be encouraged to contribute. This may be accomplished through representation on the district planning team that has already been formed or by direct input from the various stakeholders throughout the district. Procedures for both methods will be described.

District Planning Team

The procedure for identifying beliefs among district planning team members is similar to that described in the previous chapter for reaching

THE LEARNER

- Learning at all ages is a continuous process during which each person needs to develop:

  - positive attitudes and feelings of self-worth.
  - communication, problem solving, decision making, and computational skills.
  - essential knowledge.
  - an awareness of and appreciation for culture and heritage.
  - independent learning and group participation skills for self-directed learning.
  - social awareness, human relations skills, and concern for others.
  - creativity and aesthetic understandings and appreciations.
  - standards of ethical behavior.
  - physical and emotional well-being.

- Each person must have successful experiences in order to develop positive attitudes and approaches to learning.

- Each person needs to develop decision making abilities throughout life and learn to deal effectively with the consequences of his or her decisions.

- Each person needs to become an increasingly effective citizen of the home, school, community, nation, and world.

THE SCHOOL STAFF

- Each school staff member affects the individual learner's motivation, growth, and success.

- Each school staff member influences the way in which the individual learner experiences the curriculum, uses instructional time, materials, and assessment measures, and is evaluated.

- The probability of learning increases when each school staff member uses varied learning plans that provide for:

  - the unique learning styles of individual learners.
  - the individual learner's rate of learning.
  - active individual participation in learning.

- Each school staff member has a responsibility to involve the parent in the education of the child.

- Each school staff member needs to have an array of opportunities for learning and growth and that the district has a responsibility to assist in providing these staff development activities.

FIGURE 3.1 Example of a school district philosophy.

28

THE PARENT

- The parent has fundamental responsibilities for the education of the child. This requires that the parent be fully informed about the child's learning.

- The parent is responsible for a home environment which emphasizes the importance of learning.

- The parent should have a variety of opportunities to be involved in the school.

- The parent is a lifelong learner and needs opportunities to grow as a parent and as an individual.

- The parent has the responsibility to be informed about and involved in decisions that affect education throughout the community.

THE COMMUNITY

- The community has the responsibility to provide for the learning needs of all.

- These learning needs should be provided by a variety of public and private agencies and organizations.

- The community's public schools have unique responsibilities for particular dimensions of lifelong learning.

- The community should work with the schools and all other public and private, formal and informal community agencies to provide for the growth needs of citizens of all ages.

FIGURE 3.1 (continued)   Example of a school district philosophy.

consensus on a planning-to-plan document. The following steps outline the process for reaching agreement on belief statements regarding learners, school staff, parents, and community members.

Step 1

- Divide the district planning team into work groups of four to eight members so that each work group contains representatives of diverse stakeholder groups.
- Each work group selects a facilitator to keep the group on task and a recorder to take notes of the group's decisions.

Step 2

- Each work group generates lists of beliefs regarding the roles and responsibilities of learners, school staff, parents, and community members.

- Beliefs regarding each of these groups are recorded on separate sheets of paper.

Step 3

- Each work group selects one member to represent them in a consensus group whose task will be to formulate a list of beliefs about learners.
- Each work group selects three additional members to represent them in three other consensus groups with the following tasks: to formulate a list of beliefs about school staff; to formulate a list of beliefs about parents; and to formulate a list of beliefs about the community.

Step 4

- Each newly formed consensus group reviews all of the original work groups' lists of beliefs related to their own target group (learners, school staff, parents, or community).
- Each consensus group discusses and revises belief statements regarding their target group until they have developed a list of beliefs that is acceptable to the entire consensus group.

Step 5

- Members of the consensus groups return to their original work groups to present and discuss revisions made by each consensus group.
- Each work group either accepts revisions made by the consensus groups or makes additional changes and modifications to the revised belief statements.

Step 6

- If necessary, consensus groups reconvene to develop new belief statements or make new revisions that incorporate work groups' changes and modifications.
- The process continues until belief statements regarding learners, school staff, parents, and the community are acceptable to all members of the district planning team.

Direct Stakeholder Input

Receiving input directly from stakeholders throughout the district provides an alternate method for collectively identifying beliefs regarding learners, school staff, parents, and the community. While somewhat more expensive and time consuming, this method guarantees the development of a district philosophy representative of the district as a whole.

The Delphi Technique provides a method for reaching consensus among large numbers of individuals without the need for face-to-face meetings of all the participants. The following steps outline the use of the Delphi Technique to identify beliefs.

Step 1

- Identify individuals throughout the district to participate in this process. In small school districts this should include all individuals living within the district, while in larger districts one or more representatives of every stakeholder group should be included. (In either case, the number of participants should be much greater than the size of the district planning team.)

Step 2

- Request that each participant within the district write out a list of beliefs regarding learners, school staff, parents, and the community.
- Each participant submits the completed belief statements to the district planning team (or members of the team assigned to collect these statements).
- Collate and make copies of each participant's initial belief statements.

Step 3

- Distribute these initial belief statements to all participants with the request that they indicate with which statements they agree, and with which statements they disagree.
- Participants should also suggest modifications to those statements with which they could agree if minor changes were made to them.

• Participants return these initial belief statements, including their comments, to the district planning team.

Step 4

• The district planning team lists these beliefs in two columns, one for those which the majority agrees upon (with the number or percentage of participants who are in agreement) and the other for which majority agreement has not been found.

Step 5

• Distribute the two-column lists to all participants with the request that those belief statements not agreed upon by the majority be restated in such a way that they would then agree with the statement.
• Scratch off items on the list which cannot be restated in any satisfactory manner.
• Participants return these revised lists to the district planning team.

Step 6

• The district planning team restates beliefs according to participants' revisions and removes statements scratched out by a majority of the participants.
• Repeat the procedure described in Step 5 until a majority of participants agree with all of the belief statements remaining on the list.

Integrating and Prioritizing Beliefs

The resulting list will contain numerous belief statements gathered directly from stakeholders throughout the district or their representatives on the district planning team. In order to provide a clear focus for the district philosophy, however, this list must be reduced to a manageable number of beliefs that stakeholders consider most important or essential. This is accomplished by integrating or combining similar belief statements, prioritizing the resulting statements, and selecting only the eight or ten most important beliefs to comprise the district philosophy.

Step 1

- Divide the district planning team into four groups of approximately equal size—one group (learners, school staff, parents, and the community) for each set of belief statements.
- Select a facilitator and recorder for each of the four groups.

Step 2

- Each group eliminates repetitious belief statements and consolidates statements that are similar enough to be combined without significantly changing their meaning.
- Each group submits their final condensed list of belief statements to the planning team as a whole.

Step 3

- Each member of the planning team rates the strength of each belief statement (regarding learners, school staff, parents, and the community) on a five- or seven-point scale where *1* represents the weakest beliefs and *5* or *7* represents the strongest beliefs. (While the scale may contain any number of points, five- and seven-point scales are most commonly used.)
- Alternately, the planning team distributes the condensed lists of belief statements to all stakeholders within the district who participated in developing the original lists of belief statements. Each participant rates the strength of each belief statement on the same five- or seven-point scale and returns the rated lists to the planning team.

Step 4

- The district planning team (or assigned members of the team) averages all the ratings for each belief statement and positions the statements in order from the strongest beliefs to the weakest beliefs.

- Select the eight or ten strongest beliefs regarding learners, school staff, parents, and the community to comprise the district philosophy.

Integrating and prioritizing beliefs result in a district philosophy consisting of stakeholders' strongest collective beliefs regarding the educational roles and responsibilities of learners, school staff, parents, and the community. These beliefs constitute the foundation upon which the district vision, mission, and learner exit outcomes will be built.

HOW TO CONDUCT A BELIEFS ANALYSIS

A beliefs analysis assesses current educational practices in relation to stakeholders' beliefs concerning what educational practices should be implemented. The analysis identifies gaps between what is happening and what should be happening in schools and classrooms based on the beliefs expressed in the district philosophy. Gaps uncovered by the beliefs analysis should serve as an important focus for planners when making decisions regarding desired learner exit outcomes and methods to achieve those outcomes. An example of the results of a beliefs analysis for one belief regarding learners, school staff, parents, and the community is presented in Figure 3.2.

A beliefs analysis is accomplished in the following manner.

Step 1

- Divide the district planning team into four groups of approximately equal size — one group (learners, school staff, parents, and the community) for each set of belief statements comprising the district philosophy.
- Select a facilitator and recorder for each of the four groups.

Step 2

- Each group writes a statement describing what currently happens and a statement describing what should happen in relation to each of the belief statements.
- Each group shares their statements with the planning team as a whole.

LEARNERS: Learning is a continuous process during which each person needs to develop independent learning and group participation skills for self-directed learning.

WHAT HAPPENS: To maintain order and discipline, learners work individually almost all of the time and have little opportunity to work in group settings.

WHAT SHOULD HAPPEN: Learning situations must be created that provide an adequate opportunity for learners to work in group settings as well as individually to solve problems.

SCHOOL STAFF: The probability of learning increases when each school staff member uses varied learning plans that provide for active individual participation in learning.

WHAT HAPPENS: While some learners take an active part in their own learning, many choose to be passive participants in the learning process.

WHAT SHOULD HAPPEN: Through careful planning and delivery of instruction, all learners should be motivated to actively participate in the learning process occurring in the classroom.

PARENTS: The parent has the responsibility to be informed about and involved in decisions that affect education throughout the community.

WHAT HAPPENS: While a small number of parents are involved in almost every decision affecting education, most parents choose not to take part.

WHAT SHOULD HAPPEN: Numerous parental advisory committees must be formed to encourage parents to become better informed and actively involved in the educational process throughout the community.

THE COMMUNITY: The community has the responsibility to provide for the learning needs of all.

WHAT HAPPENS: While a small number of community agencies provide learning opportunities for some children and adults, learning opportunities for many more children and adults are not being provided by agencies throughout the community.

WHAT SHOULD HAPPEN: The community must form more agencies and increase the services of agencies already in existence to provide increased learning opportunities for children and adults of all ages throughout the community.

FIGURE 3.2 Example of the results of a beliefs analysis.

Step 3

- Record statements regarding what currently happens and what should happen in relation to beliefs about learners, school staff, parents, and the community and share them with the planning team as a whole.
- The planning team as a whole discusses each group's statements until a consensus has been reached regarding all of the statements, then a copy of the final results is distributed to each member of the planning team.

The beliefs analysis results in a list of discrepancies between actual and ideal educational practices related to each belief statement comprising the district philosophy. Those practices identified as ideal provide the basis for creating an outcome-based education system in which stakeholders' beliefs are translated into actual practice.

HOW TO DEVELOP A DISTRICT VISION

The district vision portrays an idea, image, or picture of what education in the district ideally will (or should) look like in the future. Incorporating previously identified significant future trends and stakeholders' collective beliefs regarding ideal educational practices (derived from the beliefs analysis), the vision represents a shared view of the preferred educational future for the district.

A well-articulated vision empowers and motivates planners and stakeholders to move in a common direction to produce the educational program depicted by the vision. It serves as a yardstick to measure progress toward the preferred future. The vision describes the activities of learners, school staff, parents, and the community within the ideal educational system. Figure 3.3 displays elements of a sample district vision that might result from belief statements comprising the district philosophy illustrated earlier in this chapter in Figure 3.1.

Creation of a district vision may be accomplished in the following manner.

Step 1

- Divide the district planning team into four groups of approximately equal size—one group (learners, school staff,

Within three years, the ABC Public School System will be a place
where ...

- learners develop positive attitudes and feeling of self-worth
  through successful experiences inside and outside the classroom.

- learners acquire independent learning and group participation
  skills through active involvement in their own learning.

- social awareness, human relations skills, and concern for
  others is generated through extensive positive interaction
  with other learners throughout the school.

- learners develop decision-making abilities through daily
  opportunities to make personal choices regarding the home,
  school, and community.

- school staff function in accordance with district beliefs and
  promote achievement of the district vision, mission, and exit
  outcomes.

- school staff serve as positive role models for all learners
  through their words and actions.

- school staff provide the maximum opportunity for growth of
  every learner by actively involving them in the learning
  process and delivering instruction that provides for
  individual learners' unique learning styles.

- every school staff member is provided with, and encouraged to
  participate in professional development activities on a
  regular basis throughout the school year and summer months.

- parents work as partners with school staff to achieve the
  district vision, mission, and exit outcomes for learners.

- parents are encouraged to spend quality time in the school
  participating in the learning activities of their children.

- parents are regularly informed of their children's progress
  through formal and informal means of communication.

- parents are provided with opportunities and encouraged to
  participate in activities designed to help them grow as
  parents and to meet their needs as lifelong learners.

- the community is actively involved in meeting the unique
  learning needs of all its members.

- cooperation among all public and private community agencies
  guarantees that the needs of every learner are met.

- cooperation between the schools and community agencies
  provides for the growth needs of citizens of all ages.

FIGURE 3.3 Example of a district vision.

parents, and the community) for each set of what-should-happen statements resulting from the beliefs analysis.
- Select a facilitator and recorder for each of the four groups.

Step 2

- Each group writes one vision statement to correspond with each of the what-should-happen statements.
- Combine similar vision statements into one integrated statement whenever possible.

Step 3

- Record the resulting vision statements and share them with the planning team as a whole.
- The planning team as a whole discusses each group's vision statements until consensus has been reached regarding all of the statements. A copy of the final district vision is distributed to each member of the planning team.

HOW TO CREATE A DISTRICT MISSION

The district mission states the overall educational purpose of the school district. A mission statement expresses in very broad and general terms why the school district exists. It sets direction and creates meaning for district educators and stakeholders. Examples of several mission statements from selected school districts are shown in Figure 3.4.

In order to effectively guide stakeholders toward a common educational destination, the district mission statement should:

- correspond to the district's philosophy and vision
- be brief enough for all stakeholders to easily remember
- use power words to motivate and inspire stakeholders
- be future-oriented to address learners' future needs
- be general enough to provide an overall framework that encompasses all learner exit outcomes

```
Evergreen School District
Vancouver, Washington

                "Empowering all students to
                 succeed in a changing world"
```

```
Rochester Public Schools
Rochester, Minnesota (draft)

                "Lifelong learning for all"
```

```
British Columbia Schools
British Columbia, Canada

      "To enable learners to develop their individual
       potential and to acquire the knowledge, skills,
       and attitudes needed to contribute to a healthy
       society and a prosperous and sustainable economy"
```

```
Aurora Public Schools,
Aurora, Colorado

           "To develop life-long learners who value
            themselves, contribute to their community,
            and succeed in a changing world"
```

FIGURE 3.4 Examples of district mission statements.

The following steps provide a guideline for developing the district mission statement.

Step 1

- Divide the district planning team into brainstorming groups of four to eight members so that each group contains representatives of diverse stakeholder groups.
- Each group selects a facilitator to keep the group on task and a recorder to take notes of the group's decisions.

Step 2

- Each brainstorming group carefully examines previously identified significant future trends and the district philosophy, beliefs analysis, and vision previously developed by the planning team. The what-should-happen statements from the beliefs analysis and district vision should be closely scrutinized.

Step 3

- Members of each brainstorming group propose mission statements and the group integrates and discusses these statements until consensus is reached on one mission statement.
- Evaluate the mission statement in terms of the five criteria for an effective mission statement listed above and, if necessary, make further modifications.
- Record the collectively agreed upon mission statement to share with the larger group.

Step 4

- The whole planning team reconvenes and each brainstorming group presents their mission statement to the group.
- The planning team as a whole discusses the proposed mission statements until they reach consensus regarding all of the statements and distribute a copy of the final district mission to each member of the planning team.

Step 5

Many school districts may already have a mission statement. In this case, the district planning team should do the following.

- Carefully examine previously identified significant future trends and the district philosophy, beliefs analysis, and vision previously developed by the planning team.
- Evaluate the current mission statement in terms of previously identified significant future trends, the district philosophy, beliefs analysis, vision, and the five criteria for an effective mission statement listed above.
- Modify the current mission statement or develop a new mission statement that better reflects previously identified significant future trends, the district philosophy, beliefs analysis, and vision.
- Record the mission statement in its final form and distribute a copy to each member of the planning team.

HOW TO DEVELOP LEARNER EXIT OUTCOMES

The final step in the strategic planning process consists of identifying a set of learner exit outcomes that describes the knowledge, skills, and attitudes that all students are expected to demonstrate upon graduation. Learner exit outcomes provide the criteria by which successful teaching and learning will be evaluated and identify the competencies required of all students for graduation. Effective learner exit outcomes:

- consist of five to ten general statements that describe learners who have the knowledge, skills, and attitudes to successfully face the challenges that await them
- include a list of competencies that each learner should be able to demonstrate in achieving each exit outcome
- emerge directly from identified significant future trends
- correspond to the district philosophy, vision, and mission
- focus on real-life roles and responsibilities
- relate to ends – not means
- provide clear enough direction to drive curriculum development and assessment
- use high-powered performance verbs
- have the capacity to impact all staff and learners, as well as the instructional process itself

An example of a set of learner exit outcomes that incorporates all of these criteria is shown in Figure 3.5.[2]

Before actually generating learner exit outcomes and the accompanying outcome competencies, members of the planning team should thoroughly familiarize themselves with previously identified significant future trends and resulting future conditions, and with the district philosophy, vision, and mission. Copies of the documents containing this information should be available to each member of the planning team.

The identification of learner exit outcomes consists of two basic processes.

1. Developing a set of general statements that broadly describes learners who have the knowledge, skills, and attitudes to live and work successfully following graduation
2. Identifying a set of competencies or performance indicators for each

PURPOSEFUL THINKER

- uses strategies to form concepts, make decisions, and solve problems
- applies a variety of integrated processes including critical and creative thinking to accomplish complex tasks
- evaluates the effectiveness of mental strategies through meaningful reflection
- demonstrates flexibility, persistence, and a sense of ethical considerations

SELF-DIRECTED LEARNER

- directs own learning
- sets well-defined goals and manages the process of achieving them
- acquires, organizes, and uses information
- initiates learning activities in the pursuit of individual interests
- applies technology to specific tasks
- applies realistic self-appraisal in selecting the content, method, and pace for learning
- integrates knowledge and skills in both familiar and new situations

EFFECTIVE COMMUNICATOR

- conveys messages through a variety of methods and materials
- adapts messages to various audiences and purposes
- engages the intended audience to understand and respond
- receives and interprets the communication of others

PRODUCTIVE WORKER

- participates as a team member in pursuit of group goals and products
- works well with individuals from diverse backgrounds
- applies conflict-management strategies
- teaches others new skills

RESPONSIBLE CITIZEN

- understands diversity and the interdependence of people in local and global communities
- demonstrates a respect for human differences
- makes informed decisions
- exercises leadership on behalf of the common good

FIGURE 3.5 Example of learner exit outcomes.

general exit outcome statement that describes what each student should be able to demonstrate in achieving that exit outcome

The following procedure outlines the steps involved in identifying learner exit outcomes.

Step 1

- Divide the district planning team into work groups of four to eight members so that each work group contains representatives of diverse stakeholder groups.
- Each work group selects a facilitator to keep the group on task and a recorder to take notes of the group's decisions.

Step 2

- Within each work group, select one future trend and carefully examine all the future conditions resulting from that trend.
- Incorporate any other relevant future trends or conditions that impact upon the selected trend. (More than one trend, or future conditions resulting from more than one trend may be incorporated into the same exit outcome when they relate closely to each other. Conversely, the same future trend may contribute to the identification of more than one exit outcome.)

Step 3

- Propose one general exit outcome that would describe a graduate possessing the ability to function effectively within the situation(s) or life role(s) described by the selected future trend and conditions. For example, *cooperation* implies that in the future:
  - work will be done collaboratively more often than competitively
  - responsibility and recognition will be given to groups more often than to individuals
  - the ability to function as a member of a group will be as important as being able to function individually
  Therefore, *productive worker* or *collaborative worker* might

be identified as one valuable exit outcome for a learner in the school district.

Step 4

- Before final acceptance of the proposed exit outcome, examine the district philosophy and vision regarding learners, and the district mission to ensure compatibility among the philosophy, vision, mission, and proposed exit outcome.
- Modify the proposed exit outcome if necessary.

Step 5

- Each work group repeats this procedure for each of the remaining future trends until each group has identified an exit outcome for each future trend on the list.
- When each work group has identified a learner exit outcome for each future trend, outcome competencies or performance indicators must be developed for each exit outcome.

Step 6

- Select one learner exit outcome and list all of the possible competencies that would indicate that a learner had achieved that outcome.
- Examine the district philosophy and vision regarding learners for other competencies that should be included.
- Integrate and discuss competencies until all members of the work group reach consensus.
- Record each learner exit outcome and accompanying competencies to share with the larger group.

Step 7

- The whole planning team reconvenes and each work group presents its exit outcomes and competencies to the larger group.
- The planning team as a whole discusses each group's proposed exit outcomes and competencies until consensus is reached on one set of learner exit outcomes and accompanying outcome competencies.

- Distribute a copy of the final set of learner exit outcomes and accompanying outcome competencies to each member of the planning team.

The relationships between future trends and conditions, the district philosophy, vision, and mission, and learner exit outcomes and outcome competencies are illustrated in Figure 3.6.

Learner exit outcomes and exit outcome competencies identified by the district planning team through this process will provide the framework for designing curriculum in all subject areas from kindergarten through grade twelve.

REVIEW ACTIVITIES

(1) As a member of the district planning team, you have been selected to explain to a group of parents from around the district how beliefs will be identified and used to develop the district philosophy.

- How would you define belief?
- What examples might you use to clarify the concept of beliefs to the parent group?
- One of the parents in the group asks you to distinguish between beliefs and values. Is there a difference between beliefs and values? If so, how would you explain the difference to the inquisitive parent?
- Why is it important to discuss future trends and their implications before trying to identify beliefs?

(2) You are facilitating a work group charged with developing a district vision that is based upon the recently completed district philosophy. Your group contains a member who is new to the district and has not participated in any of the previous activities.

- How would you explain the concept of a district vision to this new group member?
- The new group member explains that he/she has a clear vision for the school district, but the vision is contrary to some of the beliefs already contained in the district philosophy. How would you handle this situation?
- How could your group assess the school district's progress toward the vision during the next year or two?

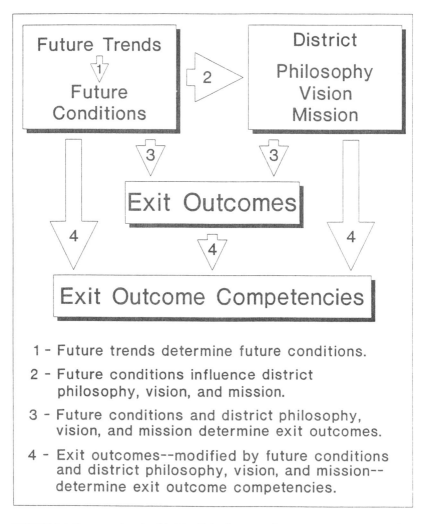

Future Trends
1
Future
Conditions

2

District
Philosophy
Vision
Mission

3   3

Exit Outcomes

4   4   4

Exit Outcome Competencies

1 - Future trends determine future conditions.

2 - Future conditions influence district philosophy, vision, and mission.

3 - Future conditions and district philosophy, vision, and mission determine exit outcomes.

4 - Exit outcomes--modified by future conditions and district philosophy, vision, and mission-- determine exit outcome competencies.

FIGURE 3.6 Processes involved in identifying learner exit outcomes and competencies.

(3) As a teacher on your district's planning team, you have been requested to head a small committee that is responsible for making sure that all district stakeholders become familiar with the newly developed mission statement.

- What other members of the planning team would you like to have on your spread-the-mission committee? Why?
- How would you ensure that all school staff members and students became familiar with the district mission?
- How would you ensure that stakeholders outside of the schools (parents, business people, and community leaders) became familiar with the district mission?
- How might your committee take advantage of the news media within the community to spread the word regarding the district mission?

(4) The district planning committee has just finalized its list of learner exit outcomes and asked you to assist in implementing these outcomes as graduation requirements for the high school in which you teach.

- Would you completely replace the current standardized graduation examination with the exit outcome competencies? If not, how would you combine them to develop a uniform set of graduation requirements for the school?
- Several teachers on staff at your high school are very uncomfortable with the idea of using exit outcome competencies as graduation requirements. How would you convince them that using exit outcome competencies as graduation requirements is in the best interest of the school's students over the long run?
- As you begin to implement the exit outcome competencies in your school, you realize that there are several critical knowledge and skill areas that have not been adequately addressed. How would you correct this oversight?
- Your principal has asked you to find several honor students in your school to help you implement the new exit outcomes as graduation requirements. However, several staff members feel uncomfortable having students work on their own graduation requirements. Would you feel uncomfortable with students identifying their own graduation requirements? Why or why not? If not, how would you convince other staff members that this situation does not create any substantial problems?

NOTES

1 The sample district philosophy is adapted from a draft produced by the Rochester Public Schools, Rochester, MN, 1991.

2 The sample learner exit outcomes are adapted from a draft of the Minnesota Department of Education Graduation Outcomes, 1993.

CHAPTER 4

Developing a Program Philosophy and Rationale Statement

THE philosophy and rationale statement for a school program, also known as a subject area curriculum or discipline, must augment a school district's philosophy, vision, mission, and exit (graduation) outcomes (see Chapter 3). The school administrator in charge of curriculum holds the responsibility to provide the destination and/or direction for the development and implementation of a comprehensive school curriculum. Curriculum development for all disciplines necessitates the establishment of a district-wide curriculum council that meets on a monthly basis during the school year.

The curriculum council should consist of professional staff in leadership positions, i.e., the curriculum director, building principals, department heads, team leaders, and others in leadership positions. Council members should be cognizant of the school district's mission, vision, philosophy, exit outcomes, program philosophies and rationale statements, program goals, program objectives, learning outcomes, learning activities, assessment, textbooks used (including publication year, edition, and condition), and so on.

A major function of the curriculum council is to develop a sequence and review cycle for district-wide curriculum development. For example, a typical five-year cycle is illustrated in Table 4.1.

The curriculum council should also select teacher representation for curriculum development. The representatives should be chosen using one of five methods: voluntary, rotation, evolvement, peer selection, or administrative selection.[1]

The procedure for developing a district-wide language arts English program philosophy and rationale statement and examples of the declarations are presented in this chapter.

PROCEDURE

To develop a sound philosophy for a language arts English program (or any school program), a language arts English program committee

Table 4.1. Typical Five-Year Curriculum Development Cycle.

1993 – 1994:	Language Arts English	1998 – 1999
1994 – 1995:	Science and Social Studies	1999 – 2000
1995 – 1996:	Fine Arts	2000 – 2001
1996 – 1997:	Mathematics and Health	2001 – 2002
1997 – 1998:	All Others	2002 – 2003

(also known as a subject area committee) must be established for the initial phase. The steps for structuring, along with responsibilities for the committee, are as follows.

Step 1

- The school district superintendent and board of education must approve the process for district-wide curriculum development.
- The curriculum council should form a language arts English program committee comprised of language arts English teachers representing all grade levels (K – 12), preferably two teachers from each grade level. In smaller districts, however, one teacher per three grade/course levels is satisfactory (with feedback from those teaching the other grade/course levels).
- Building principals (or designees) from the elementary, middle level or junior high school, and senior high school must be members of the committee as well, preferably with one principal (or designee) from each level.
- The school district curriculum director (or designee) should serve as chairperson and be responsible for organizing and directing the activities of the language arts English program committee.
- The school district's board of education should be informed by the board curriculum committee about the process used for program (curriculum) development.
- All language arts English program committee members must have a thorough understanding of the school district's philosophy, vision, mission, and exit (graduation) outcomes to enable committee members to blend them into the language arts English program philosophy and rational statement.
- The Dialogue Technique,[2] the Delphi Technique,[3] the Fishbowl Technique,[4] the Telstar Technique,[5] or the Nominal Group

Technique[6] should be used to guide the language arts English program committee in developing a program philosophy.

- The number of meetings to complete the task of writing a program philosophy by the language arts English program committee should be limited to three or four during the school year.
- The curriculum meetings should be held in a comfortable environment, i.e., comfortable work seats, circular seating arrangement, tables with room for participants to spread their papers out, and good acoustics. Name tents for the participants should be made by folding a piece of paper that will stand on its own.

Step 2

- Immediately after completion of the language arts English program philosophy, disseminate it to the language arts English staff and building administrators throughout the school district for their input. Grade- and department-level meetings should be organized by the building principals to peruse the program philosophy developed by the committee.
- A timeline for return of the program philosophy with additions, corrections, or deletions from noncommittee language arts English staff and administrators is one week.

Step 3

- After the language arts English program philosophy is returned to the curriculum director, the original language arts English program committee should re-assemble to consider the additions, corrections, and/or deletions that are suggested by noncommittee language arts English staff and administrators.

Step 4

- The completed language arts English program philosophy is now ready to be given to the school superintendent and board of education for approval.
- After approval by the school superintendent and board of education, the language arts English program philosophy is

given to the language arts English writing committee responsible for writing the language arts English program scope and sequence, program goals, objectives, learning outcomes, and authentic tasks.

The step-by-step process should be used to develop a program philosophy, followed by the same procedure to develop a program rationale statement (see Figure 4.1, which represents this top-down as well as bottom-up process).

The process heightens commitment by the district language arts English staff, building administrators, central administration, and the board of education to the language arts English program.

Sample Language Arts English Program Philosophy [7]

Learning is a complex process of discovery, cooperation, and inquiry, and is facilitated by the language arts English program. The language processes of listening, speaking, reading, writing, viewing, and representing are interrelated and interdependent. Language is not only systematic and rule-governed, but also dynamic and evolving, facilitating communication with others and flexibility of meaning. Through interaction with the social, cultural, intellectual, emotional, and physical components of the environment, the learner acquires language developmentally along a continuum.

Language learning thrives when learners are engaged in meaningful use of language. The process of constructing meaning is influenced by the learners' previous knowledge, attitudes, experiences, and abilities. All forms of communication, oral and written, expressive and receptive, are equally valuable. The language arts English program utilizes an integrated approach which treats skills as part of all subject areas. Through the study of language, literature, and media, students broaden their experiences, weigh personal values against those of others, become appreciative of the past, sensitive to the present, and inquisitive about the future.

The language arts English program accommodates each learner's abilities, interests, and background by allowing for a range of learning styles, teaching styles, instructional strategies, and resources. The program supports a classroom environment that encourages mutual respect, risk taking, and experimentation. Effective evaluation is an integral part of the learning process. Continual evaluation that encompasses both process and product and both cognitive and affective domains allows

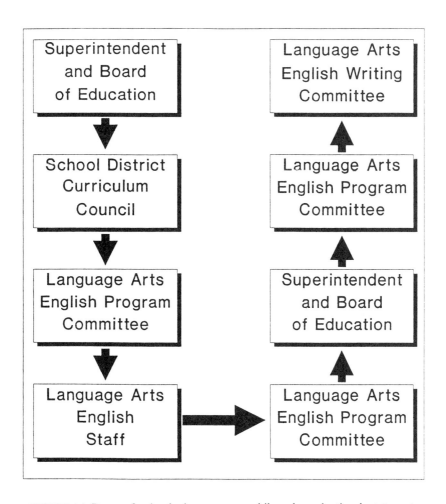

FIGURE 4.1 Process for developing a program philosophy and rationale statement.

each learner to take ownership of and responsibility for learning. The learner is already processing information and constructing meaning when formal schooling begins and continues to refine the processes of communication throughout the years of formal education and beyond.

Sample Language Arts English Program Rationale Statement [8]

The language skills and processes developed through the language arts English program are central to successful achievement in all subject areas and equip students with skills necessary to pursue learning throughout life. Students who read, write, speak, represent, view, and listen with intelligence, empathy, respect, and discrimination will develop the skills in thinking and communication, as well as the attitudes and knowledge that will prepare them for active participation in a complex society.

The language arts English program allows students to better understand themselves and others. The reading and study of literature enhance the aesthetic, imaginative, creative, and affective aspects of a person's development. Literature preserves and extends the imaginative power of individuals. It allows young people to explore imaginatively the places where they live and provides them with an understanding of cultural heritage and a historical perspective, exposing them to points of view other than the present and personal.

- Through fiction, the reader has the power to be transported in time and place, to experience vicariously places, people, and events otherwise unavailable.
- Through poems, the reader may achieve heightened perceptions of the world, sharpened senses, clarified thoughts, and broadened emotions.
- Through drama, the participant continually renews a sense of the vitality and complexity of human actions.
- Through nonfiction, the reader accesses a wide range of possibilities, opinions, and interpretations.

The electronic media provide a similar range of possibilities and furnish material for experience and study. In addition, the study of literature and of media provides models of effective and varied language use for students to draw upon in their own compositions.

The language arts English program encourages students to develop meaning, both through active response to others' work and through their own speaking and writing. Through speaking and writing, students learn to clarify thought, emotion, and experience, and to share these ideas, emotions, and experiences with others. Like reading, writing is a source of pleasure, enjoyment, and knowledge. It is a way to experience the delight and wonder in everyday life.

Writing proves the opportunity for careful organization of one's picture of reality and stimulates development of the precision, clarity, and imagination required for effective communication. In this way writing is socially valuable, one of the ways individuals engage in and contribute to the activities and knowledge of society. Writing is personally valuable, and is also an important means of learning within this program and all other subject areas. It allows students to create personal meaning out of the information offered in and out of school.

Education today increasingly emphasizes evaluation and analysis skills, critical thinking, problem-solving strategies, organizing and reference skills, synthesis, application of ideas, creativity, decision making, and communication skills through a variety of modes. All these skills and processes are based in language use; all are the material of a language program; all are developed through the language arts English program at Anytown School District, U.S.A.

REVIEW ACTIVITIES

(1) What advantages do the Dialogue Technique, the Delphi Technique, the Fishbowl Technique, the Telstar Technique, and the Nominal Group Technique have over other ways groups make decisions? What advantage does one technique have over another? What disadvantages does each technique have? (See ''Notes'' section for details on each of these techniques.)

(2) Why must a curriculum council and program committee have a thorough understanding of the school district's philosophy, vision, mission, and exit outcomes?

(3) What characterizes a program philosophy? What characterizes a program rationale statement?

NOTES

1 The five methods for choosing teacher representation for curriculum development have advantages and disadvantages. Discussion of each method of selection and recommendations as to when it should be used follow.

Voluntary

The advantages of the voluntary method are:

- people who volunteer are interested in the program
- the use of volunteers is an open, democratic process

The disadvantages of this method are:

- incompetents may volunteer
- calling for volunteers may indicate unimportance of the task

Recommended use:

- when everyone is acceptable

Rotation

The advantages of the rotation method are:

- all possible participants can eventually be involved in curriculum development
- rotating eliminates the need for selection

The disadvantages of this method are:

- there is little or no continuity
- there is an assumption that all eligible participants have equal ability

Recommended use:

- when the rotating membership will not hinder the development of an acceptable process or product

Evolvement

The advantages of the evolvement method are:

- it produces leadership from the group
- cooperation from committee members is high because they choose the leader or representative through their own process

Disadvantages of this method are:

- the evolvement process is feasible only in a long-term situation
- emerged leaders exist without recognized authority

Recommended use:

- when determining who the most competent teachers are in curriculum development

Peer Selection

The advantages of the peer selection method are:

- committee members feel that they have control over their own destiny
- cooperation is more likely

The disadvantages of this method are:

- committee representatives may be chosen for the wrong reasons
- groups do not always know the kind of leadership or representation they need

Recommended use:

- when the group has maturity and experience

Administrative Selection

The advantages of the administrative selection method are:

- it tends to legitimize a committee member's position
- administrators generally know who the best qualified people are

The disadvantages of this method are:

- administrators may not know who the best qualified people are for curriculum development
- it can have negative implications if the selections were based on politics rather than reason

Recommended use:

- when peer selection is not practical

2 The main characteristic of the Dialogue Technique is that participants in the process are expected to rely more on dialogue to make decisions and less on individual preparation.

- Participants do not deal with content decision making until they are in the actual development process with other participants.
- The dialogue approach gives participants the opportunity to listen to other views that will either contradict or support their positions.
- The dialogue approach gives participants the opportunity to acquire ownership of a group product.

3 The Delphi Technique is a method for reaching consensus without the need for face-to-face meetings of all participants.

- Each member of the program committee writes a philosophy statement which they submit to the curriculum director.
- The philosophy statement, written by each committee member, is copied and distributed to all members on the program committee.
- Each committee member reviews the written philosophy statements and indicates which ones are germane.
- The curriculum director places the philosophy statements into two columns, one for those which are mostly agreed upon and one for those which general agreement was not found.
- The most agreed-upon philosophy statements are resubmitted to committee members and the process repeated until consensus is reached.

4 The Fishbowl Technique is one where representatives from each of a large number of subgroups meet to reach consensus on a list of philosophy statements.

- Subgroups of six to eight participants meet and develop a philosophy statement.
- One elected representative from each subgroup meets with representatives from the other groups who will bring their own group's philosophy statement.
- The representatives sit in a circle facing each other while all others remain seated outside the circle.
- Representatives within the circle discuss each of the subgroup's philosophy statements until consensus is reached.

5 The Telstar Technique is similar to the Fishbowl Technique but differs in the method of involving all committee members and their degree of involvement.

- The large group is divided into subgroups with each group representing specific grade level groupings (e.g., primary grades, intermediate grades, middle level or junior high school, and senior high school).
- Two representatives are elected from each group to represent that group and bring their completed philosophy statement to the group of all representatives.
- Each two-member delegation may be joined by a small advisory committee from their constituency.
- Any member of an advisory committee can stop the discussion at any time to meet with his or her representatives regarding the issue at hand.
- This procedure continues until a general consensus is reached among all representatives.

6 The Nominal Group Technique is a process that encourages divergence by individuals.

- A small group convenes to focus on a program philosophy. Members of the group work on an identified task, which is to develop a program philosophy, in the presence of each other, but without any immediate interaction.
- Once the task of developing a program philosophy is explained by the curriculum director, group members are given time (twenty to thirty minutes), wherein each individual will write a program philosophy.
- After time has expired, the committee members present the program philosophies one at a time. The program philosophies are posted. No discussion of alternative philosophies takes place until all program philosophies have been disclosed.
- Following disclosure, committee members rank the program philosophies presented and start the process over, considering the top three program philosophies.
- After individual committee members have chosen and modified one of the three program philosophies, one is selected by the committee to be adopted as the program philosophy.
- A disadvantage of the process is that during the initial

brainstorming no interaction exists for one's idea to inspire another. However, because committee members know that each member is developing a program philosophy and that everyone's philosophy will be displayed, the competitive pressure establishes impetus.

7 The language arts English program philosophy statement was excerpted from the *Language Arts English Primary – Graduation Curriculum Guide.* 1992. Ministry of Education, Province of British Columbia, Victoria, BC, Canada, p. 12.

8 The language arts English rationale statement was excerpted from the *Language Arts English Primary – Graduation Curriculum Guide.* 1992. Ministry of Education, Province of British Columbia, Victoria, BC, Canada, p. 13.

CHAPTER 5

Developing a Scope and Sequence, Program Goals, Objectives, Learning Outcomes, and Authentic Tasks

TO make a scope and sequence for a program, program goals, objectives for the program goals, learning outcomes for the objectives, and authentic tasks (authentic tasks are explained in Chapter 7) for the learning outcomes (practical and results-centered) for students, they must be correlated with the district's philosophy, vision, mission, exit (graduation) outcomes, and the program's philosophy and rationale statement. This chapter presents procedures for developing these program elements.

THE COMMITTEE STRUCTURE

To develop a scope and sequence, program goals, objectives, learning outcomes, and authentic tasks for any school program, a subject area writing committee must be established. The steps for structuring the committee, along with responsibilities follow.

Step 1

- The writing committee is selected by and from the program committee members. It must be made up of teachers representing all grade levels (K − 12) and preferably two staff members from each grade grouping: primary, intermediate, middle level or junior high school, and high school. In smaller school districts one teacher per three-grade/course level is satisfactory so long as there is feedback from those teaching the other grade/course levels.
- A building principal or designee from the elementary, middle level or junior high school, and senior high school must be represented on the committee.
- The school district curriculum director or designee should serve

as chairperson and be responsible for organizing and directing the activities of the writing committee.

- The school district's board of education must be apprised by the board curriculum committee about the process used to write curricula.
- The writing committee work space must be in a comfortable environment, i.e., comfortable work seats, tables to spread their papers out, good acoustics, access to the district's curriculum lab containing sample courses of study and program textbooks, and clerical assistance.
- The ideal time to develop and write the program scope and sequence, program goals, objectives, learning outcomes, and authentic tasks is after the school year is completed. One week to ten days is a normal timeline for a writing committee to complete the writing exercise for a program or subject area.
- Reasonable stipends or an extended contract should be given to members of the writing committee.
- All writing committee members must understand and be able to write meaningful program goals and objectives.[1]
- The writing committee must be informed that the process for developing a course of study – the language arts program, for example – entails the following sequential tasks.
  - Review and use the school district's philosophy, vision, mission, and exit (graduation) outcomes for developing a course of study for the specified program.
  - Review and use the specified program philosophy and rationale statement developed by the language arts English program committee for developing a course of study for the language arts English program.
  - Develop a language arts English program scope and sequence matrix for the K – 12 grade levels (see illustrations on pp. 67 – 68).
  - Develop language arts English program goals (usually seven or nine) that are driven by the exit (graduation) outcomes (see examples provided in this chapter).
  - Develop language arts English program objectives (usually six to nine) for each program goal (see examples provided in this chapter).
  - Develop language arts English program learning outcomes for the objectives (i.e., primary, elementary intermediate,

middle level or junior high, and high school; see examples provided in this chapter).
   – Develop language arts English program authentic tasks for the learning outcomes (see examples provided in this chapter).
   – Develop criterion-referenced test items for the developed program (curriculum). If this is not possible, an item analysis of the standardized tests used should be made.
   – Correlate the program scope and sequence, program goals, objectives, learning outcomes, and authentic tasks with textbooks and learning materials.
   – Include learning materials for each learning outcome and authentic task.
• The Dialogue Technique should be used to guide the language arts English writing committee (see Chapter 4 for an explanation of the technique).

Step 2

• After the program scope and sequence, program goals, objectives, learning outcomes, and authentic tasks have been written, they must be distributed to all language arts English teachers and building administrators throughout the school district for additions, corrections, and/or deletions during the school year. Teachers and administrators should be given four to six weeks to return the document to the curriculum director or designee.
• During the four- to six-week district-wide review period for the program scope and sequence, program goals, objectives, learning outcomes, and authentic tasks, grade-level and department meetings at the building level must be utilized to peruse the document. Members of the writing committee should be used as consultants (to provide clarification) at the grade-level and department meetings.

Step 3

• After receiving the corrected program documents from district-wide noncommittee language arts English grade- and course-level teachers and administrators, the curriculum director (or designee) must re-assemble the writing committee to consider the additions, corrections, and/or deletions suggested.

Step 4

- After the language arts English program course of study (curriculum resource guide) is completed with suitable additions, corrections, and/or deletions suggested, the document should be given to the school superintendent and the school board curriculum committee to present it to the board of education for district-wide adoption and implementation.

Step 5

- Once the language arts English program course of study (curriculum resource guide) is adopted, a textbook review committee, encompassing members from the language arts English writing committee, is selected by that committee. Membership must include one person representing each grade and course level.
- Members on the textbook review committee must evaluate and rank each language arts English series (using a textbook selection guide)[2] from the various publishing companies for their grade level.
- The entire language arts English staff should consider for review the three highest ranked textbook series, selected by the textbook review committee.
- The language arts English program scope and sequence, program goals, objectives, learning outcomes, and authentic tasks should be submitted to the three highest-ranked publishing companies selected by the textbook review committee for their review and presentation to the district-wide language arts English staff.
- The presentations by the three selected publishing company representatives should be scheduled during the school year, preferably with one presentation each day.
- All language arts English staff and school principals must be invited to attend. Voting rights are granted only to those who attend all three presentations by the publishing company representatives.

- The textbook series preferred by a majority of staff for the language arts English program must be submitted, with rationale for the selection and cost to the district, to the school superintendent and the school board curriculum committee for presentation to the school board for adoption.

Step 6

- Appropriate in-service activities must be planned for the language arts English staff to accommodate the newly developed language arts English course of study (curriculum resource guide). Some in-service activities may need to take place before the program is implemented and some should take place after teachers have implemented the program.

Step 7

- Evaluation of the language arts English program must be an ongoing process and in-flight corrections should be made until the next five-year cycle. The curriculum director should have expertise in program (curriculum) evaluation.

The step-by-step process should be used to develop a course of study (curriculum resource guide) for all programs in the public schools. As illustrated in Figure 5.1, this top-down, bottom-up model will engage the process of planning, implementing, and evaluating in such a way that the work of content experts—the teachers—is facilitated.

The process described will consolidate the efforts of staff, district administrators, and the board of education. Teachers, especially, will be advocates of a program if the process permits them to be the decision makers.

SAMPLES OF PROGRAM SCOPE AND SEQUENCE, PROGRAM GOAL, EXIT OUTCOMES MET, OBJECTIVES, LEARNING OUTCOMES, AND AUTHENTIC TASKS[3]

The following are examples of a scope and sequence matrix, a program goal,[4] objectives for the program goal, learning outcomes for the objectives, and authentic tasks for the learning outcomes of a language arts English curriculum. The program goal is driven by exit

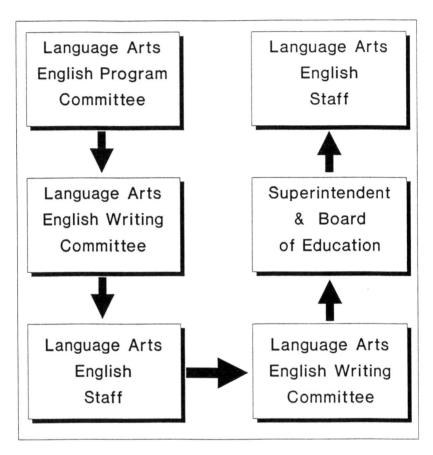

FIGURE 5.1 Process for developing a course of study for the language arts English program.

(graduation) outcomes, and the objectives, which constitute the program goal illustrated, are given specific implementation direction (scope and sequence) at the proposed groupings of primary, elementary intermediate, middle level or junior high, and high school.

Sample Scope and Sequence Matrix for the Objectives of a Language Arts English Program

P EI ML/JH HS	These indicate the proposed groupings which are primary, elementary intermediate, middle level/junior high, and high school.
O	Indicates an orientation stage. Preparatory activities are undertaken prior to the explicit teaching and learning activities suggested in the learning outcomes related to the objective. Refer to learning outcomes at the next stage if appropriate.
E	Indicates an emphasis stage. Learning outcomes are suggested in this course of study (curriculum resource guide) as examples of appropriate authentic tasks (activities) and observable behaviors. Explicit teaching and learning activities are expected.
M	Indicates a maintenance stage. Provisions are made to reinforce learning outcomes and authentic tasks related to the objective.

Continue on to the program goal and exit outcomes met that follow.

Program Goal #1

To develop the knowledge, skills, and processes needed to communicate effectively by listening, speaking, reading, writing, viewing, and representing.

Exit Outcomes Met

1. A purposeful thinker who . . . (see Figure 3.5 on p. 42)
2. A self-directed learner who . . . (see Figure 3.5 on p. 42)
3. An effective communicator who . . . (see Figure 3.5 on p. 42)
4. A responsible citizen who . . . (see Figure 3.5 on p. 42)

Continue on to the objectives that follow.

Objectives	P	EI	ML/JH	SH
Students will be able to:				
1.1 Identify reasons for communicating	E	E	E	E
1.2 Communicate ideas with clarity and precision	E	E	E	E
1.3 Experience satisfaction and confidence in the communication skills and processes	E	E	E	E
1.4 Produce, explore, and extend ideas and information	E	E	E	E
1.5 Read and examine independently, by choosing appropriate strategies and processes	O	E	E	E
1.6 Comprehend that the communication skills and processes are interrelated avenues for constructing meaning	E	E	M	M

Continue on to the learning outcomes and authentic tasks that follow.

Learning Outcomes and Authentic Tasks for a Language Arts English Program

Objective 1.1: Students will be able to identify reasons for communicating.

Primary Grades
Students will be able to:
1.1.1 Recognize why they are communicating
   Authentic task: Students will express feelings, solve problems, or confirm the meaning of a message.
1.1.2 Discuss the purposes of communicating
   Authentic task: Students will make a classroom chart on "Why We Read."
1.1.3 Plan and lead classroom activities
   Authentic task: Students will chair news time, act as spokesperson for a small group, or introduce a visitor.

1.1.4   Listen to and follow directions to perform a new activity
Authentic task: Students will playact a new game.

1.1.5   Choose to read for a variety of purposes
Authentic task: Students will read for enjoyment, to find new ideas, or to confirm ideas.

1.1.6   Choose to write for a variety of purposes
Authentic task: Students will write to request information, to express gratitude, or for entertainment.

1.1.7   Compose notes and lists to themselves
Authentic task: Students will write a list of telephone numbers or a reminder note to return library books.

1.1.8   Engage in prewriting discussion
Authentic task: Students will choose a topic, focus ideas, or clarify purpose.

1.1.9   Use a grid, chart, graph, cluster, or web to organize information
Authentic task: Students will organize collected facts from researching an animal.

Elementary Intermediate Grades
Students will be able to:

1.1.10   Describe the broad purposes that are common to communication skills and processes
Authentic task: Students will advise, command, direct, entertain, inform, persuade, or socialize.

1.1.11   Arrange their own specific purposes that identify the desired result and focus attention
Authentic task: Students will tune in to the radio news to get information on a specific item.

1.1.12   Arrange their own purposes for listening
Authentic task: Students will listen attentively to a poem to form sensory images.

1.1.13   Organize their own purposes for speaking
Authentic task: Students will make a speech to express a personal point of view.

1.1.14   Determine their own purposes for reading
Authentic task: Students will read a selection to answer specific questions.

1.1.15   Determine their own purposes for writing
Authentic task: Students will record observations to write a science report.

1.1.16 Arrange their own purposes for viewing
  Authentic task: Students will analyze T.V. commercials to identify persuasive techniques.
1.1.17 Determine their own purposes for representing
  Authentic task: Students will develop a diagram to organize similarities when comparing two opinions.
1.1.18 Identify the purposes of other people's communication
  Authentic task: Students will recognize propaganda and the desire to convince in a biased presentation.
1.1.19 Recognize the purposes of various media
  Authentic task: Students will infer that television aims to entertain, to inform, and to persuade.

Middle Level/Junior High
Students will be able to:
1.1.20 Recognize the broad purposes that are common to communication skills and processes
  Authentic task: Students will do controlling, imaging, informing, and socializing.
1.1.21 Identify the audience at which communication is addressed
  Authentic task: Students will communicate with adults, friends, or relatives.
1.1.22 Recognize and focus attention on the desired result of communication
  Authentic task: Students will write a letter of complaint or speak to a group in order to raise funds for a project.
1.1.23 Engage in preparatory activities for listening, speaking, and viewing
  Authentic task: Students will recall prior knowledge of the topic or predict what could be learned about a topic.
1.1.24 Establish a purpose for speaking
  Authentic task: Students will give a formal speech to persuade a group to accept a personal point of view.
1.1.25 Create a purpose for representing
  Authentic task: Students will use a chart to show similarities of themes in American literature.

1.1.26 Recognize persuasive techniques
    Authentic task: Students will recognize bias, propaganda, use of connotation, and use of emotive language.

High School
Students will be able to:
1.1.27 Employ language strategies and processes that are most likely to elicit the desired results
    Authentic task: Students will choose between a telephone call or letter to deal with business.
1.1.28 Identify the audience at which a communication is to be directed
    Authentic task: Students will choose peers, adults, or special interest groups as the appropriate audience.
1.1.29 Select the desired result of a communication
    Authentic task: Students will write a letter of application or a student council letter of request to the principal.
1.1.30 Appraise the difference between active and passive listening by discussing which activities require no effort on the part of the listener and which will demand full attention
    Authentic task: Students will decide that background music is passive listening and listening for a main idea is active listening.
1.1.31 Develop and apply criteria to evaluate what is heard
    Authentic task: Students will utilize criteria agreed to by the class, such as the main idea, details, and examples to be applied to class speeches.
1.1.32 Identify main ideas
    Authentic task: Students will write down the main ideas after hearing a passage read or paraphrasing a speaker's message orally or in written form.
1.1.33 Distinguish fact from opinion
    Authentic task: Students will, after listening to a reading, list orally or in writing what is fact and what is opinion.
1.1.34 Recognize the influence of the listener's bias or perception
    Authentic task: Students will examine possible preconceived ideas on a topic before the class hears a speech.

1.1.35 Recognize a speaker's purpose and bias
    Authentic task: Students will peruse differences between
                         speeches from the opposing sides on an issue
                         as such capital punishment.

Each program goal should also list a wide variety of resources, accessible to the staff, to help students accomplish the exit outcomes. Examples of resources include textbooks, textbook activities, novels, nonfiction books, anthologies, collections, handbooks, dramas, selected readings from reserved material in the library or classroom, printed handouts, kits, periodicals, transparency sets, filmstrips, films, video recordings, audio recordings, and computer software. The language arts English staff should have an updated inventory of materials available that lists where each is located, such as in the classroom, departmental media center, school media center, district media center, regional media center, or state media center.

The program (curriculum) development process described is a design-down, deliver-up model (see Figure 5.2). Samples of scope and sequence, program goal, objectives for the program goal, learning outcomes, and authentic tasks provided should enable a school district to develop an outcome-based education program. Once a program is developed, teachers can easily develop unit plans and daily lesson plans for their students. A variety of teaching strategies that teachers can use to connect students with subject matter are presented in Chapter 6; ways to assess student performance are provided in Chapter 7; and considering alternative approaches for restructuring school organization are illuminated in Chapter 8.

INDICATORS OF EFFECTIVE CURRICULUM DEVELOPMENT[5]

How can a developed and implemented curriculum be measured for effectiveness? The ten indicators listed below should be considered when measuring curriculum effectiveness.

1. *Vertical curriculum continuity* – The course of study reflects a K – 12 format which enables teachers to have quick and constant access to what is being taught in the grade levels below and above them. Also, upward spiraling prevents undue or useless curricular repetition.
2. *Horizontal curriculum continuity* – The course of study developed

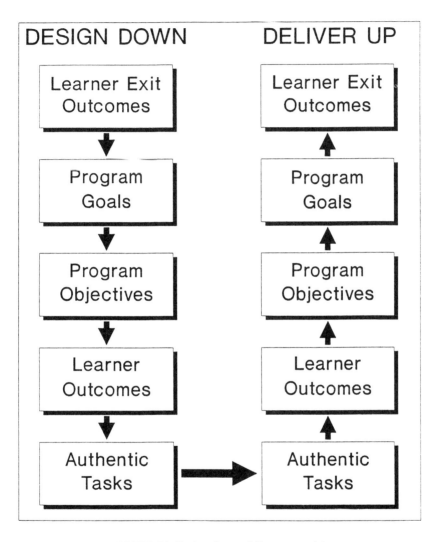

FIGURE 5.2 Design-down, deliver-up model.

provides content and objectives which are common to all classrooms of the same grade level. Also, daily lesson plans reflect a commonality for the same grade level.

3. *Instruction based on curriculum* — Lesson plans are derived from the course of study, and curriculum materials used are correlated with the content, objectives, and authentic tasks developed.

4. *Curriculum priority* — Philosophical and financial commitments are evident. Clerical assistance is provided and reasonable stipends are paid to teachers for work during the summer months. Additionally, curriculum topics appear on school board agendas, administrative meeting agendas, and building-staff meeting agendas.

5. *Broad involvement* — Buildings in the district have teacher representatives on the curricular committees; elementary, middle level or junior high, and high school principals (or designees) are represented; and school board members are apprised of and approve the course of study.

6. *Long-range planning* — Each program in the district is included in the five-year sequence and review cycle. Also, a philosophy of education and theory of curriculum permeate the entire school district.

7. *Decision-making clarity* — Controversies that occur during the development of a program center on the nature of the decision, and not on who makes the decision.

8. *Positive human relations* — All participating members are willing to risk disagreeing with anyone else; however, communication lines are not allowed to break down. Also, the initial thoughts about the curriculum come from teachers, principals, and the curriculum leader.

9. *Theory-into-practice approach* — The district philosophy, vision, mission, exit (graduation) outcomes, program philosophy, rationale statement, program goals, program objectives, learning outcomes, and authentic tasks are consistent and recognizable.

10. *Planned change* — There is tangible evidence that the internal and external publics accept the developed program course of study for the school district.

The process of developing a course of study for each program or discipline in a school district is no longer one of determining how to do it, but one of determining how to do it better. Developing a program's course of study assures continuity of instruction across grade levels and, subsequently, allows a smoother transition from one grade level to the next. It is a road map for staff and students in a district.

REVIEW ACTIVITIES

(1) Identify interrelationships that exist between scope and sequence, program goals, objectives, learning outcomes, and authentic tasks.

(2) Explain how developing a course of study (curriculum resource guide) facilitates the teacher as content expert.

(3) Outline responsibilities for the program committee.

(4) Distinguish the responsibilities of the subject writing committee from those of the program committee.

(5) Plan an in-service activity for the staff to accommodate a newly developed course of study.

(6) Assess the indicators of effective curriculum development.

NOTES

1 A taxonomy of thinking guide is often useful in developing new programs (see Figure 5.3).

2 An example of a textbook selection guide to be used by a textbook review committee is illustrated in Figure 5.4.

3 The language arts English program scope and sequence, program goal, objectives, and learning outcomes were excerpted from the *Language Arts English Primary – Graduation Curriculum Guide.* 1992. Ministry of Education, Province of British Columbia, Victoria, BC, Canada, pp. 18 – 30.

4 The program goals listed, including Program Goal #1 listed in this chapter, were excerpted from the *Language Arts English – Primary Graduation Curriculum Guide.* 1992. Ministry of Education, Province of British Columbia, Victoria, BC, Canada, pp. 19 – 27. The nine goals for the language arts English program are as follows.

- Program Goal #1 develops the knowledge, skills, and processes needed to communicate effectively by listening, speaking, reading, writing, and representing.

CATEGORIES	CUE WORDS	
KNOWLEDGE Recall Remembering previously learned information	Cluster Define Label List Match Memorize Name Observe	Outline/ Format stated Recall Recognize Record Recount State
COMPREHENSION Translate Grasping the meaning	Cite Describe Document/ Support Explain Express Give Examples Identify	Locate Paraphrase Recognize Restate Report Review Summarize Tell
APPLICATION Generalize Using learning in new and concrete situations	Apply Dramatize Frame How to Illustrate Imagine Imitate	Imagine Manipulate Organize Sequence Show/Demonstrate Solve Use

ANALYSIS
Break Down/Discover
Breaking down an idea
into component parts so
that it may be more
easily understood
	Analyze
	Characterize
	Classify/
	  Categorize
	Compare/
	  Contrast
	Dissect
	Distinguish/
	  Differentiate
		Examine
		Infer
		Map
		Outline/No
		  format given
		Relate to
		Select
		Survey

SYNTHESIS Compose Putting together to form a new whole	Combine Compose Construct Design Develop Emulate Formulate Hypothesize	Imagine/ Speculate Invent Plan Produce Propose Revise

EVALUATION
Judge
Judging value for
a given purpose
	Appraise
	Argue
	Assess
	Compare/
	  Pros-Cons
	Consider
	Criticize
	Decide
	Evaluate
		Justify
		Judge
		Prioritize/
		  Rank
		Recommend
		Summarize
		Support
		Value

FIGURE 5.3 Taxonomy of thinking.

```
              ANY  SCHOOL  DISTRICT   NO.  3
                     Any  Town,  USA
       LANGUAGE  ARTS  ENGLISH  TEXTBOOK  SELECTION  GUIDE


    (Textbook)          (Publishing Company)      (Grade Level)

Rate each characteristic listed for the textbook on a scale of
1 to 5.  Circle your choice and total your ratings to obtain a
single overall measure for each textbook reviewed.

CONTENT                                       Low         High

1. Matches the program objectives             1   2   3   4   5

2. Presents up-to-date accurate information    1   2   3   4   5

3. Avoids stereotyping by race, ethnicity,     1   2   3   4   5
   and gender

4. Stimulates student interest                 1   2   3   4   5

ORGANIZATION AND STYLE

1. Is clearly written                          1   2   3   4   5

2. Use language and style appropriate for      1   2   3   4   5
   students

3. Develops a logical sequence                 1   2   3   4   5

4. Contains useful practical exercises         1   2   3   4   5

5. Provides thorough reviews and summaries     1   2   3   4   5

6. Includes clearly outlined table of          1   2   3   4   5
   contents and index

7. Includes helpful student aids such as       1   2   3   4   5
   illustrations, charts, etc.

8. Provides practical teacher aids such as     1   2   3   4   5
   lesson plans, test questions, etc

PHYSICAL FEATURES

1. Has attractive cover                        1   2   3   4   5

2. Presents up-to-date, interesting            1   2   3   4   5
   illustrations and photographs

3. Has well designed page layout               1   2   3   4   5

4. Uses clear type appropriate for students    1   2   3   4   5

5. Has durable binding                         1   2   3   4   5

                           Sub Totals  =

                           TOTAL       =       _____

Evaluator _____    Grade Level/Subject _____
```

FIGURE 5.4 Sample textbook selection guide.

- Program Goal #2 develops knowledge, understanding, and appreciation of language and how it is used.
- Program Goal #3 develops knowledge, understanding, and appreciation of a wide variety of literary genres and media forms.
- Program Goal #4 develops knowledge, understanding, and appreciation of American and other world literature.
- Program Goal #5 develops and extends knowledge of self, the world, and our multicultural heritage through language, literature, and media.
- Program Goal #6 extends capacity for creative thought and expression within the context of language, literature, and media.
- Program Goal #7 extends capacity for critical thought and expression within the context of language, literature, and media.
- Program Goal #8 develops the wide variety of strategies for learning.
- Program Goal #9 develops attributes of wonder, curiosity, independence, and interdependence necessary for lifelong learning.

5 The ten indicators of effective curriculum development were excerpted from Bradley, L. H. 1985. *Curriculum Leadership and Development Handbook.* Englewood, NJ: Prentice-Hall, Inc.

CHAPTER 6

Delivering Outcome-Based Education

TO connect the student with subject matter, which one of the two statements listed below would you select?

- The instructional strategy is thc tool of the teacher's trade.
- Instructional strategies are the tools of the teacher's trade.

If you selected the first statement, which is singular, chances are that you believe that teaching is a one-dimensional form of behavior. If your choice was the second statement, which is plural, you are the richer teacher because you have a large repertoire of behavior models.

Cognitive psychologists like Ausubel, Bruner, Glasser, Piaget, Taba, Torrance, and others contend that people prefer to learn in creative ways through problem-solving activities. Their research shows that learning can be achieved more effectively and economically in creative ways rather than by authority. In contrast, some teachers continue to insist that it is more prudent to learn by authority.

The argument for authoritarian-type teaching is meaningless because students are not one-dimensional creatures. Consequently, no single form of teaching behavior, no single plan, and no single device will accommodate students' full development. To deny students the multiplicity of teaching strategies ignores the individuality of students. When we as teachers curb the complexness of students, we diminish their intellectual, social, and emotional growth. When we as teachers facilitate the complexness of students, we augment their intellectual, social, and emotional growth.

If the strategies of instruction that engage students in using their minds are scorned, there is a high probability that students will not connect with the subject matter, the curriculum is likely to be artificial and irrelevant, and concrete activities are apt to be turned into abstract exercises. No school will want to admit to being unproductive. The cost is too great to students and society, and research on productive learning is spurned.

TEACHING STRATEGIES THAT ENHANCE
AUTHENTIC LEARNING

The purpose of this segment on teaching strategies is to offer all teachers, preservice as well as experienced, the opportunity for introspection and growth. Since many teachers have used one or more of the teaching strategies presented, they are encouraged to continue. For those teachers who are one-dimensional, they are enlisted to use one or more of the teaching strategies to amplify their students' intellectual, emotional, and social growth.

Production-Driven Learning

When students create a real product or perform before a live audience they are involved in production-driven learning. Examples of this strategy are, among others, a class-produced newspaper and a classroom circus performed by the members in the class. What do students learn from putting on a circus? In addition to vocabulary words, first-grade students practiced reading, writing, oral language, counting, and number recognition. As Sprague[1] attests, the students "learned with intensity. Two months of instruction were enhanced because of a two-hour event."

Problem-Based Learning

Problem-based learning engages students in solving problems by having them take on the roles of scientists, lawyers, doctors, teachers, historians, artists, and other roles in the workplace. To make an authentic learning condition, the problem statement is the key to problem-based learning. For example, a problem statement could focus on "Why We Read"; "How Television Aims to Entertain, to Inform, or Persuade"; "How to Recognize Bias, Propaganda, Use of Connotation, or Use of Emotive Language"; or "How to Choose between a Telephone Call or Letter to Deal with Business." Teachers can also use the brainstorming technique to help students find problems or research ideas connected to interests they already have.

Research on the problem-based learning approach shows that students master "essential content equally as well as students in the traditional track even though they were not 'covering the material' in the same way."[2] Students are also less threatened by such a learning environment and are more able to pursue learning independently. An added positive result of problem-based learning is that it equips students to be lifelong learners.

Authentic Research and Learning

When research is mentioned in a typical classroom, the students' responses are usually "How long does the paper have to be?" "How many sources do we need?" and "Do we have to do an outline first?" To make matters more difficult for students, the research topics are usually teacher-decided, which generate negative attitudes from students and gives them an unrealistic picture of research in the real world.

Schack[3] indicates that students at all grade levels can do correlational, descriptive, developmental, experimental, and historical research, while case, casual, comparative, and field research is more successful with older students. Authentic research, in contrast to traditional library research using secondary sources such as note-taking, outlining, and bibliography skills, is more likely to use the data-gathering techniques of primary research which include observations, surveys, document analysis, and interviews. Students will also learn a variety of ways to select samples.

After the data have been collected, students learn how to analyze and interpret data, how to use quantitative methods, and how to make a qualitative analysis. As Schack found, upper-elementary and middle-grade students can successfully use statistical methods for analyzing data.

By doing authentic research, students learn that their questions and interests matter; it demonstrates that students have the skills and abilities to pursue their interests in a high-quality way; and it shows young people that their work has value in the real world. Also, when students are given the opportunity to share the results of their research, they learn how to communicate in an effective form.

Off-the-Page Learning

To provide students with realistic situations to practice solving meaningful problems, we need to disjoin from the word-problem paradigm and focus on problem-solving conditions organized around authentic tasks that connect to students' everyday lives. As Bottge and Hasselbring[4] experienced, one of the most practical and pleasant ways for students to use video anchors (the Jasper series) is by using small (cooperative) groups, with three or four students assigned to each group according to teacher judgment, which should be based on reliable data as constructed by *The Small Grouper* (see structuring small groups). The steps are as follows.

1. The teacher asks students to view the video anchor without interruption.
2. During the second viewing, students record in their notebooks information from scenes that depict details for solving the challenge problem.
3. In their small groups, students compare notes, discuss possible solutions, and search the episode for more detail.

Deficiencies apparent in standard word problems are not present in the Jasper videos. The videos provide a rich, realistic context from which students can search for relevant clues to the challenge problem. The results are that students are motivated, they gain practice in using mathematics as a tool for solving problems encountered in real-world contexts, and achievement levels increased while behavior problems decreased.

Students with lower reading abilities prefer these types of math problems over word problems. As in real life, students learn to distinguish relevant from irrelevant information embedded in a natural way throughout the video.

Reenactment Learning

The past must have personal relevance for students if they are to find meaning in it.[5] The *reenactment learning* strategy has students participate in various ways by:

- donning authentic dress of the era studied (e.g., The Roaring Twenties)
- conducting primary research using newspapers, letters, diaries, and photographs
- presenting programs before school groups, historical societies, and civic organizations
- taking part in preservation efforts involving original documents

The lasting effects on students of the reenactment learning strategy is that it contributes to their body of knowledge about a historic era and they see the people of that era as real.

The authentic learning movement is neither totally new, nor should it discourage teachers from exploring the potential of the approach. It is a strategy that lets students encounter and master situations that resemble real life. If "learning to remember" is an accepted axiom, something that is true and universal for effective teaching, it should be reflected in what we do in the classroom. The data on learning and remembering, illustrated in Figure 6.1,[6] are applicable to all ages.

Teaching for thinking, problem solving, and understanding has more positive effects on student achievement than traditional teaching. Therefore, the types of instructional strategies that effectively engage students in using their minds must reflect higher-order thinking, depth of knowledge, connectedness to the world, substantive conversation, and social support for student achievement.[7]

Technology and Learning

Teachers do not need to change what they teach, they need to change how they teach. Technology is the bridge that enables students to see

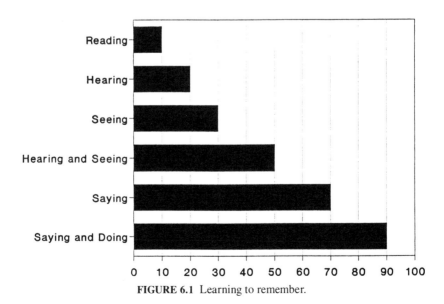

Percentage people generally remember when they learn by:

FIGURE 6.1 Learning to remember.

relationships and experience the interconnectivity of subject areas and the outside world. Students in all classrooms use the same thinking skills that are applied in both mathematics and writing. The ability to link the classroom to the outside world prevents the teacher and textbook from becoming the only knowledge source for a subject area.

For example, students in a French class can connect directly with students in France by using a computer and a modem. This technology enables students to use their foreign language skills to communicate with contemporaries and to explore common problems in the two countries.

To use technology effectively and efficiently in our schools, teamwork is needed. The most effective use of computers is when students work in small groups. This way team members can "specialize in different aspects of activities that include computation, writing, or analysis of data from the perspective of history, the arts, and/or science.[8]

Authentic learning vehicles, like real-life activities, also range from fun to mundane. "The point of authentic learning is to let students encounter and master situations that resemble real life."[9] Authentic tasks can allow students to learn fractions by using common household measuring cups and spoons to produce a batch of no-bake cookies; to write a resumé or simulate an interview for a summer job; to create recycling plans for school, home, or community; to interview a nursing home resident; or give a speech about the Great Depression. Just as life's experiences are varied, so are the learning styles of students; thus the potential for learning opportunities must extend the teacher's creativity.

STRUCTURES TO ENHANCE AUTHENTIC LEARNING

A carpenter building a house will need materials to commence construction, just as will a teacher for the development of teaching strategies. The procedures for structuring small groups, brainstorming, and student heterogeneity will assist in accomplishing enriching and authentic learning experiences for *all* students.

Structuring Small Groups [10]

To group students within a classroom for cooperative learning, obvious behaviors are necessary. The guidelines for establishing small groups in a classroom are as follows.

1. Teachers must exhibit a positive attitude for this type of learning. A benefit of small group learning is that it multiplies the opportunities for student interaction and responsibility.

2. Teachers should know the composition of the students in the classroom. For example, who are the group leaders? Who are the neglectees? Who are the isolates? Using a computer program, a sociomatrix and student-choice sociogram constructed by *The Small Grouper*[11] (see Figures 6.2 and 6.3) are designed to group students into groups of four, five, or six and to identify class group leaders, neglectees, and isolates. It is available and its use is recommended for all teachers.

3. Teachers should plan the learning outcomes and authentic tasks for the class by considering the exit (graduation) outcomes, program goals, and objectives that are to be learned by students. Teachers who are analysts and facilitators know how much information must be given before the small groups are able to function.

4. The task to be completed should determine the length of meeting time for small groups.

5. Teachers should determine the size of small groups according to the content goals and objectives, and according to individual needs. For example, all students may be assigned to small groups to work on an assignment, or some students may be grouped to work on special assignments. It is important, however, that students, whether a dyad or a group of three, four, five, or six students, be grouped with someone or others they have selected.

6. Student leaders for the groups are important. Using the information from the sociomatrix, the students chosen most often are natural choices as group leaders. As the quarter, semester, or year progresses, all students should be given the responsibility of being group leaders. The assigning of group leaders should be correlated with the task to be completed. The need for group recorders and presenters should be determined by the content covered and the task to be completed. If the assignment is to have the groups make reports, then there is a need for a recorder and a presenter.

7. The small groups should be physically separated as much as possible to develop cohesiveness and to reduce the noise level.

8. Teachers should intervene only to keep group interaction going, to provide positive feedback, and when asked to join the group.

By following these guidelines, the task(s) is clearly defined for

```
                         Sociomatrix
   Sociometric Report for  _____

                       School . . . . . . . Any Elementary School
                       Teacher  . . . . . . Any Teacher
                       Grade Level  . . . . 2
                       No. Students . . . . 24
                       Date . . . . . . . . 2/14/91

                                                           #Times
   Student List          _____ Choices _____         Chosen
   _____         _____         _____

    1. Ryan Block         8    13    16     2    12            7

    2. Susan Brady       15    16    17    12    19            3

    3. Jennifer Bumstead 24    15     7    10    12            2

    4. Gary Christenson   9    10    23    14     5            8

    5. Jeremy Crawford    9    10     4    11    21            7

    6. Karla Erickson    10     8     1     3    12            0

    7. Jane Gross         8     1    17    24    12            4

    8. Marsha Handover   17     1    12    19    24            7

    9. Joseph Jackson     4    18    10    11     5            9

   10. Michael Kemp       9     4    11     5    18            9

   11. John Langley      10    22     1     7    21            6

   12. Kathy Meyer       19    13     8    17    24           13

   13. Cindy Nelson      17    19    12     7     1            5

   14. Jerry Nixon       23    22     4     8    12            2

   15. Mindy North        2     5     8    17    13            3

   16. Karen Sails       10    20     5     4     9            2

   17. Lisa Smith        13    12    19    24    15            9

   18. Ronald Snow        9     4    12    22    10            3

   19. Kristin Stone     12    17    13     7     1            5

   20. Charles Toft       5     9    11    21    12            2

   21. Brian Trimble     10     9    11    17     4            4

   22. Mitch Underwood   18     9    11     1    20            3

   23. Timothy Vail      14    21     4     5     9            2

   24. Amy Waters         8    12     2    17     3            5
```

FIGURE 6.2 Compilation of student choices.

```
Sociometric Report for    _____

                          School . . . . . . . Any Elementary School
                          Teacher  . . . . . . Any Teacher
                          Grade Level  . . . . 2
                          No. Students . . . . 24
                          Date . . . . . . . . 2/14/91

Suggested Grouping for Group Size = 4

Group One
                              Kathy Meyer (star)
                              Kristin Stone
                              Susan Brady (neglectee)
                              Mindy North (neglectee)

Group Two

                              Lisa Smith (star)
                              Cindy Nelson
                              Jennifer Bumstead (neglectee)
                              Amy Waters

Group Three

                              Michael Kemp (star)
                              John Langley
                              Ronald Snow (neglectee)
                              Mitch Underwood (neglectee)

Group Four

                              Joseph Jackson (star)
                              Jeremy Crawford
                              Karen Salis (neglectee)
                              Charles Toft (neglectee)

Group Five

                              Gary Christenson (star)
                              Timothy Vail (neglectee)
                              Jerry Nixon (neglectee)
                              Brian Trimble

Group Six

                              Marsha Handover (star)
                              Ryan Block
                              Karla Erickson (isolate)
                              Jane Gross
```

FIGURE 6.3 Student choice sociogram.

students; individual assignments and each student's role in the group are elucidated; the necessary resources, or information about where to obtain the resources, will be provided; the progress of each group is checked, and the groups are held to a realistic schedule; and teachers will provide feedback to individual groups and to the larger group during the time small groups are working and after the groups have completed their task(s).

The strategy of using small groups in the classroom is an effective way of involving students in active, meaningful learning, and each student in class will have an opportunity to make significant contributions. Each small group allows for differences as students must explore, talk, and come to tentative conclusions.

Brainstorming

Brainstorming literally means using the brain to storm a problem. It is a technique by which the group, large or small, attempts to find a solution to a specific problem. The basic rules for brainstorming are:

- No criticism of an idea or proposal will be allowed.
- Freewheeling of ideas or proposals is desirable.
- A quantity of ideas or proposal is essential.
- A combination and improvement of ideas or proposal presented should be sought.

After the ideas or proposals have been assembled, they should be placed in appropriate categories. A committee of three or five students, with teacher assistance, should do the editing and placement of ideas or proposals.

Heterogeneous Grouping

The purpose of heterogeneous grouping is to help all students success-fully accomplish both academic and nonacademic tasks. As O'Leary and Dishon[12] point out, ''Effective student groups are those that are heterogeneous, including students of different genders, social back-grounds, skill levels, and physical capabilities.''

The specific advantages claimed for heterogeneous grouping are:

- The interaction of the various ability levels contributes to all aspects of development and achievement.

- Heterogeneous groups are more analogous to the relationships of life.
- The instructional models and participation alternatives available to pupils and teachers are more numerous.
- Some research studies generally favor social, affective, and maturational advantages for children in heterogeneous groups.[13]

Grouping of students is a delicate and complicated process, which can have a significant impact on student performance and student attitude toward the learning process. Done incorrectly, grouping can stigmatize and demoralize students. But if done with care and intelligence, grouping can stimulate students and provide them with a positive attitude toward school and learning that will last a lifetime.

An IBM-compatible computer program, *The Classmate*,[14] assists elementary school principals in systematically making heterogeneous student placement in classes, which maximizes the learning for *all* students. Figures 6.4, 6.5, and 6.6 illustrate a student data characteristics form to be completed by teachers for placement, student class priority criteria, and *The Classmate*'s edition of placing students into a class. The following should be noted.

- Six sections of third grade students were assigned to classes in the fourth grade with *The Classmate*.
- Each class had about the same mix of students among the twelve categories.
- *The Classmate* creates heterogeneous class groups based on students' abilities and traits.

The claims for heterogeneous grouping are contrary to the beliefs of many administrators and teachers. However, literally hundreds of research studies have been conducted which evidence that homogeneous grouping does *not* contribute to the academic achievement and social-emotional growth of children. The statement by Montaigne provides a sound rationale for heterogeneous grouping by stating that "it is good to rub and polish our brain against that of others."

REVIEW ACTIVITIES

(1) Select a learning outcome and plan a one-dimensional lesson approach and a multi-dimensional strategy to teach the same learning outcome. Discuss the difference between one-dimensional and multi-

Student Data Worksheet

Student Last Name: _____   First Name: _____   Initial: ___

Grade Level: _____   School: _____

Teacher: _____   Date: ___/___/___

Gender:

[ ] Male
[ ] Female

Reading:

[ ] High
[ ] High Average
[ ] Average
[ ] Low Average
[ ] Low

Math:

[ ] High
[ ] High Average
[ ] Average
[ ] Low Average
[ ] Low

Special Program:

[ ] None
[ ] Chapter 1
[ ] Communication Disorder
[ ] Learning Disabilities
[ ] Behavioral Disabilities
[ ] Cognitive Disabilities (MR)
[ ] Physical/Health/Sensory

Minority:

[ ] No
[ ] Yes

Pull Out:

[ ] No
[ ] Yes

Leader:

[ ] No
[ ] Yes

Gifted:

[ ] No
[ ] Yes

Learning Rate:

[ ] Fast
[ ] Average
[ ] Slow

Reteaching Frequency:

[ ] Never
[ ] Seldom
[ ] Usually

Birthdate:

[ ] Sept   [ ] Dec   [ ] Mar   [ ] Jun
[ ] Oct   [ ] Jan   [ ] Apr   [ ] Jly
[ ] Nov   [ ] Feb   [ ] May   [ ] Aug

Sibling Order:

[ ] First   [ ] Third   [ ] Fifth
[ ] Second   [ ] Fourth   [ ] Sixth

FIGURE 6.4 Student data characteristics.

```
Current Priority                    New Priority
─────────────────────────────────────────────────────
[ 1]  Gender                    [ 8]  Gender
[ 2]  Reading Performance       [ 1]  Reading Performance
[ 3]  Math Performance          [ 2]  Math Performance
[ 4]  Special Programs          [ 5]  Special Programs
[ 5]  Minority                  [ 7]  Minority
[ 6]  Pull Out                  [10]  Pull Out
[ 7]  Leader                    [ 6]  Leader
[ 8]  Gifted                    [12]  Gifted
[ 9]  Learning Rate             [ 3]  Learning Rate
[10]  Reteaching Frequency      [ 4]  Reteaching Frequency
[11]  Birthdate                 [ 9]  Birthdate
[12]  Sibling Order             [11]  Sibling Order

Note: The "New Priority" column configuration was used to assign
      third grade students into fourth grade class sections.
```

FIGURE 6.5 Student class priority criteria.

```
Class Grouping for _____ School Third Grade  Date _____
Group One
```

Nme	Gndr	Rdng	Mth	Spcl	Min	Plot	Ldr	Gft	Lrn	Rtch	Bd	Sib
A	F	L	LA	Cl	N	Y	N	N	S	A	AG	3
B	M	L	LA	Cl	N	Y	N	N	S	A	AP	2
C	M	L	L	Cl	N	Y	N	N	S	A	AG	1
D	M	HA	A	CD	N	Y	N	N	A	S	JN	1
E	M	A	HA	CD	Y	Y	Y	Y	F	N	OC	1
F	F	H	H	N	N	Y	Y	Y	F	N	SP	1
G	M	LA	LA	Cl	N	Y	N	N	S	A	AG	2
H	M	A	A	N	N	N	N	N	A	S	MR	2
I	F	L	L	Cl	N	Y	N	N	S	A	JN	4
J	F	H	H	N	N	N	Y	N	F	S	FB	3
K	M	A	A	N	N	N	N	N	N	S	DC	2
L	F	A	LA	N	N	N	N	N	S	A	AG	1
M	F	HA	HA	N	N	N	Y	N	A	A	AG	5
N	M	LA	LA	N	N	N	N	N	A	S	MY	1
O	M	H	H	N	N	N	Y	N	F	N	AG	3
P	M	H	H	CD	N	Y	Y	Y	F	N	FB	3
Q	M	HA	HA	N	N	N	N	N	A	S	JY	2
R	M	HA	A	N	N	N	N	N	A	S	NV	1
S	M	H	H	N	Y	N	N	N	F	N	JY	1
T	M	A	A	N	N	N	N	N	A	S	SP	1
U	F	L	L	CD	Y	Y	N	N	S	A	NV	3
V	M	HA	HA	N	N	N	Y	N	F	S	JA	1
W	M	A	A	N	Y	N	N	N	A	A	OC	1
X	F	LA	A	N	N	N	N	N	A	A	JY	4
Y	M	HA	A	CD	N	Y	N	N	A	S	JA	3
Z	M	H	HA	N	Y	N	Y	N	F	S	MY	2

```
Note: The names of students have been omitted for usual reasons.
      The Classmate printout provides a key for abbreviated terms
      (e.g., BD = Birthdate, CD = Communication Disorder, etc.).
```

FIGURE 6.6 Class grouping computed by *The Classmate*.

dimensional teaching strategies. What advantages/disadvantages does each teaching strategy hold? What advantages/disadvantages does the learner have with each approach?

(2) Create five lessons using each of the teaching strategies that enhance authentic learning. Design lessons that would involve production-driven learning, problem-based learning, authentic research and learning, off-the-page learning, and reenactment learning.

(3) Brainstorm a list of possibilities to utilize technology within the classroom.

(4) What advantages exist when students work in teams on computers rather than when students work alone with a computer?

NOTES

1 Sprague, M. M. 1993. "From Newspapers to Circuses—The Benefits of Production Driven Learning," *Educational Leadership*, 50(7):68–70.

2 Aspy, D. N., C. B. Aspy and P. M. Quinby. 1993. "What Doctors Can Teach Teachers about Problem-Based Learning," *Educational Leadership*, 50(7):22–24.

3 Schack, G. D. 1993. "Involving Students in Authentic Research," *Educational Leadership*, 50(7):29–31.

4 Bottge, B. A. and T. S. Hasselbring. 1993. "Taking Word Problems off the Page," *Educational Leadership*, 50(7):36–38.

5 See LaRocca, C. 1993. "Civil War Reenactments—'A Real and Complete Image,'" *Educational Leadership*, 50(7):42–44.

6 Alcorn, M. D., J. S. Kinder and J. R. Schunert. 1970. *Better Teaching in Secondary Schools*. Chicago, IL: Holt, Rinehart and Winston, Inc., p. 216.

7 Newmann, F. M. and G. G. Wehlage. 1993. "Five Standards of Authentic Instruction," *Educational Leadership*, 50(7):8–12.

8 Avots, J. 1993. "Technology as a Bridge," *Educational Leadership*, 50(7):83–84.

9 Cronin, J. F. 1993. "Four Misconceptions about Authentic Learning," *Educational Leadership*, 50(7):78–80.

10 For a complete description of small groups and their benefits, see

Boschee, F. 1989. *Grouping = Growth*. Dubuque, IA: Kendall/Hunt Publishing Company.

11 To order *The Small Grouper,* send $140.00 to Pat Snow, P.O. Box 201, Yankton, SD 57078. Please indicate 3-1/2″ or 5-1/4″ IBM-compatible (with 640K RAM, hard disk, and mouse recommended) or Apple II, IIe, IIc; or Macintosh.

12 O'Leary, P. W. and D. Dishon. 1985. *Cooperative Learning: Developing Minds*. Alexandria, VA: Association for Supervision and Curriculum Development, p. 179.

13 Shepherd, G. O. and W. B. Ragan. 1982. *Modern Elementary Curriculum*. Chicago, IL: Holt, Rinehart and Winston, pp. 57−58.

14 To order *The Classmate,* send $400.00 plus 25¢ per student enrolled district-wide in grades K−5, to Excelltech, Inc., 300 West Third St., Yankton, SD 57078. Please indicate 3-1/2″ or 5-1/4″ floppy disk size.

CHAPTER 7

Assessing Outcome-Based Education

WHEN considering the most effective process for assessing students' learning and progress toward established outcomes, the following key questions must be addressed.

- Does assessment focus on what is important, what is of value, and what students will need to succeed in the future?
- Does the assessment process serve students by giving them useful information that will make a meaningful difference to them?
- Are assessment results being used fairly, meaningfully, and in a manner that empowers students?
- Does the assessment process incorporate multiple strategies that encourage students to demonstrate learning and outcomes through a variety of acceptable means?

Authentic tasks and authentic assessment[1,2] provide an outcome-based system for evaluating student learning that effectively addresses all of these questions. This chapter describes authentic tasks and authentic assessment, examines the components of an authentic assessment system, and provides a model for a grading system based on authentic assessment.

DEVELOPING AUTHENTIC TASKS

Authentic tasks consist of student-centered activities that focus on content and skills that are useful in real life. While authentic tasks often involve the acquisition of knowledge and skills, their major focus relates to the application of that knowledge and those skills. Authentic tasks serve simultaneously as both instructional and assessment tools; they provide a direct link between what is taught and what is assessed.

An authentic task:

- includes concepts, generalizations, and processes critical to specific content areas
- is often interdisciplinary in nature
- requires a variety of information sources and gathering methods
- allows for multiple and varied products or outcomes
- provides maximum student control and regulation
- focuses on issues relevant to the student and the community
- provides opportunities for cooperation and collaboration
- is long term in nature
- requires the use of complex thinking processes

While some authentic tasks may incorporate all of these characteristics, due to practical reasons, most single tasks will not include all of them. However, all authentic tasks should contain the following elements.

1. *Learner outcomes* — Students will demonstrate specific content knowledge and skills that relate to the topic being studied.
2. *Learner exit outcomes* — Students will achieve one or more learner exit outcomes (already developed by the district or school) that particularly lend themselves to the knowledge and skills related to the topic being studied.
3. *Complex thinking processes* — Students will use one or more complex thinking processes as they relate to the specific knowledge and skills associated with the topic being studied (see Figure 7.1 for a description of complex thinking processes and how to evaluate them[3]).

These elements provide the basis both for developing the authentic task and assessing student outcomes demonstrated during completion of the task. Specific examples of developing and assessing authentic tasks will be provided in the following section.

ASSESSING AUTHENTIC TASKS

Authentic assessment consists of various performance-based methods of measuring and reporting the degree to which students demonstrate significant learning results related to content and skills that are useful in real life. Authentic assessment uses authentic tasks to measure how well

Complex Thinking Processes	Key Questions Answered	Criteria for Evaluation
COMPARING: Articulating the similarities and differences between two or more items/elements on specific characteristics.	• Based on specific characteristics, how are these things alike or different?	• Did the student select appropriate items/elements to be compared? • Did the student select appropriate characteristics on which to compare the selected items/elements? • Was the student accurate in the assessment of the extent to which the identified items/elements possess or do not possess the identified characteristics? • Did the student come to a conclusion about the comparison?
CLASSIFYING: Organizing items/elements into categories based on specific characteristics.	• What groups can items/elements be put into? • Why are items/elements put into these groups?	• Were the items/elements identified for classification important to the topic? • Were the categories the student selected to organize the items/elements useful and important? • Were the defining characteristics of the categories useful and important? • Did the student accurately assess the extent to which each item/element possesses each defining characteristic?
STRUCTURAL ANALYSIS: Describing in detail the overall structure along with details relating to that structure.	• What is the critical theme, concept, or idea? • What details support this? • What information is irrelevant?	• Was the student accurate in the identification of the central structure, theme, or pattern? • Did the student accurately identify the structures subordinate to the central theme or structure? • Did the student accurately identify information not related to the central structure, theme, or pattern, or its supporting structures?

FIGURE 7.1 Complex thinking processes and how to evaluate them.

97

Complex Thinking Processes	Key Questions Answered	Criteria for Evaluation
SUPPORTED INDUCTION: Creating a generalization from information within the whole and then articulating that information along with the reasoning leading to the generalization.	• What conclusions or generalizations can be drawn from these specific instances?	• Were the specific pieces of information from which the student made inductions important to the general topic about which inductions were made? • Did the student understand the information or premises from which the inductions were made? • Did the conclusions (inductions) naturally follow from the specific pieces of information used to draw the conclusions?
SUPPORTED DEDUCTION: Identifying a generalization within information or an incident and then articulating the consequences of the generalization.	• What examples can I give of this generalization? • What has to be true given the validity of this principle?	• Did the student base the deduction on an important or useful generalization or governing principle? • Was the student accurate in the interpretation of the generalization or principle? • Were the conclusions drawn by the student logical consequences of the identified generalization or principle?
ERROR ANALYSIS: Identifying and articulating specific types of errors.	• What is wrong with this? • Why is it wrong? • How can it be corrected?	• Did the student select important or critical errors in the information or process? • Was the student accurate in the analysis of the manner and extent to which errors affect the information or process within which they exist? • Was the student's description about how to correct the errors valid?

FIGURE 7.1 (continued) Complex thinking processes and how to evaluate them.

Complex Thinking Processes	Key Questions Answered	Criteria for Evaluation
CONSTRUCTING SUPPORT: Developing a well-articulated argument for or against a specific claim.	• What is the issue? • What are the reasons for this argument? • What evidence supports or refutes claim? • What conclusions have you reached?	• Was the student accurate in the identification of information that needs support versus information that does not need support? • Was the student's claim supported by a sufficient amount and appropriate types of information? • Was the student accurate in the description of the limitations of the claim and the support provided?
EXTENDING: Identifying how the pattern within one piece of information is similar or different from the pattern within another piece of information and providing support for the reasoning leading to the relationship.	• What is the pattern in the information? • Where else does it apply?	• To what extent was the information identified from the original source important and useful as a subject for the abstraction process? • Did the abstract pattern the student identified represent the pattern of important information from the literal source? • To what extent did the related information contain the key characteristics of the abstract pattern?
DECISION MAKING: Choosing among alternatives which appear to be equal.	• What are the important criteria to use in making the decision? • Based on the specific criteria, which of the alternatives is best or worse?	• Did the student select appropriate and important alternatives to be considered? • Did the student select appropriate and important criteria with which to assess the identified alternatives? • Was the student accurate in the assessment of the extent to which the alternatives possess the identified characteristics? • Did the final selection adequately meet decision criteria and answer the initial decision question?

FIGURE 7.1 (continued) Complex thinking processes and how to evaluate them.

Complex Thinking Processes	Key Questions Answered	Criteria for Evaluation

INVESTIGATION: There are three basic types of investigation:
Definitive - constructs a definition or description for a concept when this definition or description is not available or not accepted.
Historical - constructs an explanation for some past event for which there is no definite explanation.
Projective - makes a prediction about some future event.
	• What are the defining characteristics (definitive)?
	• Why/how did this happen (historical)?
	• What would happen/would have happened if (projective)?
		• Was the student accurate and complete in the assessment of what is already known or accepted about:
		  ▪ the concept (definitive)?
		  ▪ the past event (historical)?
		  ▪ the hypothetical event (projective)?
		• Was the student accurate and complete in the assessment of a confusion or contradiction about:
		  ▪ the concept (definitive)?
		  ▪ the past event (historical)?
		  ▪ the hypothetical event (projective)?
		• Was the resolution to the confusion/contradiction logical and plausible about:
		  ▪ the concept (definitive)?
		  ▪ the past event (historical)?
		  ▪ the hypothetical event (projective)?

SYSTEMS ANALYSIS: Identifying and describing the internal structure of a system, its operation, and how it interfaces with what lies outside the system.	• How does this operate? • What are the relationships between the components? • What effect does one part have on another?	• Did the student accurately and clearly identify the boundaries of the system? • Did the student accurately and completely identify and articulate how the component parts interact? • Did the student accurately and completely describe how the system can fail? • Did the student accurately describe how the system interfaces with the world outside it across the system boundaries?

FIGURE 7.1 (continued) Complex thinking processes and how to evaluate them.

Complex Thinking Processes	Key Questions Answered	Criteria for Evaluation
PROBLEM SOLVING: Developing, testing, and evaluating a method or product for overcoming an obstacle.	• What is the obstacle? • What are the alternatives? • Which alternative best overcomes the obstacle?	• Were the obstacles to the goal identified by the student? • Were the alternative ways of overcoming the obstacles identified by the student viable and important to the situation? • Did the student adequately try out a selected alternative before trying another? • If other alternatives were tried, how well did the student articulate the reasoning behind the order of the selection and the extent to which each alternative overcame the obstacles?
EXPERIMENTAL INQUIRY: Generating, testing, and evaluating the effectiveness of a theory to explain a phenomenon and then using those theories to predict future events.	• What is observable? • How can the observations be explained? • What predictions can be made from the observations? • How can the predictions be tested? • What are the results and generalizations?	• Did the student accurately explain the phenomenon using appropriate and accepted facts, concepts, and principles? • To what extent did the prediction made by the student logically follow from the student's explanation? • To what extent did the experiment truly test the prediction? • To what extent did the explanation of the outcome of the experiment adequately relate to the student's initial explanation?

FIGURE 7.1 (continued) Complex thinking processes and how to evaluate them.

Complex Thinking Processes	Key Questions Answered	Criteria for Evaluation
INVENTION: Developing a unique product or process which fulfills some expressed need.	• What needs to be improved? • What needs to be created? • What standards will be met? • What is the final product? • Does the final product meet the standards?	• To what extent would the invention proposed by the student improve upon the identified situation or meet the need that was identified? • How rigorous and important were the identified standards or criteria the final invention should meet? • How detailed and important were the revisions the student made on the initial model or draft? • To what extent did the final product meet the standards and criteria that had been identified?
COMBINATION TASKS: Analyzing or generating information via the explicit use of two or more of the previously described types of tasks or thinking processes.	• The specific question(s) answered are those related to the specific tasks or thinking processes being used.	• Criteria for evaluation are those related to the specific tasks or thinking processes being used.

FIGURE 7.1 (continued) Complex thinking processes and how to evaluate them.

102

students are achieving learner outcomes and utilizing complex thinking skills to achieve those outcomes.

Before developing authentic tasks for the purpose of assessing student progress, remember the following.

- All learning activities and tasks in the classroom do not have to be authentic tasks – there is still a need and a place for covering some basic knowledge and skills in a more traditional manner.
- All authentic tasks do not have to be assessed – some of them may be employed primarily as instructional tools that are not formally assessed.

However, when creating authentic tasks for assessment purposes, the following guidelines will be helpful.

- Identify a few important issues within the topic students are studying.
- Identify learner outcomes for the task – that is, the knowledge and skills students shall demonstrate in completing the task.
- Identify the criteria that will be assessed for the learner outcome(s) selected. Focus on several important criteria rather than trying to assess all the possible criteria for each outcome. In general, the criteria to be assessed for learner outcome(s) include the degree to which
  – the student understood the content area facts, concepts, and principles important to the task
  – the student effectively used the content skills and processes important to the task
- Use a rating scale of *1* (lowest degree of proficiency) to *4* (highest degree of proficiency) to record results for each criterion.
- Select one or more learner exit outcomes to incorporate into the task. Choose exit outcomes that appear particularly relevant to the knowledge and skills related to the topic students are studying.
- Select one or two different types of complex thinking processes to incorporate into the task. Do not try to assess too many thinking processes for each task.
- Identify the criteria that will be assessed for the thinking process(es) selected. Focus on several important criteria rather than trying to assess all the possible criteria for each thinking

process. A general criterion to be assessed for all of the thinking processes would be the degree to which the student used all important components of the thinking process necessary to complete the task. Specific criteria to be assessed for each particular complex thinking skill are listed in Figure 7.1. Use a rating scale of *1* (lowest degree of proficiency) to *4* (highest degree of proficiency) to record results for each criterion.

- Review the authentic task that has been created to make certain that:
  - it will provide all the necessary information needed to assess the criteria that have been selected
  - it is interesting and relevant enough to engage students and maintain their involvement
- If necessary, modify the task to ensure that it provides the necessary information for assessment purposes and is relevant and interesting for students.
- Construct an assessment scoring sheet for the authentic task that includes:
  - the topic students are studying
  - the learner exit outcome(s)
  - the learner outcome(s)
  - the criteria to be assessed indicating to what degree students have achieved the learner outcome(s) and the rating scale for recording results
  - the task students are to complete
  - the complex thinking process(es) students will use to complete the task
  - the criteria to be assessed indicating to what degree students have used the thinking process(es) and the rating scale for recording results
- If desired, assign weights to the selected criteria to reflect what students should emphasize in the task. Communicate the criteria and weights to the students so they know what is being emphasized in the assessment.
- Select an appropriate assessment tool(s) to measure or observe student outcomes for the task (various assessment tools will be presented in the next section).
- Guide students through the completion of the task and assess each student's performance using the assessment tool(s) you selected and the assessment scoring sheet you constructed.

One suggestion for developing an authentic task and assessment is to start with a project or activity that has been used before and make it authentic by redesigning it in a manner that includes all of the elements described above. A sample authentic task assignment is illustrated in Figure 7.2, and a general assessment model for evaluating student performance on that task is shown in Figure 7.3.

For the sake of simplicity, the task depicted in Figure 7.2 focuses primarily on classification skills within the context of life science. This task could easily be transformed into an interdisciplinary task by emphasizing and assessing presentation skills, oral and written communication skills, and collaborative group skills using content material from several subject areas. Individual teachers should determine the exact content and skill assessment for each authentic task based upon their own instructional needs and desired focus for the task.

School districts and individual schools should consider developing standardized formats for authentic tasks and assessment scoring sheets. Standardized formats save classroom teachers valuable planning time and permit them to spend more time on developing the task content and skills.

DEVELOPING AUTHENTIC ASSESSMENT SYSTEMS

Employing an assortment of different authentic assessment tools to evaluate student learning greatly enhances the overall validity of the assessment process. An assessment system model that incorporates three different types of authentic assessments – multiple validations, student portfolios, and secured tasks – provides a wealth of information for assessing learner exit outcomes as well as content knowledge and skills.

Multiple Validations

Multiple validations include a variety of authentic assessments made over time by individual teachers and trained evaluators on the knowledge and skills identified as important. Employing multiple validations places assessment in the hands of teachers and students rather than outside test developers and scorers. Multiple validations include authentic tasks assessed by the following.

- activity checklists
- contracts

```
                    AUTHENTIC TASK
                    ASSIGNMENT SHEET


GRADE LEVEL:  Middle School

SUBJECT AREA:  Life Science

TOPIC:  Classification of Living Organisms

EXIT OUTCOME(S):  Purposeful Thinker

LEARNER OUTCOME(S):

    The student will demonstrate the ability to classify
    living organisms into groupings based upon the defining
    characteristics of those groupings.

COMPLEX THINKING SKILL(S):  Classification

TASK:  You and three colleagues have landed on an uncharted
    island in the Caribbean to explore for previously unidentified
    life forms.  Your group has several taxonomy manuals that
    identify and describe the characteristics of almost every
    known species of living organism.  Unfortunately, all of your
    photographic equipment was lost during a fierce storm at sea.

    Your assignment is to describe to the class at least three
    previously unknown animal species and determine to what
    biological grouping each belongs.  Your report to the class
    may be done however you choose, but must include at least the
    following elements for each unknown species of animal you are
    reporting:

    1. A display of photographs or films of at least two familiar
       animals that belong to the same grouping as the unknown
       animal.

    2. A list of at least four observable characteristics that
       support your decision regarding the grouping to which you
       are assigning the unknown animal.

    3. A description of the unknown animal's likely habitat based
       upon what you know about the habitat of familiar animals
       belonging to the same group.
```

FIGURE 7.2 Sample authentic task assignment sheet.

106

AUTHENTIC TASK ASSESSMENT SHEET			
Criteria for Evaluation	**Evaluation**	**Weight**	**Score**
Understanding and use of topic-specific information:		1/3/5	
Did the student understand the content area facts, concepts, and principles important to the task?	1 2 3 4	_____	_____
Did the student effectively use the content skills and processes important to the task?	1 2 3 4	_____	_____
Use of the process of classification:			
Did the student use all important components of the process necessary to complete the task?	1 2 3 4	_____	_____
Were the elements identified for classification important to the topic?	1 2 3 4	_____	_____
Were the categories the student selected to organize the elements useful and important?	1 2 3 4	_____	_____
Were the defining characteristics of the categories important and useful?	1 2 3 4	_____	_____
Did the student accurately assess the extent to which each element possesses each defining characteristic?	1 2 3 4	_____	_____
OBSERVATIONS/COMMENTS:			

FIGURE 7.3 Sample of a generalized authentic task assessment sheet.

107

- culminating exhibitions and presentations
- hands-on demonstrations
- oral interviews
- reflective journals/learning logs
- student observations/anecdotal records
- student self-appraisal
- writing tests (including traditional paper-and-pencil tests and standardized tests)

Activity Checklists

A checklist is composed of activities, behaviors, or steps that an observer records when monitoring student performance. Checklists may focus on a single event or may be cumulative. The teacher may use a checklist when observing individuals or groups, or students may use a checklist for self or peer evaluation. Checklist items must be clear, precise, and understandable by all. The elements of a student activities checklist are presented in Figure 7.4.

```
_____              _____
      Student Name                         Person Rating

_____
                  Activity                          Date

_____  Reads and carefully follows directions

_____  Works well with others in a group

_____  Remains on task throughout activity

_____  Uses a variety of problem-solving strategies

_____  Gives relevant and complete answers to questions

_____  Shares information with others

_____  Incorporates previous learning into present task

_____  Suggests problems worth investigating

_____  Uses a variety of thinking processes to complete activity

_____  Prefers active learning to passive learning

Rate the student on this activity using a scale of:

1 = rarely    2 = occasionally    3 = frequently    4 = consistently
```

FIGURE 7.4 Elements of a sample activities checklist.

Contracts

A contract sets the academic expectations and responsibilities for the student entering into an agreement with the school or teacher regarding a specific task. The contract specifies the task that both parties agree to complete within a given period of time. The teacher carefully poses problems with varying degrees of difficulty and the students, with guidance from the teacher, select the problems they will work on and the amount of time they will spend in fulfilling the agreement. The contract also provides the teacher an opportunity to assess each student's level of responsibility, reliability, accuracy, and precision. Figure 7.5 illustrates a sample contract for the development of a student portfolio.

Culminating Exhibitions and Presentations

Culminating exhibitions and presentations provide students an opportunity to demonstrate that they have learned the content and skills required for a particular task or project. Students make oral and/or written presentations to explain or defend their projects before a class or committee composed of staff, students, and outside adults. Evaluation of the presentation should include ratings for each of the following components.

- Introduction to the presentation
  - It gained attention of the audience.
  - It established importance of the subject matter.
  - It outlined the objectives clearly.
- Subject matter included in the presentation
  - The material was practical and important.
  - The information was accurate and complete.
- Adequacy of the presentation
  - Information and materials were selected and presented well.
  - Information and materials were effectively used and organized.
  - Information and materials were adequately explained.
  - Performance was easy and smooth.
  - Manner was pleasant and confident.
  - Speech was clear and distinct.
  - Teamwork and division of responsibility were evident (group presentation).
- Results of the presentation
  - Finished products or principles were developed.

```
                        PORTFOLIO CONTRACT

This agreement is hereby entered into this _____ day of

_____, 199___, between _____

(the teacher) and _____ (the learner).


The parties hereby agree to the following:

    1.  The learner shall provide all of the required informa-
tion, skills, and effort needed to complete a portfolio that
demonstrates _____
_____
_____.

    2.  The teacher agrees to assist, confer, and help the
learner in acquiring the needed materials, skills, space, and
equipment.  And, the learner agrees to make his/her needs known
to the teacher so assistance can be given in a timely manner.

    3.  The learner agrees to complete the portfolio for final
presentation on or before _____, and at that time
arrange with the teacher a date and time for presentation.  If
the learner is unable to complete the portfolio by the agreed
upon time because of unavoidable causes, neglect by the teacher,
or changes in the requirements for the portfolio, the learner
must negotiate with the teacher a new completion date and
presentation time.

    4.  The learner agrees to include in his/her portfolio the
following information and evidence of work:

        a.  all necessary preliminary planning documents,
        b.  the initial representation--first draft--unedited,
        c.  evidence of responses and reactions of others,
        d.  evidence of revision and refinement, and
        e.  the final product and a plan for presentation,
            distribution, and/or display--logistics of time,
            place, space, and needed equipment.

    5.  All changes in the portfolio and work to be included
within the portfolio must be negotiated with the teacher and
and be in writing appended to this contract.  All additional
work not specified in this contract, but deemed necessary to
ensure a high quality of work, will be recognized and rewarded.

    6.  The learner agrees to correct any and all work that
does not conform to the specifications agreed upon in this
contract in a timely fashion--not to exceed one week after
the original due date and time.


_____        _____
        Learner                       Teacher
```

FIGURE 7.5 Sample contract for creating a portfolio.

 — Presentation had positive effect upon audience.
 — Summary was effective and accurate.

Hands-On Demonstrations

Students use manipulatives to demonstrate such skills as measuring and classifying. They also formulate hypotheses, and design and conduct experiments to test their hypotheses. While hands-on demonstrations are particularly well suited to science projects, they may also be used in other subject areas and for interdisciplinary projects. Evaluation of hands-on demonstrations should include evaluation of the following criteria.

- logic and precision of the hypothesis(es)
- accuracy of data collection and recording
- proficiency of data analysis
- logic of the conclusion drawn from the data
- understanding of the concepts involved
- application of concepts to nonscientific situations (i.e., everyday life)

Oral Interviews

Oral interviews provide an effective means of observing students' thinking processes and their readiness to progress to new or more advanced topics. The oral interview may be a structured or unstructured dialogue with an individual or group of students. Questioning and open discussion provide an opportunity to determine the student's depth of understanding rather than whether or not the student can produce the "right" answer. The following are suggested guidelines for the oral interview as an authentic assessment tool.

- Try to remain neutral – allow learners to control the flow of the conversation.
- Be empathetic and encouraging by being attentive.
- Allow plenty of wait time.
- Encourage elaboration of ideas by requesting evidence or support for statements made.
- Encourage learners to bring journals or logs to the interview to record their thoughts and results of the conversation.
- Prepare a chart or form to note and assess learner responses.

Reflective Journals/Learning Logs

A learning log is a journal in which students write about and respond to what they have learned, record questions, and make notes of what they do not understand. Students should make entries once or twice a week in their journals or at the end of an instructional cycle. The teacher should read journals periodically to assess students' thought processes and perceptions, and to inform instruction. Examples of the information students may record in the journal include:

- predictions about what they are going to learn in a chapter of the textbook or an instructional cycle
- reflections about what they learned in a particular lesson
- feelings about the subject
- estimates of how well they are performing
- statements about their level of effort in class
- problems and/or questions they have for the teacher

Student Observations/Anecdotal Records

The teacher observes individual and group behavior related to academic tasks, work habits, thinking processes, and other activities related to student performance. Observations may be overt or subtle, and may focus on a single event or an accumulation of abilities over time. Anecdotal records are made to document what students say and do, as well as to keep track of student progress.

Student Self-Appraisal

Self-appraisal requires students to think about what they are doing, why they are doing it, and how they can improve. Results of self-appraisal may be included in journal entries, discussed in small groups, or recorded on teacher-designed forms. Self-appraisal encourages students to learn more about themselves through introspection and reflection, and permits the teacher to assess where the student is in class.

Writing Tests

Writing tests generally require students to write on assigned topics. Student essays or stories are then rated by teams of readers who assign grades according to standard criteria. Writing tests can be assigned periodically to provide a pre- and post-comparison of thinking and writing abilities or knowledge or particular content for planning subsequent instruction.

Portfolios

Portfolios provide tangible evidence of a student's knowledge, abilities, and academic growth that affords the teacher opportunities for formative and summative evaluation. Effectively designed portfolios give students, teachers, and parents rich, authentic evidence of a student's performance capabilities. Increasing numbers of state departments of education, including those in Michigan, Florida, California, and Vermont, have adopted the portfolio as one indication for parents, employers, and colleges that students have learned.

Purposes

The primary purposes for using portfolios as one type of authentic assessment tool include:

- assessing students' accomplishment of learner (content) outcomes and learner exit outcomes
- assessing the quality of students' sustained work
- allowing students to showcase their own special interests and abilities
- encouraging the development of qualities such as pride in quality workmanship, ability to self evaluate, and the ability to accomplish meaningful tasks
- providing a collection of work students may use in the future for college application and job seeking
- documenting improvement of students' work

Contents of the Portfolio

The portfolio contents will be student selected and based on the student's stated purpose for developing the portfolio. Important decisions regarding the contents and presentation of the portfolio should be made with advisement from the student's mentor. Generally, the faculty or staff member who works most closely with a student over a given period of time will serve as the student's mentor. The mentor may be the student's homeroom teacher, a subject area teacher, classroom teacher, team teacher, or a member of the support staff such as a counselor or special needs teacher.

Portfolios may represent a student's cumulative efforts over a long period of time (a year or more) or focus on a more specific task or assignment. A comprehensive portfolio will contain all the student's planning, research, and development documents, as well as the finished products. A limited-focus portfolio will be more selective, containing only documents directly related to a specific project, content area, or limited time period. Specific documents and records that would appropriately comprise a portfolio include:

- traditional test results
- writing tests, projects, and essays
- journal pages and entries
- records of student self-appraisal
- sketches and drawings
- evidence of knowledge acquisition and skill development in specific content areas
- indicators of student growth
- literacy milestones
- evidence of progress toward achievement of specific learner exit outcomes
- observational records
- anecdotal notes

Evaluating the Portfolio

Periodic evaluation of the portfolio should be conducted at a time predetermined by the student and the student's mentor. Logical times for evaluation would be at the conclusion of a project, the end of a grading period, semester, or academic year, or during the senior year in high school for graduation requirement purposes. The panel of evaluators that assesses the portfolio should include:

- two teachers from different grade levels or subject areas
- one teacher of the student's choosing
- one community member
- one other student

Invited guests, including the student's parents, mentor, and peers may also be asked to examine the portfolio.

Criteria for evaluating the portfolio should include:

- one or more meaningful purposes set by the student for use of the portfolio (for example—seeking employment, applying to college, documenting academic/personal growth, or setting personal/academic goals)
- the degree to which portfolio contents are quality products and are congruent with the student's stated purpose(s) for the portfolio
- evidence in the portfolio of the student having demonstrated achievement of learner (content) outcomes, program goals, or learner exit outcomes
- effectiveness of the student's portfolio presentation to the evaluation panel, that should include the degree to which
  - the student provides a rationale for the items included (based on the stated purpose of the portfolio)
  - the student communicates clearly and effectively

Secured Tasks

Secured tasks include assessments of individual student performance under controlled conditions. Secured tasks consist of paper-and-pencil tests, as well as student performances, simulations, and problem-solving activities. Paper-and-pencil tests differ from standardized tests in that they are open book, and designed to measure higher order thinking skills and the meaningful use of concepts and principles across content areas. Among the characteristics of secured tasks are the following.

- Assessment is administered under controlled conditions (have time limits, completed without help, monitored by a teacher/evaluator, etc.).
- Tasks are designed to assess specific content knowledge and/or skills.
- Although the student knows what knowledge and/or skills will be assessed and what criteria applied, the exact content of the assessment is not known ahead of time.
- Scoring is completed by trained graders, including teachers or outside evaluators.

- Assessment of secured tasks matches learner (content) outcomes (that is, assessment has criterion- or content-related validity).
- Students are provided feedback on task performance.
- Secured tasks provide multiple opportunities for meeting promotion and/or graduation standards.

DEVELOPING AN OUTCOME-BASED GRADING SYSTEM[4]

Within an outcome-based education system, students are assigned grades on the basis of demonstrated achievement rather than the amount of material covered during a grading period, semester, or academic year. Evidence of achievement from all three types of authentic assessments — multiple validations, portfolios, and secured tasks — should be used to determine grades. The specific emphasis on each of these three types of authentic assessment will be determined by the purpose for computing the grade (that is, interim grading, grade-level promotion, or meeting graduation requirements).

A four-point scale is recommended for scoring learner outcomes whether assessed via multiple validation tasks, portfolios, or secured tasks. The specific scores should be interpreted as follows.

- A score of *1* indicates inadequate performance on the task (equivalent to a grade letter of D).
- A score of *2* indicates the student has mastered the basic competencies of the outcome (equivalent to a C).
- A score of *3* indicates the student has met all the expectations for the outcome (equivalent to a B).
- A score of *4* indicates the student has exceeded the expectations for that outcome (equivalent to an A).

Grade-point average (GPA) for each program (subject area) may be calculated by combining and averaging scores from multiple validations and secured tasks. However, acceptable levels of achievement should be required for each individual validation or task. Overall GPA is calculated by averaging the GPA in all subject areas.

Interim Grading

Interim grading refers to assigning grades at the end of a specified grading period (six-week period, nine-week period, quarter, or semester). Interim grade assignments should reflect each student's demonstrated level of achievement and progress regarding only the specific content knowledge and skills addressed during that grading period. Each type of authentic assessment should be used in the following manner.

Multiple Validations

Each student must earn validations in every learner outcome assigned during the grading period. A score of 2 or better (on the four-point scale described above) should be required for validation of each outcome. Prior to the end of the grading period, each student should be given the opportunity to demonstrate an acceptable level of achievement (that is, a score of 2 or better) on any learner outcomes for which validation was lacking.

Portfolios

All students, in conjunction with their teacher or mentor, select which subject areas to include for the grading period based on the students' purposes for the portfolio. An acceptable score should be based on how well the student meets all of the criteria outlined above for portfolio evaluation.

Secured Tasks

Each student must pass an assessment on the knowledge and skills in each of the content areas covered during the grading period. A score of 2 or better should be required on each assessment.

Grade-Level Promotion

Grades assigned at the end of the academic year for the purpose of promotion to the next grade level also should be based upon evidence of student achievement accumulated through all three types of authentic assessments. Naturally, final grades must reflect cumulative student accomplishments made throughout the academic year. Additionally, assessment of students' progress toward achieving learner exit outcomes should be documented.

Multiple Validations

Each student must earn validations in every learner outcome assigned throughout the academic year. A score of 2 or better should be required for validation of each outcome. Prior to the end of the year, each student should be given the opportunity to demonstrate an acceptable level of achievement on any learner outcomes for which validation was lacking.

Portfolios

Each student, in conjunction with their teacher or mentor, determines which subject areas to include in the portfolio for the academic year based on the student's purpose for the portfolio. Alternatively, each student may be required to include materials for all subject areas studied during the year in the portfolio. An acceptable score should be based on how well the student meets all of the criteria outlined above for portfolio evaluation.

Secured Tasks

Each student must pass an assessment on the knowledge and skills in each of the content areas covered during the academic year. Alternatively, each student may be required to pass an assessment only on those subject areas deemed necessary through agreement between the student and teacher (mentor). A score of 2 or better should be required on each required assessment.

Progress toward Exit Outcomes

One component of each student's annual evaluation should focus on the student's progress toward achieving the district's learner exit outcomes. While specific evidence of proficiency in all learner exit outcomes eventually will be required for graduation, an annual checklist of proficiencies demonstrated throughout the academic year assists the student and teacher in identifying areas needing attention for the coming academic year(s). A sample evaluation using one learner exit outcome and related competencies is provided in Figure 7.6.

Graduation Requirements

Requirements for graduation should reflect student demonstration of proficiency in all subject (program) areas and learner exit outcomes.

```
┌─────────────────────────────────────────────────────────────────────┐
│              PROGRESS TOWARD LEARNER EXIT OUTCOMES:                   │
│                         ANNUAL REVIEW                                 │
│                                                                       │
│   Student _____    Grade Level _____         │
│                                                                       │
│   Reviewer _____    Date _____           │
│  ┌──────────────────────────────────────────────────────────────┐   │
│  │ Exit Outcomes/Competencies                       Evaluation    │   │
│  │                                                                │   │
│  │ PURPOSEFUL THINKER:                                            │   │
│  │                                                                │   │
│  │ • uses strategies to form concepts, make          _____      │   │
│  │   decisions, and solve problems                                │   │
│  │                                                                │   │
│  │ • applies a variety of integrated processes,      _____      │   │
│  │   including critical and creative thinking                     │   │
│  │   to accomplish complex tasks                                  │   │
│  │                                                                │   │
│  │ • evaluates the effectiveness of mental           _____      │   │
│  │   strategies through meaningful reflection                     │   │
│  │                                                                │   │
│  │ • demonstrates flexibility, persistence, and      _____      │   │
│  │   a sense of ethical considerations                            │   │
│  │                                                                │   │
│  │                                                                │   │
│  │ Evaluate the degree to which the student demonstrated each of  │   │
│  │ the above competencies using a scale of:                       │   │
│  │                                                                │   │
│  │ 1 = Rarely  2 = Occasionally  3 = Frequently  4 = Consistently  │   │
│  └──────────────────────────────────────────────────────────────┘   │
│  ┌──────────────────────────────────────────────────────────────┐   │
│  │ Comments/Observations:                                         │   │
│  │                                                                │   │
│  │                                                                │   │
│  │                                                                │   │
│  └──────────────────────────────────────────────────────────────┘   │
└─────────────────────────────────────────────────────────────────────┘
```

FIGURE 7.6 Sample annual evaluation of student progress toward achievement of learner exit outcomes.

Evidence of student proficiency in each of the subject areas should be based on authentic assessments using multiple validations, portfolios, and secured tasks. Multiple validations and portfolios should be utilized to provide evidence of proficiency for all of the competencies (performance indicators) associated with each of the learner exit outcomes.

Program Goals

Recommended procedures for assessing student proficiencies in each of the subject areas include the following.

1. *Multiple validations* — Each student must earn validations in every program objective that comprises each program goal. A score of *2* or better should be required for validation of each program objective.

Any low score earned by a student may be replaced (not averaged with) a higher quality performance on the same objective.

2. *Portfolios*—Each student's portfolio must contain tangible evidence of the student's achievements and accomplishments as they relate to each program area. As an alternative, each student may select which programs to include in the portfolio based on the student's purpose for the portfolio. An acceptable score should be based on how well the student meets all of the criteria outlined above for portfolio evaluation.

3. *Secured tasks*—Each student must pass an assessment in each of the program areas included in the student's program of studies. Alternatively, each student may be required to pass an assessment only on those program areas deemed necessary through agreement between the student and teacher (mentor). A score of 2 or better should be required on each required assessment.

Learner Exit Outcomes

Recommended procedures for assessing student proficiencies for each learner exit outcome include the following.

1. *Multiple validations*—Each student must earn at least two validations (or a reasonable number of validations as determined by the district) on each of the learner exit outcome competencies. A score of *3* or better on the following generalized scale should be required for validation of each of the learner exit outcome competencies.
   - A score of *1* indicates that the student seldom, if ever, demonstrates the knowledge or skills associated with the learner exit outcome competency.
   - A score of *2* indicates that the student only occasionally and inconsistently demonstrates the knowledge or skills associated with the learner exit outcome competency.
   - A score of *3* indicates that the student frequently demonstrates the knowledge or skills associated with the learner exit outcome competency.
   - A score of *4* indicates that the student consistently demonstrates the knowledge or skills associated with the learner exit outcome competency.

2. *Portfolios*—Each student must include in the portfolio evidence of proficiency in each of the learner exit outcomes. In order to graduate,

the student should present a portfolio that meets or exceeds a *3* as determined by the district standards for portfolio evaluation.

REVIEW ACTIVITIES

(1) You have just been appointed head of the district committee for developing and integrating authentic tasks into the curriculum for kindergarten through grade twelve.

- What are some of the pedagogical advantages of using authentic tasks for instruction instead of the traditional learning activities currently used in your district?
- How would you convince other teachers on the committee and in the schools that using authentic tasks could improve the effectiveness of their teaching?
- Select one classroom activity or project that you have used successfully and with which you are comfortable. How could you convert the lesson or project into an authentic task?

(2) Unlike many forms of traditional assessment, authentic assessment requires students to demonstrate proficiency regarding knowledge and skills related to the topic being evaluated.

- What are some of the benefits of changing to more authentic forms of assessments?
- What are some of the drawbacks of changing to more authentic forms of assessments?
- Select one test or assessment that you have used to evaluate students on a given task. How might you transform that evaluation into an authentic assessment of the same task?

(3) Using multiple validations to assess student performance allows students to demonstrate achievement in a variety of ways, which increases the validity of the assessment process.

- What are some of the potential benefits of using a variety of student-centered and teacher-centered ways of assessing student achievement and performance?
- Do you envision any drawbacks to using a multiple system of validating student achievement and performance? If so, what are they?
- Please study the list of different ways to validate student achievement and performance included in the section on

multiple validations. What are some other methods of assessment that you can think of that are not included on that list?

- How might you work with one or more of your colleagues to develop a system of multiple validations?

(4) The use of student portfolios is gaining approval all over the country as one way to evaluate student progress and ability.

- What are some of the advantages of using student portfolios as an adjunct to traditional methods of assessing student achievement and ability?
- What are some of the drawbacks of using student portfolios as an adjunct to traditional methods of assessing student achievement and ability?
- Is it educationally sound to allow students to decide what materials they will include for evaluation in their portfolios? Why or why not?
- What role should the teacher play in deciding what materials students should include in their portfolios?
- If you were charged with appointing a portfolio evaluation team, who would you include on the team? Please give your rationale for selecting each of the members.

(5) Your school district has decided to implement an authentic assessment system of grading and you have been asked to chair the committee that will determine how to transform the current grading system into an authentic assessment system.

- How would you convince other teachers on the committee and throughout the district that an authentic assessment system of grading will be more valid than the system currently used in your district?
- What role would you envision for traditional paper-and-pencil tests within the new system of assessment?
- Should the new system of authentic assessment be implemented differently in the elementary, middle/junior high, and senior high schools throughout your district? If so, how would the system differ at each of these instructional levels?

NOTES

1 Authentic tasks and authentic assessment models and information were adapted from Marzano, R. J., D. J. Pickering, J. S. Whisler,

J. S. Kendall, F. Mayeski, and D. E. Painter. 1993. *Authentic Assessment*. Aurora, CO: McREL Institute.

2 Authentic tasks and authentic assessment models and information also were adapted from Aurora Public Schools, Aurora, CO, 1992.

3 Descriptions of complex thinking processes, key questions answered, and criteria for evaluation were adapted from Marzano, R. J., D. J. Pickering, J. S. Whisler, J. S. Kendall, F. Mayeski, and D. E. Painter. 1993. *Authentic Assessment*. Aurora, CO: McREL Institute.

4 Essential elements of the outcome-based grading system are adapted from the ''Proposed Graduation Requirements,'' Aurora Public Schools, Aurora, CO, 1992.

CHAPTER 8

Considering Alternative Approaches for Restructuring the School Organization

THE decision to adopt an outcome-based education system represents a commitment to restructure educational planning, curriculum development, instructional delivery, and assessment of learner outcomes. Inherent in the outcome-based educational philosophy is the belief that all individuals can learn successfully and that schools create the conditions within which learners succeed. Therefore, the following questions should be asked.

- Do present conditions within the school building and district organization promote successful learning for all students?
- What alternatives are available that create conditions that promote successful learning for all students?

Educational research and practice suggest that traditional approaches to organizing and delivering instruction may not provide all students with equal opportunities for success. Numerous alternative approaches — many of which are compatible with, and supportive of an outcome-based education system — have been suggested to equalize and promote learning opportunities for all students. The following represent some of the more promising alternative approaches.

- site-based management
- nongraded organization
- school-within-a-school organization
- flexible-block scheduling plan
- Copernican plan
- year-round education
- interdisciplinary approach

This chapter describes each of these alternative approaches to restructuring the school organization and examines how each relates to outcome-based education.

125

SITE-BASED MANAGEMENT

Site-based (or school-site) management suggests that individual school sites assume greater autonomy over their own planning and decision making. In reality, site-based management encompasses two related concepts—decentralized decision making and participatory management.

The basic principle underlying decentralized decision making is that overcentralized management may be too far removed from conditions within a given school to respond adequately to the individual needs of staff and students within that school. Decentralized decision making, on the other hand, permits the development of policies and procedures that address the specific needs of each individual school or site.

Participatory management gives local stakeholders a voice in making decisions regarding a wide range of educational policies and issues that directly affect their school. Greater commitment to change, increased satisfaction with the school's educational program, and generally higher quality decisions represent only a few of the potential benefits resulting from participatory management practices.

The formation of a school-site council or advisory board provides a mechanism for simultaneously implementing decentralized decision making and participatory management. A school-site council or advisory board composed of teachers, staff, parents, community members, and students represents all of the school's stakeholders.

Coordination of the school-site council and site-based planning team (see Chapter 2) provides an excellent opportunity to integrate strategic planning and outcome-based education into the overall organization of the school. Dual membership of at least several individuals on both the school-site council and site-based planning team ensures open communication and effective coordination of both groups' efforts. Integrating elements of site-based management and strategic planning results in an outcome-based education program that provides the framework for decentralized and participatory planning and decision making.

NONGRADED ORGANIZATION

Traditionally, children have been separated into discrete grade levels based solely on their chronological age, with little regard for individual learning differences and abilities. Nongraded organization, on the other hand, groups students from different grade levels for instruction based upon similar levels of academic achievement, ability, or interests. Among the benefits that have been associated with nongraded instruction – particularly at the elementary level – are higher student achievement scores, more positive attitudes toward school, and fewer students repeating grades (especially among minority students, males, and underachievers).[1]

Depending upon the desired level of organizational complexity and availability of faculty and staff, several options exist for implementing nongraded instruction.[2]

Nongrading within the Self-Contained Classroom

Teachers, independently of one another, organize materials and deliver instruction differently for students whose placement spans two or three grade levels within a single classroom.

Nongraded Grouping within the Same Grade Level

Two or more teachers at the same grade level collaboratively develop materials and teach students whose placement spans two or more grade levels. Students may be grouped and regrouped, as appropriate, to maximize the number of potential instructional groups.

Multi-Grade Level, Cross-Grade Grouping

Two or more teachers from different grade levels collaboratively organize materials and teach students whose placement spans two or more grade levels. Students may be grouped and regrouped, as appropriate, to maximize groupings in accordance with the subject matter expertise of the teachers.

School-Wide Nongraded Organization

All staff members participate in a multi-grade level, cross-grade instructional grouping design.

Many of the characteristics of effectively implemented nongraded instructional systems lend themselves to outcome-based education. The following represent some of the most obvious characteristics.

- Instructional grouping based on student ability, achievement, or interest (rather than age or grade level) provides an ideal structure for addressing individual student needs. Therefore, nongraded organization creates a success-for-all environment.
- Nongraded instruction permits students to advance when they have demonstrated mastery of learner outcomes regardless of whether or not other students in the same classroom or grade level have achieved mastery of the same content or skills.
- Collaborative planning and instructional delivery promote interdisciplinary approaches to teaching and promote creativity among staff members.
- Regular regrouping of students for instruction encourages positive interpersonal interaction and promotes development of students' communication skills.
- Nongraded instructional systems rely upon frequent formative evaluation using criterion-referenced tests and other forms of authentic assessment.

SCHOOL-WITHIN-A-SCHOOL ORGANIZATION

School district consolidation as well as rapid urbanization and suburbanization of the population during the 1950s and 1960s produced schools (particularly at the secondary level) having enrollments of 2,000 or more students. Individual school organizations that deal with thousands of students are incapable of addressing individual student needs and rarely are able to create the conditions under which most learners succeed.

The school-within-a-school organizational plan strives to create success for individual learners by dividing all the staff and students into smaller units or subschools. Each subschool remains as self-contained as possible, having its own administrators, support staff, teachers, and, whenever possible, its own area of the building. Characteristics of the school-within-a-school design include the following.

- The larger school is subdivided into two to four subschools, depending on student enrollment, the building size and layout, and available staff.
- Each subschool contains its own
  - administrator (principal or assistant principal)

- guidance counselor(s)
- office staff
- teachers of basic subjects such as English, math, social studies, and science
- separate classroom facilities and homerooms

- Students are randomly assigned to each subschool so that the composition of each subschool is as similar as possible to all of the others.
- Each subschool serves as the home base for students assigned to it, with students spending as much as three-fourths of their time there.
- Students share common areas such as the cafeteria, gymnasium, auditorium, library, and specialized classrooms such as science laboratories and vocational rooms.
- Students remain in the same subschool for the duration of their time at the school.
- The faculty assigned to each subschool is multidisciplinary, facilitating the formation of teaching teams and interdisciplinary programs.

The school-within-a-school design represents another alternative approach to restructuring the traditional school organization to support outcome-based education programs. Self-contained subschools provide a structure that facilitates individualized learning, empowering students to better meet their own learning needs. In addition, school climate is enhanced by providing students a more personalized educational experience than they could possibly experience in a larger school setting.

FLEXIBLE-BLOCK SCHEDULING PLAN

Despite the enormous social, political, economic, and technological changes that have characterized American society during the past several decades, the basic organizational pattern in secondary schools has remained essentially unchanged. The school day is typically divided into seven periods of about fifty minutes each, plus homeroom and lunch, and most students are expected to enroll in almost every class that is offered every day. Convenience, rather than concern for individual student or faculty needs and interests, perpetuates this traditional approach to organizing the school day.

A flexible-block scheduling plan that organizes the school day into four instructional blocks of approximately ninety minutes offers a promising alternative to the traditional seven-period day. Although the length of the school day remains essentially unchanged, longer blocks of instructional time permit a greater percentage of the day to be spent in class. Potential advantages of the four-period flexible-block design include the following.

- Fewer class assignments during any given semester enable students and teachers to prepare more thoroughly for each class.
- Offering each of four classes on alternating days or during alternating semesters enables students to complete eight different classes during the year (compared to six or seven under the traditional plan).
- The inclusion of eight classes (rather than six or seven) in an annual cycle may actually reduce the number of students in any given class during any given semester.
- Teachers have fewer preparations each day, facilitating the possibility of interdisciplinary team teaching.
- Flexibility in course offerings allows students to earn extra credits by scheduling additional elective and enrichment courses during the course of a semester.
- Reduced time spent in passing from class to class permits a larger percentage of each day to be spent as learning time.
- Longer blocks of time assigned to each class period facilitate completion of activities and projects, as well as encourage teachers to employ a variety of teaching strategies.

Flexible-block scheduling plans provide another student-centered strategy for restructuring the traditional school organization. Flexible scheduling and availability of a wide range of course offerings support outcome-based education by affording students an opportunity to identify and fulfill their own diverse learning needs.

The organization of instruction into fewer, but longer blocks of time throughout the day greatly facilitates the incorporation of authentic tasks and assessment techniques into the curriculum. Students have more uninterrupted class time to complete projects and activities that demonstrate their real abilities and accomplishments. Block scheduling also permits a greater depth of content coverage which allows students a more profound understanding of basic concepts and how they may effectively be applied to real-life situations. The increased quantity and quality of instructional time provided by flexible-block scheduling creates an environment where all students have the opportunity to become successful learners.

THE COPERNICAN PLAN

The Copernican plan[3] proposes a major restructuring of high school organization in which students enroll in only one or two major subjects at a time. Students are given the option of either enrolling in one four-hour class each day for a period of thirty days or enrolling in two two-hour classes each day for sixty days. Under the first option, each student would enroll in six of these four-hour classes each year, while the second option requires students to enroll in three two-course trimesters each year (totalling 180 instructional days per year for both options). In both options, the remainder of the school day is composed of a seminar class, an elective class, and a lunch period. The optional schedules of classes under the Copernican plan are illustrated in Figure 8.1.

Under the Copernican plan, each teacher has to prepare for and deliver only one or two classes at a time. Each teacher instructs six classes per year (rather than five under the traditional system), resulting in a 20 percent increase in the number of classes offered per year. Assuming that the number of classes chosen by students and the number of teachers on staff remain constant, a 20 percent reduction in class size becomes possible.

Reduction of the teacher's daily load and smaller average class sizes enable teachers to make much more effective use of individualized instruction. Greater individualization of instruction enables each teacher to better plan for specific needs of each student in the class and to monitor more closely each student's progress. The ability to concentrate on smaller numbers of students also facilitates the employment of performance-based or mastery-based instruction. Working with students on an individual basis lets teachers more accurately assess student progress and achievement — an important condition for assigning performance-based grades.

The daily seminar class is designed to give students the opportunity to discuss complex issues related to the subject matter they are studying. Global and national issues that will impact students' lives when they have completed their schooling (or any topics of interest to class members) may also be explored during the seminar classes.

TIME	SCHEDULE A	SCHEDULE B
7:46		Macroclass I
	Macroclass	(110 min.)
		for 60 days
9:36	(226 min.)	
		Passing (6 min.)
9:42	for	Macroclass II
	30 days	(110 min.)
		for 60 days
11:32		
	Passing (6 min.)	Passing (6 min.)
11:38	First Lunch	
	(35 min.)	Seminar I/Music/P.E.
12:13		(70 min.)
12:48	Seminar II/Music/P.E.	
	(70 min.)	Second Lunch
		(35 min.)
1:23		
	Passing (6 min.)	Passing (6 min.)
1:29	Preparation/Help/ Study/P.E./Music	Preparation/Help/ Study/P.E./Music
	(70 min.)	(70 min.)
2:39		
	Departure (6 min.)	Departure (6 min.)
2:45		
	Activities/Sports	Activities/Sports
	(135 min.)	(135 min.)
5:00		

FIGURE 8.1 Two proposed schedules for the Copernican plan.

The restructured high school organization proposed by the Copernican plan provides an ideal instructional arrangement for outcome-based education. Reduced class sizes and a limited number of daily preparations greatly enhance the teacher's ability to assist students in identifying and meeting their individual needs. Lengthened class periods foster variety in teaching strategies and empower students to become active participants in their own learning.

Discussion of complex issues during seminar classes facilitates the development of critical thinking skills that are crucial for achieving learner exit outcomes. The opportunity to apply basic knowledge and concepts to real-world problems enables students to prepare themselves for life outside the classroom—a basic goal of outcome-based education.

YEAR-ROUND EDUCATION

Year-round education offers another alternative to the traditional school organization by utilizing physical facilities and staff on a continuous basis throughout the calendar year. Twelve-month calendars can be tailored to fit individual learner, family, and community needs by permitting vacation and other nonschool activities to be scheduled throughout the year. Differential scheduling of vacations also reduces the number of students enrolled in classes at any given time by 20 to 35 percent. Other potential benefits offered by year-round education include the following.

- Year-round education enables students to learn in any of the twelve months.
- Students needing or desiring additional learning opportunities may enroll in classes during all or part of their vacation times.
- Shorter, but more frequent vacations enable students to pursue projects or short-term employment in the community more easily than fixed three-month summer vacations.
- Unlike traditional scheduling that forces most students out of school for three months every summer, year-round education assures that no student is out of class for more than one month out of every four.
- Vacations of fifteen, twenty, and thirty days interspersed throughout the year provide maximum flexibility for families unable to take vacation leave during the summer months.
- Community education programs and activities can use the local school building throughout the year.
- School districts can save up to one-third of their capital outlay for new buildings by utilizing existing buildings during all twelve months of the year.
- Where space is not an extreme hardship, utilizing school buildings throughout the year reduces the number of students enrolled in classes at any given time by up to one-third.
- Children from lower-income families can make use of federally

funded programs administered through the local school on a
year-round basis.
- Year-round calendars permit scheduling common vacation
  periods when all students and teachers are out of the building.

The tremendous flexibility built into a year-round education schedule
provides an excellent framework for implementing an outcome-based
education program. Individual needs—academic and social—can be
accommodated easily within a schedule that permits differential vacation
periods throughout the year.

Year-round education also provides for continuous learning by making
instruction available to all students twelve months of the year and by
limiting vacation time to a maximum of thirty days at a time. Continuous
learning promotes consistent acquisition of knowledge and skills without
the problem of beginning again at the end of each three-month summer
vacation. Varying levels of remediation are available for all students
during one or more of their vacation periods throughout the year.

Short, but frequent vacation periods provide students with multiple
opportunities to learn through experience by completing projects and
activities in the community. Community input into classroom instruction
is also facilitated by a year-round education schedule.

Year-round education also supports outcome-based education by enabling the school's stakeholders to adopt other alternative approaches
such as the nongraded organization or school-within-a-school model.
Either of these alternative models can easily be combined with year-
round education to foster a learning environment in which all students
have the opportunity to succeed.

INTERDISCIPLINARY APPROACH

Another long-standing tradition in school organization is the com-
partmentalization of content areas. Despite the importance of understanding the connectedness of related bits and pieces of information from
various disciplines, school personnel (especially at the high school level)
are slow to break down the barriers that separate subject areas.

The interdisciplinary approach to curriculum development and instructional delivery is gaining widespread attention as an alternative
approach to the traditional compartmentalized curriculum. An interdisciplinary approach to content enables students to make connections
between subjects and apply their knowledge and skills to real problems.

Basically, an interdisciplinary approach teams two or more content teachers for organizing materials and delivering instruction on a topic or theme that integrates content information from both of the teachers' disciplines. Ideally, the interdisciplinary unit or activity incorporates content from a wide variety of subject areas into a well-integrated learning experience. Integrating content to produce a thematic or interdisciplinary unit or activity will enhance the teaching/learning experience when the following occurs.

- District and school philosophy support an interdisciplinary approach as an integral part of the overall instructional program.
- Integration incorporates logical, natural elements of associated content areas.
- Integrated material from each content area is appropriate to the learners' age.
- Critical learning outcomes are identified for each content area in addition to the overall learning outcomes for the interdisciplinary unit or activity.
- Interdisciplinary units or activities encourage the development of basic skills such as communication, critical thinking, problem solving, and decision making.
- Interdisciplinary units or activities are designed and delivered by a team of teachers whose expertise covers all of the constituent content areas.
- Members of interdisciplinary teaching teams are allocated common planning time to develop quality instructional units and activities.
- Interdisciplinary or thematic units focus on topics of high interest or recognized importance to students.
- It is understood that content area integration is not an end in itself, but a means for achieving a quality learning experience.

An interdisciplinary approach to curriculum development and instructional delivery is an indispensable element of an outcome-based education program. A well-developed interdisciplinary unit or activity encourages the development of real-life skills, such as problem solving and decision making, that students will use constantly after they have completed their formal education.

The inclusion of content from a variety of subject areas in an interdisciplinary unit stimulates the interest of students who come from diverse backgrounds and have a wide range of abilities. In addition, almost every student will achieve some degree of success or be good at some aspect of the unit. Outcome-based education is predicated upon the premise that success breeds success, and exposing students to a variety of interdisciplinary units and activities provides numerous opportunities for success.

The holistic or integrated nature of interdisciplinary activities lends itself extremely well to authentic learning and assessment. By focusing on various aspects of important or high-interest topics, the interdisciplinary approach encourages students to employ complex thinking processes to relate textbook material to real-life problems and situations. A learning environment that stimulates students to develop and expand their complex thinking skills inherently creates conditions in which all learners can succeed.

REVIEW ACTIVITIES

(1) Carefully review each of the alternative approaches to school organization discussed in this chapter and how each relates to, or supports outcome-based education.

- Which of these alternative approaches do you believe could be reasonably implemented in your own district or school? Why?
- What would be the first step to be taken in order to successfully implement each of these alternative approaches?
- Who within the district or school would have to be involved in the process to assure successful implementation of the alternative approach?

(2) As a member of the district planning team, you have been asked to study the potential benefits of implementing *one* of the alternative approaches discussed in this chapter as a support system for the district's newly adopted outcome-based education program.

- Which one of the alternative approaches to school organization would you recommend to support outcome-based education in your district?
- What benefit does that particular approach offer for an outcome-based education program that none of the other approaches seem to offer?
- Would it be a mistake to try to implement both outcome-based education and an alternative approach to school organization at the same time? Why or why not?

NOTES

1 Martin, L. S. and B. N. Pavin. 1973. "Current Research on Open Space, Nongrading, Vertical Grouping, and Team Teaching," *Phi Delta Kappan*, 57(5):310 – 315.

2 Worner, R. B. 1991. "Graded/Nongraded Organization," in *Instructional Leadership Handbook, Second Edition*, J. W. Keefe and J. M. Jenkins, eds., Reston, VA: National Association of Secondary School Principals, pp. 33 – 34.

3 Carroll, J. M. 1989. *The Copernican Plan: Restructuring the American High School.* Andover, MA: Regional Laboratory for Educational Improvement of the Northeast and Islands, p. 27.

FLOYD BOSCHEE is an associate professor, Division of Educational Administration, School of Education, University of South Dakota, where he teaches and conducts research in educational leadership, supervision, curriculum, and outcome-based education. Over the past eighteen years he has been a teacher, coach, athletic director, and assistant superintendent for curriculum and instruction. He has also served as chairman of departments of education, published extensively in national journals, and authored the books, *Grouping = Growth* and *Effective Reading Programs: The Administrator's Role.*

MARK A. BARON is an assistant professor, Division of Educational Administration, School of Education, University of South Dakota, where he teaches graduate courses in educational administration, educational research, curriculum, and outcome-based education. He also serves as regional coordinator and member of the advisory board for the South Dakota Leadership in Educational Administration (LEAD) Project. He began his career in education as a Peace Corps Volunteer in West Africa, and has been a teacher and principal in schools within the United States and American-sponsored overseas schools in Latin America.

T5-DHI-142

I've travelled the world twice over,
Met the famous: saints and sinners,
Poets and artists, kings and queens,
Old stars and hopeful beginners,
I've been where no-one's been before,
Learned secrets from writers and cooks
All with one library ticket
To the wonderful world of books.

© JANICE JAMES.

THE BUFFALO BOX

Private Detective Simon Lash, a collector of Americana, is not very impressed when confronted with a Desert Rat calling himself Lansford Hastings, who has in his possession a small box and asks Lash to find the owner. Lash is reluctant to help. As he points out to his assistant, Eddie Slocum, a Lansford Hastings was part of the Donner Party, who in 1846 crossed the plains and mountains to California by wagon train — but he died in 1870. So who is this other Lansford Hastings?

Books by Frank Gruber
in the Ulverscroft Large Print Series:

FRANK GRUBER

THE
BUFFALO BOX

Complete and Unabridged

ULVERSCROFT
Leicester

First published in the
United States of America

First Large Print Edition
published October 1994

Copyright © 1942 by Frank Gruber

British Library CIP Data

Gruber, Frank
  The buffalo box: a Simon Lash mystery.
  —Large print ed.—
  Ulverscroft large print series: mystery
  I. Title
  823.912 [F]

  ISBN 0–7089–3165–0

Published by
F. A. Thorpe (Publishing) Ltd.
Anstey, Leicestershire
Set by Words & Graphics Ltd.
Anstey, Leicestershire
Printed and bound in Great Britain by
T. J. Press (Padstow) Ltd., Padstow, Cornwall

This book is printed on acid-free paper

1

HOLLYWOOD is the place where a man who wears shorts and has a long white beard runs down Sunset Boulevard every afternoon. It's where they don't allow pinball games, but more than fifty psychics, seers, astrologers, and fortunetellers advertise in the newspapers and claim they can tell you everything about yourself and you don't even have to tell them your name.

In a town like that the man riding the burro down Hollywood Boulevard attracted no attention whatever, even though the burro was a rather small one and the man's long legs dragged on the street. The burro proceeded placidly past the Roosevelt Hotel at a gait of about two miles an hour. The rider, who had a ragged, red beard and was dressed like a desert rat, seemed in no haste. He smoked a short clay pipe and when the tobacco was all gone tapped out the ashes and refilled the hot bowl with a coarse, black mixture.

After some time the burro reached Harper Avenue, and the rider, taking the pipe out of his mouth for a moment, said, "Haw, Daisy."

The burro turned left, and the desert rat began scanning the numbers on the two-story apartment houses. About halfway down the hill he kneed his mount and it moved to the curb. There the desert rat dismounted and took off an alkali-stained jute sack that had been balanced over the burro's shoulders. Carrying the sack, he crossed the sidewalk to a door, where he pressed a pearl button.

After a minute or two the door was opened by a slender man in his middle thirties.

The desert rat took the pipe from his mouth. "You Simon Lash?"

"No," was the reply. "I'm Eddie Slocum. What did you want to see Mr. Lash about?"

"'Bout some private detective work."

Eddie Slocum shook his head. "Sorry, old-timer, but I don't think Mr. Lash would be interested."

"*You* think," snapped the desert rat. "Can't Lash talk for himself?"

"He can, but he won't. He never sees anyone without an appointment and he doesn't make appoint — "

"I've got an appointment with him! My name's Hastings."

Eddie Slocum blinked. "When did you make it?"

"A long time ago. Now, lead the way . . ."

Slocum hesitated a moment, then shrugged and, turning, trotted up a flight of stairs. The desert rat followed, climbing heavily. At the top of the stairs Slocum led him into an office furnished meagerly with a desk and swivel chair, a couple of red leather armchairs and a stack of steel files.

"Wait in here, please," Slocum said and walked out of the room, closing the door behind him.

In the hall, Slocum turned to a closed door and drew a deep breath. Then he opened the door and stepped into a large room lined with bookshelves that reached to the ceiling. Simon Lash was sprawled on a red leather couch, reading a copy of Burton Rascoe's *Belle Starr*.

"Chief," said Eddie Slocum, "there's a character here, says he's got an appointment with you."

"Send him away," Lash replied without taking his eyes off the book.

"I don't think he'll go, chief. I said he was a character."

"You're a character yourself, Eddie," Simon Lash retorted. "Throw him down the stairs. Or entertain him yourself, since you made the appointment."

"I didn't make the appointment. He says he made it with you . . . a long time ago."

Lash lowered the copy of *Belle Starr*. "I didn't make any appointment with anyone."

"He says his name is Hastings."

Lash shook his head. "I don't know anyone named Hastings. Get rid of him."

Eddie Slocum shrugged and left. A moment later Lash heard a violent commotion in the other room and throwing down his book sprang to his feet. The library door burst open and the desert rat filled the doorway.

"Lash!" he snarled.

4

Beyond Hastings, Eddie Slocum's voice said tensely: "I've got the brass knuckles now, chief. I'll take him."

"Hold it," Lash said. Then to Hastings, "What do you want?"

"I want to talk to you."

"You can talk but you can't make me listen."

"You'll listen. My name is Lansford Hastings — "

"And mine is Simon Lash. Hello and good-bye."

Hastings lowered his head as if about to make a charge, but changed his mind and let his glance wander about the book-lined room. He said:

"You've got a lot of books here. Maybe you've read about me."

"I haven't had that pleasure," Lash said, sarcastically.

Hastings was still not deterred. "I even wrote a book. It's called *The Emigrant's Route to Oregon and California*. Are you interested now?"

Simon Lash did a double take, an automatic nod of his head then a quick jerk up. "Eddie," he called. "Get ready . . . "

Hastings grunted. "You think I'm crazy."

"Well, aren't you?"

"No," Hastings said. "And I can make my point in three minutes . . ."

"Three minutes?"

"Yes."

"All right," said Lash. "I'll give you three minutes. Step aside, Eddie."

Hastings retreated to the office and plumped himself down in one of the leather chairs. Lash entered the office cautiously and got into the swivel chair behind his desk. He opened the top right hand drawer, a movement that Hastings did not miss. Eddie Slocum came to the door and leaned against the jamb. He held his right hand behind his back.

Hastings dropped the jute sack on the floor at his feet and stooping over it reached in and brought out a box. It was about three inches tall, four inches wide and six long. It was made entirely of redwood and ornately hand-carved. Although Hastings retained the box in his hand, Lash could see that the relief carvings consisted of a series of buffaloes, each exquisitely carved and about a half inch in size.

Hastings regarded Lash in silence for a moment. Then he said: "I want you to find the owner of the box."

"I'm a detective," Lash said, "but I don't take every case that comes along — "

"I know," Hastings cut in. "You only take the cases that interest you. This one will."

"Not yet it doesn't."

"Then I'll tell you the name of the man who originally owned this box. He carved it himself during a certain winter. The man's name was Isaac Eckert."

Hastings shot a triumphant glance at Simon Lash, but when he saw the latter's face, calm and unperturbed, a scowl twisted his features. "You said you'd read my book. Then you must have read about the Donner Party."

"I have."

"And you don't remember the name of Isaac Eckert?"

"Of course I remember it."

Hastings exploded. "Then you know that Eckert was the richest man in the party. He had fifty thousand dollars in gold in his wagon box."

Simon Lash said deliberately, "Your three minutes are up, Mr. Hastings."

"What?" cried Hastings, aghast. "You'd let me go now?"

"I said I'd listen for three minutes. I did. I'm not interested in your case."

Hastings sprang to his feet and Eddie Slocum darted forward, bringing his right hand from behind his back. Brass gleamed on his knuckles. Hastings did not seem to see the brass. He goggled once more at Simon Lash, then rushed past Eddie Slocum.

They could hear his heavy boots pound down the stairs.

"Take a look out the window, boss," said Eddie Slocum. "You'll see something. A jackass. He came up on it."

"Naturally," said Simon Lash.

"What do you mean — naturally?"

"The build-up. The man's suffering from hallucinations."

"You mean the fifty thousand bucks in gold he was talking about is baloney?"

Simon Lash groaned. "Some day one of my books is going to jump right down

8

from a shelf and bite you, Eddie. The Donner Party was snowbound during the winter of 1846 – 47."

Eddie Slocum looked blank.

Lash shook his head. "The Donner Party were emigrants, who took a short cut that had been recommended to them by a man who wrote a book about it. The book was published in 1845 and the name of the man who wrote it was . . . Lansford Hastings!"

Eddie Slocum exclaimed in chagrin. "Hey, that's the same name as the guy who was here."

"That's right."

"But that's ninety-seven years ago."

"You get sixty-four dollars for that one, Eddie. Would you like to try for the jackpot question?"

"I don't get it," said Eddie Slocum, slowly. "If he wrote a book in 1845, he'd be over a hundred years old . . . "

Simon Lash got up and moved to the door. There he said, "You're getting close, Eddie. He'd be a pretty old man by now . . . if he hadn't died in 1870 . . . "

After the departure of the desert rat Simon Lash returned to his library and tried to recapture interest in the book he had been reading. But he found the words blurred on the pages and after a while he put the book down.

Eddie Slocum found him sprawled on the couch, staring at the ceiling. "What we need to do, chief," he said, "is go out and get drunk. We don't get out enough."

"You can go out any time, Eddie."

"Yeah, but what about you? You don't get out of the house sometimes in two or three weeks. You don't do a damn thing but lay around here and read. What difference does it make today if Buffalo Bill killed sixteen redskins at the battle of Gettysburg."

"You have a remarkable flair for history," Lash said.

"That's what my teacher said when I was a kid in Brooklyn. Which reminds me, we used to pay forty and fifty cents for a brand-new history book. How come you have to pay forty and fifty bucks for secondhand books? The dope in them ain't any better than in the new books, is it?"

"Sometimes not as good. I've tried

to explain it to you before. I like old books, particularly the rare ones. I collect Americana like some people collect china or pipes. But I like to read my books."

"What's the percentage in reading history. You're a detective."

"Ah," said Lash. "Now, you're getting down to it. You take that fellow who was here a few minutes ago. I knew he was a phony the moment he mentioned his name. I knew it because I'm posted on American history. Not just the important events that you learn about in school, but the other things that happened in this country that by themselves were not so very important, but on the whole helped to make this country. You take the Donner Party — "

"You take them; I never even heard of them."

"Then this is a good time. The Donner Party consisted of eighty-some people who started from Missouri in 1846 and crossed the plains and mountains to California. This was two years before gold was discovered in California. Not very many people had gone overland to California before. The trip was a hard one later when there were a lot of people on the trails; in 1846 it took real courage. These people had it. They crossed the plains in wagons. When they got to Utah they had to cut paths through miles of woods and practically lift the big wagons up the sides of mountains. They got on the other side and had to cross the salt desert, about the worst stretch of country in all the world. Then they had all of Nevada and at last, when they thought they were about at the end of the trip, they hit the worst stretch of all, the Sierra Nevada Mountains in winter. They couldn't make it."

Lash sighed. "They became snowbound, locked in a little valley, the snow twenty feet deep . . . and no food . . . "

"What did they eat?"

"That," said Lash, "is the story of the Donner Party."

"What do you mean? They couldn't live without food."

"Some of them didn't live. To put it briefly only half of the party survived. More than forty members starved to death . . . and made it possible for the others to get out."

"Huh?"

"The survivors ate the bodies of the others . . ."

Eddie Slocum recoiled. "You mean . . . they turned cannibal?"

"It took a million years to develop civilization, Eddie. Five days without food and people revert to the primal instincts of the savage. The experiences of the Donner Party aren't without parallel in American history. There were a number of other cases of cannibalism on the frontier. Boone Helm, who was hanged by the Vigilantes in Virginia City, Montana, boasted that he had eaten human flesh. Quantrill, the notorious Missouri guerrilla of the Civil War, was suspected of cannibalism in Utah, before the war. He went prospecting in the Wasatch Mountains with a group of men. Some of the men disappeared and Quantrill was reported wandering around the mountains carrying the leg of a man."

Eddie Slocum rubbed his chin with the back of his hand. "This fellow Lansford Hastings who was here was a cannibal?"

Lash blinked. "I told you that the original Lansford Hasting died in 1870."

"He belonged to the Donner Party?"

"No. He was a man who'd crossed the mountains before and had written a book. He claimed to have found a short cut to California and the Donner Party followed his trail. They blamed their difficulties on him and, to an extent, they were right. If they'd followed the known trails, they probably would have got through all right."

"So the Donner Party was pretty sore at Hastings. Mmm, suppose this guy was the son maybe of the first Hastings and there were some of the Donners or their children alive . . . "

"What're you trying to do, Eddie?" Lash exclaimed irritably.

"Nothing, chief. Only the idea has possibilities, don't you think?"

"You're about as subtle as a buzz saw. You're trying to rouse my interest in this case."

"And you're not interested?"

"No!"

Lash looked at Eddie Slocum's grinning face, then sprang to his feet. He rushed out of the room. He caught up his hat on the way to the stairs.

14

2

THERE were better-looking book-stores in Hollywood than Oscar Eisenschiml's hole-in-the-wall on Wilcox, but Simon Lash never patronized the other stores. They sold the latest novels and best sellers, and Lash seldom bought a book that wasn't at least twenty years old.

Eisenschiml was in his late fifties, a heavy-set man with a fringe of gray hair running around a bald spot like a hedge. He was studying a first edition with a reading glass when Lash entered the store.

He put down the glass. "Ah, Simon, I haven't seen you in some time. So you've been working."

"Is there any law says I have to work?" Lash retorted.

Eisenschiml was oblivious of Lash's ill temper. "No, but you only come in here when you want to buy books or sell. And you haven't got any books with you. So you want to buy. That means you've been working. Simple deduction."

"You should have been a detective."

"And you should own a bookstore," Eisenschiml grunted. "You've got enough books to start one. What're you interested in today?"

"The Donner Party. What've you got on it?"

"Stewart's *Ordeal of Hunger*. It's the best."

"It's too new. I'm interested only in the old ones."

"As a matter of fact," said Eisenschiml, "your coming in here is quite a coincidence. A party was in here this morning with a very fine book. Lansford Hastings' *The Emigrant's Trail to Oregon and California*."

Lash's face became sullen. "A man with red whiskers . . . ?"

"Oh no, a young woman."

"Let's see the book."

Eisenschiml winced. "I haven't got it. I turned it down. She wanted too much money."

"How much?"

"For . . . I mean seventy-five dollars.

16

That means I would have had to sell it for a hundred and you can't get that much money around here for a book like that."

"Why not? You can always find a sucker — like me."

"You'd pay a hundred dollars for it?"

"Right now I would. Tomorrow I might not want it for ten cents. Did you get the woman's address?"

"No, I didn't. I told her to try some of the other stores. Then if she couldn't get what she wanted to come back here."

Lash groaned. "She may not return."

Eisenschiml shrugged. "If you really want a copy, I can advertise for it in the trade papers. It's not too rare. I ought to be able to get a copy in three or four weeks."

"Three or four weeks! I want it now — today."

"Why such a hurry? . . . Say . . . !" Eisenschiml's jaw suddenly became slack. Simon Lash turned quickly to the door and saw a girl enter. She was in her early twenties, rather tall and slender, and wore a mustard-colored suit with the collar of a tan sport shirt laid over the suit collar. Her shimmering blond hair was uncovered.

She carried a small, flat parcel under her arm.

"Mr. Eisenschiml," she said in a clear voice, "I'm going to give you one more chance to buy this book."

Eisenschiml's eyes rolled and he swallowed with difficulty. "Ah, yes, Miss, uh, would you care to come into my office . . . in back?"

"What for?" asked the girl. "You examined it before. It's still the same book . . . and I'm still asking the same price."

"Yes, I know, but — "

"Let's see the book," Lash cut in.

Eisenschiml groaned. "This gentleman collects Americana. I was telling him about your book and he thought he might possibly be interested in it. Mr. Lash, Miss . . . ?"

"Elizabeth Dunlap."

"Ah yes, Miss Dunlap."

The girl peeled the wrapping paper from the book and handed it to Lash. "It's autographed."

Lash opened the front cover and looked

at the autograph. "A forgery, of course."

Elizabeth Dunlap exclaimed, "I beg your pardon!"

"This inscription — 'to George Donner, with the best wishes of Lansford Warren Hastings' — it's not legitimate."

The girl's nostrils flared. She held out her hand. "D'you mind?"

Lash paid no attention to her. He turned to the title page.

"The book," the girl said, firmly. "It's not for sale."

"But Miss Dunlap," cried Eisenschiml. "You just said . . . "

"I've changed my mind."

"Fifty dollars," said Lash.

Eisenschiml struck his forehead with the palm of his hand. Lash looked at him coldly. "The flies bothering you, Eisenschiml?"

"Miss Dunlap," said Eisenschiml, "if you'd step into my office for a moment . . . "

"That won't be necessary," Elizabeth Dunlap said. "The book's no longer for sale."

"All right," said Lash, "the autograph is genuine. I'll give you fifty dollars for

19

the book, which is ten dollars more than you offered it to Eisenschiml for."

Elizabeth Dunlap gestured impatiently for the book. "Please!"

Lash sneered. "You've been around to every bookdealer in town. There're a couple over in Pasadena. If you want to waste some more time, go on over there, but you'll find that this is still the best offer you'll get."

"But it's not good enough. The price is . . . five hundred dollars . . . "

"Miss Dunlap!" cried Eisenschiml, in horror.

Lash looked at the girl steadily for a moment. "Will an apology knock off four hundred and fifty dollars?"

"Your apology, Mr. Lash," Elizabeth Dunlap said, coldly, "is worth something. I shall be glad to deduct for it. The book is now four hundred and ninety-nine dollars and ninety-five cents."

Lash handed back the book, nodded and started to the door. Eisenschiml called after him, but even though his hand was on the knob, Lash didn't hear the girl's voice. He opened the door and turned.

"One hundred dollars," he snarled.

"It's a pleasure to have met you, Mr. Simon Lash," the girl said.

Lash let the door swing shut and came back into the store. "The man with the red whiskers put you up to this."

The girl's eyebrows arched in a question. "Red whiskers?"

"How did you know my name was Simon Lash?"

"Mr. Eisenschiml introduced you."

"He didn't give my first name."

"Oh, didn't he? Then I must have heard it somewhere. Don't tell me — you're some sort of celebrity, aren't you? Yes, of course. A motion picture star."

"All right," said Lash, through gritted teeth. "Now we're even. Shall we talk business?"

"But that's what we've been doing, Mr. Lash."

Lash reached out deliberately and took the book from her hand. "You win. I'll pay . . . your price."

"Five hundred dollars?"

"If that's what you want — yes!"

She suddenly smiled. "Shall we go

somewhere where we can talk?"

"Yes."

Eisenschiml banged on his glass show-case. "But Simon . . . Miss Dunlap . . . !"

"It's all right, Eisenschiml," Lash said. "You'll get your commission. Twenty-five percent."

"Twenty-five percent!" cried Eisenschiml.

Lash followed the girl out of the store. "Musso Frank's is just around the corner. It won't be crowded this time of the afternoon."

"Very well, let's go there."

A few minutes later they seated themselves in a booth in Musso Franks' Restaurant. A waiter came to take their order and Lash looked inquiringly at the girl.

"A glass of sherry, please."

"And a beer," Lash added.

The waiter went off and Lash leaned back against the padded booth partition. "Now, about the price for the book."

"Yes, of course. I've just been thinking. You mentioned a man with a red beard . . . "

"Yeah," said Lash.

"Was he a tall, well-built man, wearing

22

rough . . . well, prospector's apparel?"

"D'you mind?" said Lash.

"I beg your pardon?"

"The routine. You don't have to give it to me. I said I'd pay the price. What do you want?"

Color came into her cheeks, but the arrival of the waiter with the drinks prevented an outburst. After the man had gone, Elizabeth Dunlap had mastered her control.

"Very well, you're a private detective. I want you to conduct an investigation for me. I'll give you the book as a — a retainer."

"And if I get the box?"

"Five — what box?"

"The box with the buffaloes."

The girl's eyes widened in horror. "Wh-what . . . what do you know about that box?"

"Redbeard."

"*He* asked you to find the box for him?"

"No, he had the box . . . "

The girl had the beauty to be a great actress and she most certainly had acting ability. If he hadn't known better, Lash would have been convinced that she wasn't acting.

"If he had the box . . . wha-what did he want you to do?"

"He wanted me to find the owner."

"But *I'm* the owner!"

She had made Lash grovel. Now he repaid her with interest. "Swell, then all you two have to do is get together and you'll both be happy."

"No! It's not that simple. I'm sure it isn't. There's something about this . . . what did this redbearded man say his name was?"

"Lansford Hastings."

"What?"

"The same name that's on the book."

"But Lansford Hastings had no descendants."

"Miss Dunlap," said Lash. "Drink your sherry. You may need it. I'm about to tell you a shocking story . . . a shockingly funny story. Ha-ha. The man with the red whiskers says he wrote the book!"

Elizabeth Dunlap looked puzzled for a moment, then her eyes widened. "But that's absurd."

"Isn't it? Ha-ha-ha!" Lash laughed

mirthlessly. "Lansford Hastings is the nineteenth century Flying Dutchman, the Wandering Jew. He led emigrant trains across the plains and mountains. He was a Confederate during the Civil War and afterwards he started a Confederate colony in Brazil. But this is the funniest of all — ha-ha-ha! He died in Brazil in 1870 . . . but he doesn't know it. Isn't that a scream?"

"It's ridiculous!" Betty Dunlap burst out. "The man's an imposter, or — "

"Or balmy. And of course he ain't. He rode up to my house on a jackass, but that didn't necessarily indicate that he was fresh out of the bughouse. And now, what can I do for you, Miss Dunlap?"

"You can act civilly."

Lash made an impatient gesture. "All right, all right. I'll apologize again. But I've got a witness. You can go over there to the telephone booth and I'll stay right here. Call my apartment and ask my assistant, Eddie Slocum, about the man who was there yesterday afternoon."

"No, I don't have to do that. Perhaps this man did tell you that fantastic story.

It's in character. He told Harold one almost as wild."

"Harold?"

"Harold Wade — a friend."

"What did he tell him?"

"About the box."

"Well, what about the box?"

Elizabeth Dunlap frowned. "I don't believe that matters. The point is simply that the box rightfully belongs to me and I want to acquire it."

"And you want me to get it for you?"

"That's right."

Lash shook his head. "No."

"No, what? You agreed — "

"I agreed to perform a job for you. But I don't believe I can, after all."

"Don't you want this book?"

"Yes," said Lash, "I want it. But I don't want it as badly as you seem to think."

"I don't understand."

Lash glowered at the girl for a moment. Then he said: "Do I look to be as big a fool as all that?"

Elizabeth Dunlap gasped. "What are you talking about?"

"You. You think because you've got blue eyes and a pretty face you can get away with anything."

"You're the worst-tempered man I've ever met in my life," Elizabeth Dunlap said furiously.

"I didn't hunt *you* up," Lash reminded.

The girl started to get up, then suddenly dropped back. "All right," she said, "let's start all over."

"At the beginning? Very well, who sent you to me?"

"No one sent me. It was my own idea."

Lash shook his head angrily. "It so happens that I have absolutely no conceit. I don't give a damn what anybody in this world thinks of me. So don't give me that routine about coming to me because you'd heard I was a great detective. I'm not that well known. I don't want to be. Too many people annoy me as it is. Now, answer my questions or forget the whole business. Who sent you to me?"

"Harold Wade."

"Your fiancé?"

"Friend."

"Who told him about me?"

"You mean to say you've never heard of Harold Wade? Haven't you got a radio?"

"No, what is he — a singer?"

Elizabeth Dunlap regarded Lash through lowered lids. "Are you really as obtuse as all that? Harold said you were eccentric . . . "

"I'm not. I live my own life. I don't happen to care for radio programs. Who is Harold Wade and how did he hear about me?"

Elizabeth Dunlap sighed wearily. "I'm going to recommend that Harold get you on his program."

"Shall I start taking singing lessons?"

"Harold doesn't use singers. He's the Oddity Man. He collects odd facts and information, queer people. I imagine that's how he heard about you. At any rate, he told me you were a capable detective, despite you — "

"Despite my eccentricities."

"That's right."

Lash tapped the book. "And how did you know about this?"

"That has to do with the investigation. Once you tell me definitely that you'll take the case, I'll tell you."

"You'll tell me everything?"

There was a shade of hesitation before she answered, "Yes."

"That means *almost* everything. Well, go ahead."

"Very well. You know what this book is about?"

"I've read it."

"You have? Then why do you want it so badly?"

"Because I collect Americana. As a matter of fact, I once owned a copy of that book. I thought I'd like to have one again."

"You've read about the Donner Party?"

"Yes, and to save time, I'll add that Hastings — rather, the man who called himself Hastings — declared that the buffalo box was carved by Isaac Eckert."

"It was. And Isaac Eckert was my great-grand-father."

3

LASH leaned back against the booth cushion. "You might as well give me the genealogy."

"Isaac Eckert died, as you know, in 1847. But three of his children were rescued — Isaac, Junior, George Pearson Eckert, and Elizabeth, my grandmother. I'm named after her."

"She was the youngest, wasn't she?"

"That's right. Isaac, Junior, at the time was thirteen, George Pearson was eleven, and Elizabeth only three. Isaac was killed in a California mining camp in 1856, before he was married. George Pearson married a girl named Hester Lupton. He served in the Union Army in the Civil War and was wounded so seriously at Cold Harbor that he died a few months later. He never returned to California. At the time he went to war he had two sons, Isaac Eckert, III, and Fremont Eckert. Isaac was born in 1860 and Fremont in 1862, after his father had already gone east. Cousin Fremont died only three years ago . . . "

"And Cousin Isaac?"

"He ran away from home when he was sixteen and no one's ever heard a word from him."

"Did Fremont have any children?"

"Two. One died in infancy, and the survivor is my cousin Sheridan Eckert."

"Where does he live?"

"In Santa Monica. He's an attorney."

Lash grimaced. "What about your own tree?"

"My grandmother, Elizabeth, was born in 1843. She did not marry until 1869; Grandfather Jim Dunlap was the superintendent of a silver mine in Virginia City. He made a great deal of money, but lost it all when the bonanza petered out. My father, also named Jim, was born in 1882."

"Your grandmother was thirty-nine when he was born?"

"That's right."

"And your mother — I mean, is she still alive?"

"No, she died when I was born."

"What is your father's occupation?"

"He's an inventor."

Lash grunted. "Yes, but what does he do for a living?"

Elizabeth Dunlap flushed. "It so happens that some of father's inventions paid off."

"Sorry," said Lash. "Well, that takes care of the genealogy. Let's get down to the box, now. How did you become the owner?"

"My grandmother gave it to me. Her father made it during that horrible winter." A shudder ran through her. "You know, of course, how her father died?"

"He starved. So did forty-some others of the Donner Party."

"Yes." Elizabeth Dunlap hesitated and frowned. "Of course I've known the story since I was in my teens. It's always had a strange fascination . . . and horror . . . for me. The incredible suffering and hardships they all endured . . . "

"I know the story," said Lash. "I know, too, that the emigrants blamed Lansford Hastings for their plight. He got them to take the short cut to California, the southern route across the salt flats of Utah, the wastes of Nevada and finally the pass over the Sierras, which they reached too late in the season. They became snowed in and one half of the party never got out. Your grandmother and two greatuncles were rescued, however. Now, which of them carried out the box?"

"Grandmother. Her father had carved it during the long weeks and had given it to Elizabeth, the baby, as a toy. She carried it with her when she was taken out."

"What was in the box?"

"Nothing. It was empty."

"What's in it now?"

"It's still empty."

Lash bit his lower lip. "All right; now what about this red-bearded man who calls himself Lansford Hastings? Where does he come into the picture — and how did he get the box?"

"That's one of the things I want you to find out. Harold had him on the program one night — "

"What for?"

"An oddity — a genuine desert rat."

"You saw him?"

33

"Yes, I often go to the studio."

"How'd you find out that he had the box?"

"I didn't! I hadn't the slightest suspicion until you told me so yourself a few minutes ago."

Lash drummed on the table with his fingers. "You still haven't cleared up the matter of the box. You say your grandmother carried it out of the mountains away back there in '47. When did it leave her possession?"

"It never did. It was in her effects when she died in 1919."

"Then how did you come into possession of it?"

"She willed everything to me. I was only one year old at the time."

"Then you've seen the box yourself?"

"Oh, yes, I played with it as a child. But just like a child I lost interest in it. I probably haven't seen it since I was seven or eight years old."

"Then what brought back your interest in it?"

Elizabeth Dunlap frowned. "I can't tell you that."

"You can't or won't?"

34

"It has nothing to do with this. It's sufficient to say that I discovered the box was missing and that I have reason to believe it was stolen. I've told you more than enough to get you started. Now, I want you to find the box."

"Very well. Just one more question. Your father . . . does he know about the box? I mean, that you're searching for it?"

"Yes, of course. In fact, I told him I was going to engage a detective."

"And he approved?"

"Yes."

"Then it's all right if I talk to him myself?"

"Well, he's terribly busy right now . . . "

"Inventing?"

"Yes."

Simon Lash slid out from behind the table, then pulled it a little toward him so Elizabeth Dunlap could get up more easily.

"Where do you live?"

"In Laurel Canyon." She gave him the number. "You'll get right to work on it?"

"As soon as I read this book."

"But why . . . ?" she began, then shook her head and left him.

Lash paid the check and followed to the door. Elizabeth Dunlap, however, did not wait for him. She stepped out and walked swiftly in the direction of Highland.

Lash walked to Ivar and was about to step into a taxi when he changed his mind. He crossed the street to a drugstore and telephoned his apartment.

"Eddie," he said, when his assistant answered. "We're on a case. Get out the car and pick me up in front of the Roosevelt Hotel. Right away."

Leaving the drugstore, Lash walked west to Highland. He bought a *Herald-Express* at the corner and said casually to the newise:

"Did you see a nut going by here this morning, riding a jackass?"

"I don't come on until noon," replied the newsie, "but I see plenty of nuts; what kind do you want?"

Lash chucked the newspaper into the street and continued up Hollywood Boulevard. In front of the Roosevelt he said to the doorman, "Look, George,

36

to settle an argument, did a man wearing a prospector's outfit go by here this morning, riding a jackass?"

"Yeah," replied the doorman. "Only it wasn't a jackass; it was a burro. The guy's feet were dragging the street. I didn't notice though — what was he advertising?"

"Himself," said Lash. Nodding thanks, he stepped into the cigar store and looked at the magazines on the rack until a familiar horn beeped outside. He went out and climbed into the coupé that Eddie Slocum had at the curb.

"Where to?" Eddie asked.

"Santa Monica."

Lash slid down in the leather seat and opened the book he had received from Elizabeth Dunlap.

Slocum turned right at the corner and barely touching the gas pedal zoomed the car toward Sunset Boulevard. The motor was a stepped-up one. The car was four years old, of a small make. It could do one hundred and eight miles an hour.

Reaching Sunset, Eddie turned right. At LaBrea he made a left turn and went to Santa Monica Boulevard. When he had the car purring along he asked casually:

"Is it an interesting case, chief?"

"No," replied Lash, keeping his eyes on the book. "We're supposed to find the box the jackass man brought to the office this morning."

Eddie Slocum exclaimed softly. "How'd you get such an assignment?"

"It walked up and bit me."

Eddie Slocum winced and remained quiet. He rolled the car along Santa Monica Boulevard, whipping in and out of traffic. At Beverly Hills he turned into Wilshire and swished down the broad boulevard at precisely five miles an hour above the speed limit.

Passing Sepulveda, just west of Westwood, he finally spoke again, "Any particular section of Santa Monica?"

"Stop at a drugstore and look up the address of Sheridan Eckert. He's a lawyer."

"Eckert. Isn't that the name . . . ah, never mind."

Eddie Slocum continued on for several blocks, then pulled to the curb before the drugstore. He got out of the car and was gone about two minutes. When he returned Lash was still engrossed in Lansford Hastings' book.

"His office is on Wilshire, but since it's ten minutes to six, we might have better luck at his home. That's on Twenty-second just three blocks from here. Okay?"

"Okay."

4

FIVE minutes later Slocum stopped the car again before a rambling California-style stucco house. Lash closed the book and stepped out of the car. "You wait, Eddie."

He crossed the sidewalk and rang the doorbell. A thin, gray-haired woman opened the door after a moment. She held one hand to her ear.

"Mr. Eckert," Lash said.

"We don't want any," the woman replied.

"I want to see Sheridan Eckert," Lash said in a voice loud enough for the neighbors across the street to hear.

A deep voice spoke from inside the house. "What is it?"

Lash brushed past the woman and stepped into a shaded living room. A lean, ascetic-looking man, holding a newspaper on his lap, sat in an overstuffed chair.

"Yes?"

"I'm a member of the State Historical

40

Society," Lash said, "we're collecting data on the Donner Party and I understand one of your ancestors — "

Sheridan Eckert groaned. "Again?"

"Eh?"

Eckert fanned the atmosphere with his newspaper. "They come right along, the State Historical Society, the W.P.A. writers' group, every hack writer who happens to come across the story and doesn't know that it's been done a dozen times."

"In that case I'll change my approach. I'm a private detective."

Eckert gave a start. "A detective . . . ?"

"Yes, and I know all about the hardships of the Donner Party, so we can skip that. I'm interested only in a certain object that one of the members of the party brought out, a small wooden box . . . "

Eckert looked blank. "What kind of a box?"

"It was carved out of redwood by your grandfather, Isaac Eckert. Your great-aunt Elizabeth Eckert carried it with her when she was rescued."

"That's the first I ever heard of it.

What was in the box?"

"Nothing."

"Then why worry about the box? It couldn't have been worth very much."

"It seems to have an intrinsic value . . . "

"To whom?"

"I'm not permitted to tell."

"You don't have to; there are only two other descendants of Isaac Eckert alive, Jim Dunlap and his daughter Elizabeth. Jim has about as much sentiment as this newspaper. So it must be the girl. She's reached the romantic age."

"Did you ever hear of a man named Lansford Hastings?"

"The name is vaguely familiar. He had something to do with the old affair, didn't he?"

"Something. You don't know what?"

"No. I'm not really up on the story. I was never greatly interested. Every family has a skeleton in the closet, but I see no point in dragging ours out continually."

Lash looked steadily at Sheridan Eckert. "You're an attorney, aren't you, Mr. Eckert?"

"Yes, but what's that got to do with it?"

"Nothing, I was just wondering . . . Well, suppose your great-grandfather had left some money . . . "

Eckert laughed shortly. "He was supposed to have had fifty thousand dollars. And ever since 1847 treasure hunters have been digging up Donner Pass, looking for it. No thanks; if I want to do any digging, I'll spade up my back yard and plant a few potatoes. It'd be more profitable than digging for my great-grandfather's gold."

"How do you know it was gold?"

"They liked hard money in those days."

Lash nodded thoughtfully. "I wonder if you can straigten me out on the genealogy of the family. Your great-grandfather and great-grandmother both died that winter. The three children were rescued, however. Their names were Isaac, Junior, George Pearson, and Elizabeth."

"That's right. I'm descended from George P. Eckert. The Dunlaps are descendants of Elizabeth."

"And Isaac?"

"He had no descendants. He died at an early age."

"In the middle '50's, if I got it correctly. He was over twenty at the time."

"Yes, but he didn't marry."

"And your grandfather, George Pearson Eckert, had two sons — your father Fremont, and his older brother Isaac III."

"That's right."

"Your father died in the last few years, but I seem to have lost his brother somewhere, Isaac III — "

"No one knows how he died. He ran off to sea when he was a mere boy."

"But you don't know for sure if he died? He might be alive today."

"He might be, but that's unlikely. After all, he was older than Dad, who was born in 1862. Isaac would be around eighty now . . . and why didn't he ever get in touch with the family?"

Lash had no reply for that. He shrugged. "Well, thanks, Mr. Eckert."

"No trouble, but I'm surprised that the Dunlaps didn't give you this information. Did they tell you to come to me?"

"I didn't say that they were my clients."

"You didn't, but I assumed . . . "

"As an attorney, Mr. Eckert," Lash said ironically, "you shouldn't jump to conclusions . . . "

"Eh?"

"I was an attorney myself once," said Lash. He moved to the door. "Until I reformed." Then he stepped out.

Eddie Slocum had the motor running by the time Lash climbed into the car. "Where to, now?"

"You're always listening to the radio, Eddie. Ever hear a chap who calls himself the Oddity Man?"

"Sure, he's good. He gets the darnest people and things on his program . . . "

"When does his program go on?"

"Every Tuesday evening . . . say, that's today. At seven thirty."

"It's almost six-thirty. Let's run over to the studio and see if we can grab him before his program goes on."

"Sure," Eddie Slocum assented eagerly. "I've been wanting to see the inside of one of those studios for a long time. Hang on!"

Eddie raced the car back to Wilshire and up to Sepulveda. He took the latter street to Sunset, then ripped the car up the winding climb through Brentwood and Beverly Hills. When he reached West Hollywood, he cut over to Fountain merely because there was less likelihood of encountering traffic policemen and he could exceed the speed limit.

It was ten minutes to seven when he parked the car on Vine near the big building that housed the broadcasting station.

There was a little difficulty getting into the studio, but Lash effected the entry by sending in his card to Harold Wade, who was already in the rehearsal hall.

5

WADE was a slender man of about thirty-five. His hair was black and glistened with pomade. He had an olive-tinted complexion that made him look Latin.

He smiled, showing a mouthful of even, white teeth. "How do you do, Mr. Lash? I was just talking to Betty Dunlap on the phone. She said I ought to have you on the program."

"I don't sing," Lash snapped. "And I'm a lousy dancer. What do you know about the desert rat who calls himself Lansford Hastings?"

"Very little," Wade said. "I'm not up on my frontier history, and I took him at his word. I've discovered since that he was a gosh-awful liar."

"You mean he sprung that stuff about being the original Lansford Hastings?"

"Yes, but he didn't put it exactly that way. He just said his name was Lansford Hastings and that he used to guide

47

emigrant parties across the Sierras."

"Hastings isn't much over fifty," Lash said, sarcastically. "If he guided emigrants, they must have been Iowa farmers who came to California in their flivvers twenty-five years ago."

Wade's face twitched. "I know. I received twenty or thirty complaints about his spiel. I told you that I didn't know frontier history very well."

"How'd you get Hastings in the first place?"

"Why, he was parked outside the studio last Tuesday. One of my other attractions had taken sick at the last moment and I pulled Hastings in as a substitute . . . "

"That didn't strike you as a coincidence? The one act taking sick and another waiting outside to go on."

Wade stared at Lash. "I never thought of that."

"Who was the sick act?"

"A man named Luke Lupton; he has four singing owls. They sang the 'St. Louis Blues'."

"Hey," exclaimed Eddie Slocum. "Owls can't sing."

"These can. Each screeches in a

different pitch. They're well-trained and the general effect sounds very much like the 'St. Louis Blues'."

"If it wasn't your program, Mr. Wade," said Eddie Slocum, "I wouldn't believe it."

"Eddie's a fan of yours," Lash explained. "My assistant, Eddie Slocum."

"How do. Well, what else can I do for you, Mr. Lash?"

"You can give me the address of this owl trainer, Luke Lupton."

"I can do better than that. Since he couldn't go on last week, I asked him to do his act tonight. He's probably in the rehearsal hall right now. You can talk to him . . . "

"In a moment. What about the buffalo box that Betty Dunlap claims was stolen from her?"

"I never saw it," Wade declared. "But in a way I — rather the program — is responsible for Betty discovering that her box was gone. You see, Betty was listening in from the control room. When Hastings began telling about himself, she was reminded of her family history. She wanted to talk to Hastings after we went off the air, but he slipped away. However, she went home and looked for the box — "

"Why? Was the box mentioned on the program?"

Harold Wade's forehead furrowed. "I really don't remember. I have so many different people on my program — "

"Don't you use a script?"

"To a certain extent, but since I'm actually interviewing these people, I do a good deal of ad-libbing; and they do, too, in their replies. But . . . "

"Yes?"

"As a matter of fact, all programs are waxed."

"You mean you make a recording?" Lash asked eagerly.

Wade nodded. "Would you like to hear it?"

"I most certainly would. When can you play it for me?"

"Why, I'm going on the air myself in about ten minutes. But I can take you into one of the rehearsal rooms and have a man run it off for you."

"Do that. Then when you're off, I want to talk to this Lupton."

"Very well; this way."

Wade led Lash and Slocum into a sound-proofed room and signaled to one of several men in a glass-enclosed control room. The man came into the sound-proofed room, and Wade requested him to get the recording of his previous program.

"He'll have it for you in a minute or two and play it; now I've got to be running. I'll see you after the program."

Eddie Slocum looked eagerly at Simon Lash, but the latter shook his head. "The hell with the owls; I want you to hear this."

Wade left the room, and Lash and Slocum found seats. After a couple of moments the radio technician came into the room with a large platter and put it on a phonograph.

"If you want any of it played over, just signal," he said, and returned to the control room.

The announcer's enthusiastic voice extolled the virtues of Scrubo Soap Chips. Lash slouched in his chair, an expression of disgust on his face, which did not change much when the announcer's voice gave way to Harold Wade's. Wade gave himself quite a build-up, threw in a couple of additional plugs for the soap chips, then interviewed a woman who raised bullfrogs in her bathtub. After her, four hillbillies played 'Deep in the Heart of Texas' on washboards.

Then Wade introduced Lansford Hastings:

"And now, ladies and gentleman, I want to introduce a genuine desert rat. He is here in the studio tonight straight from Death Valley. He is wearing a blue flannel shirt, a pair of alkali-stained Levis, scuffed and worn boots and a floppy, black felt hat. He has a bristling red beard. I understand he has a burro tied right outside the studio. Isn't that right, Mr. Lansford Hastings?"

"It shore is," rumbled the deep voice of Lansford Hastings. "I wouldn't go anywhere without Daisy. She's my family."

"Can she cook and sew?" Wade asked, adding a hearty forced laugh. "No? Well, Mr. Hastings, will you tell the radio audience something about yourself? Exactly what do you do for a living?"

"Why, I prospect most of the time," replied Lansford Hastings, "but in the old days I used to guide emigrants across the Sierras."

"That's very interesting, Mr. Hastings," said Harold Wade, "but can you tell us something about your prospecting? What are you looking for? Gold?"

"Any precious mineral, gold, silver, or tungsten, but naturally the prospector's favorite is gold, and there's plenty of it out there in the desert and mountains. The trouble is finding it."

"Have you ever made a strike, Mr. Lansford?"

"Oh yes, several. None really big, though. Not like the one I'm on the trail of now."

"Oh!" exclaimed Harold Wade. "You're on the verge of making a big strike?"

"Yep," Hastings replied.

"Do you mind telling us — well, you don't have to tell us exactly — but could you *hint* at the general vicinity of this strike you're about to make?"

"Sure, I don't mind. It's up in the high Sierras. You know, the old-timers were so doggone eager to get to the known gold fields, they rushed right over the mountains without stopping to prospect. None of them wanted to linger around Donner Pass, not after what happened there to the Donner Party . . . "

"What did happen to the Donner Party, Mr. Hastings?"

"Why, they was snowbound all winter, and when their food was gone, they et one another . . . "

Harold Wade gasped and spoke hurriedly. "Yes, yes, of course, Mr. Hastings. We're all familiar with that tragic episode in our pioneer history. It's been a pleasure having you on this program. Thank you . . . And now, folks, I'd like to introduce a man who has invented a machine by which you can hear a fly walk . . . "

Lash got up and waved his hand back and forth until he caught the attention of the man in the control room. He pointed to the phonograph to have it played again. The man nodded and came into the room and made the necessary adjustment. Lash listened once more to the interview with Lansford Hastings. He finally nodded.

"All right, Eddie, let's go."

"Did you get anything?"

"A little. Now, let's go and listen to the owls sing."

But they were too late. Leaving their own studio, they walked down a corridor and encountered Harold Wade just coming out of another with a group of people.

"Lupton," Lash said to Wade.

"Oh, yes," the radio man said. "He's right . . . well, he seems to have disappeared. I had him on right at the beginning and I guess he didn't wait."

"You've got his address?" Lash snapped.

Wade took a handful of cards from his pocket and riffled through them. "Here it is, Longridge Avenue, in Van Nuys . . . Did you hear last week's program?"

"Yes," said Lash, "and I think the lady with the bullfrogs was simply divine."

He walked away from Wade, with Eddie Slocum at his heels.

Outside they got the car. "Van Nuys?" Eddie Slocum asked.

"Yes, and drive as fast as you can without getting pinched."

Eddie clucked his tongue against the

roof of his mouth and made a quick U turn in Vine. He hurtled the car to Sunset, cut west to Cahuenga, and a few minutes later zoomed the car over Cahuenga Pass into San Fernando Valley.

Five minutes later he turned left into Longridge Avenue and began scanning the houses for numbers. It was a dark street, and he had to drive more than a block before he came across an illuminated house number.

"About three blocks," he guessed. "Pretty well up in the canyon."

"Hurry it up."

"Eh? You think something's . . . ?"

"Yes." Lash opened the glove compartment and took out a .32 automatic. He slipped out the clip, saw that it contained cartridges, and, putting it back into the butt, worked a cartridge into the chamber.

Eddie Slocum sent the car hurtling up the street, into the canyon. For a couple of blocks there were big houses on both sides of the street, then they became more sparse, and in the third block there was only a single house.

As Eddie braked the coupé, Lash glanced at the house. There was a light in an upper window, but the entire lower floor was dark.

He swung open the car door and stepped to the street. At that moment a car without headlights shot out of the drive and careened into the street. It passed within six feet of Lash, but it was too dark for him to make out the occupant.

Holding the small automatic in his hand, Lash ran swiftly across a stretch of lawn to the front door of the house. He groped for the door button and, finding it, pressed it savagely. Inside the house bells chimed.

He waited until he heard Eddie Slocum coming across the lawn, then pressed the button again. As the chimes went off once more, he tested the door and found it unlocked. As he pushed it open, Eddie Slocum flicked on a flashlight and sent the ray of light into the dark house. Lash stepped in, listened a moment, then proceeded directly to a carpeted staircase. Eddie crowded at his heels sending the flashlight spot ahead of Lash.

They padded to the second floor and discovered that the door of the lighted room was open. Lash looked into the room and stopped.

"We're too late, Eddie."

Eddie jostled Lash so he could look into the room. He inhaled sharply.

"Jeez!"

The body lay on the floor, feet and legs protruding around the end of a bed. Lash suddenly sprang forward, so he could see the entire body. A low cry was torn from his throat.

"It's Hastings!"

"Yeah," said Eddie Slocum. "Were you expecting him?"

"No, I'd counted on Lupton . . . "

"But Lupton only left the studio a couple minutes ahead of us . . . "

"That's why I said to hurry . . . I don't get it."

An automobile spotlight suddenly flashed through the window. Lash stepped quickly forward and looked out.

"This'll be Lupton now."

He stepped to the hall, and by that time Luke Lupton was already yelling outside the door, "Hey, what's the idea?"

Lash started for the stairs and when he was half-way down the hall light went on. He looked down at a heavy-set man who had a tire iron in his hand.

"Hey!" the man cried. "Who're you?"

"A detective," Lash snapped.

Lupton gasped. "You're a what?"

"A detective; we just got here a moment ago. A car dashed out of the driveway and — prepare yourself for a shock — there's a dead man upstairs."

Lupton cried out in horror. "In my house?"

"A man named Lansford Hastings . . ."

"Hastings! Holy cow! How'd he get in here?"

"You know him?"

"Yeah, sure, but I don't see how he got in. He wouldn't just walk into the house when I'm not at home. I didn't know him *that* well."

"Where's your telephone?" Lash asked. "I want to call the police."

"The police! You just said you were a cop."

"I said I was a detective; I'm a private detective. I have to notify the police as well as anyone else, when I find a dead person — a murdered one."

Lupton pointed to a telephone at the rear of the hall. Lash went to it and asked for police headquarters. A gruff voice came on in a moment.

"I want to report a murder," Lash said. He gave the address and, ignoring the desk sergeant's excited inquiries, hung up.

He turned back to Lupton. "Lansford Hastings paid you to let him take his place on the radio show last week, didn't he?"

Lupton started to nod, caught himself, then shrugged. "So what? I got on this week."

"How much did he pay you?"

"What's the diff . . . Well, two hundred dollars."

"How'd he proposition you?"

"What do you mean?"

"Did he come here to your house, or did he get in touch with you at the studio?"

"Oh, he came here."

"How'd he know about you?"

"Oh, Harold Wade — that's the Oddity Man — announces the week before who's going to be on his program the next week. Didn't you ever hear his program?"

"Not all of it," Lash replied, thinking of the partial recording he had heard that evening. He frowned. "Where are your owls?"

"In the car; when I saw the light on here, I didn't know what to make of it, so I bust right in."

"You might as well bring in the owls. The police will want to see them."

"Yeah," said Eddie Slocum. "Let's hear them sing."

Lupton hesitated a moment, then went outside. He returned in a moment with a wicker cage, containing four screech owls. Eddie Slocum moved forward.

"Why, they look just like regular owls," he said.

"They *are* owls," Lupton said, looking annoyed.

"And they really sing?"

"Of course they do. Didn't you hear them on the program tonight? They were a sensation."

"I don't believe it," said Eddie Slocum, shaking his head.

Lupton put the cage on the hall table

and clapped his hands twice. He waited a moment, then began waving his hand like an orchestra leader.

One of the owls began hooting, "Woo-woo-woo," then another joined in, and finally the other two. The secret of their 'singing' was quickly revealed. Each owl was trained to hoot a certain number of times, then pause and come in again. The total effect of the four different series of hootings could have been construed as harmony by a not too literal-minded listener.

"They stink," said Lash.

Lupton whirled on him, and the owls stopped their hooting. "No one asked for your opinion," he snapped. "And if you ask me, I don't think you have any right in my house."

"I haven't," Lash said, honestly retorted. "But you haven't any right to murder people here . . ."

"Me?" cried Lupton. "Why, you . . . !"

He stopped as an automobile siren wailed outside. Flashlights winked outside and suddenly a concerted rush of men assaulted the open door.

The leader, a swarthy, powerful man

of medium height, skidded to a stop.

"Simon Lash!" he cried. "Of all the . . . "

"Sergeant Coons," Lash said. "The pride of the sheriff's office."

Sergeant Coons scowled. "Where's the dead man?"

"Upstairs."

Sergeant Coons gestured to one of the uniformed policemen. "Keep an eye on them." He bounded for the staircase, followed by two or three men and leaving that many behind.

"I don't know a thing about this," Lupton said loudly. "I was at the radio station, and when I came home I found these men . . . "

"Save it for the sergeant," one of the policemen said, covering a yawn.

6

LASH leaned against the wall and whistled tunelessly. Eddie Slocum examined the singing owls. He walked around the cage a couple of times and even stooped to examine them closely. He was still looking at them when Sergeant Coons clumped down the stairs.

"How'd you know it was murder, Lash?" he asked.

"Wasn't it?"

"Yeah, but how'd *you* know?"

"He was shot, wasn't he?"

"Uh-huh, and there's a gun, too."

"Prints?"

"Didn't you look?"

"No."

"Then how'd you know it was murder?"

Lash shook his head. "Would a man go into a stranger's house, just to shoot himself?"

Sergeant Coons turned to Luke Lupton. "He's a stranger?"

"Not exactly. I saw him once before. Last week."

"How come?"

Lupton shot an angry look at Lash. "I suppose I might as well tell. If I don't, he will. I was supposed to go on Harold Wade's Oddity Man program last week. Just as I was ready to start out this fellow came here and offered me two hundred dollars if I'd stay home. Said he wanted to go on in my place."

"What for?"

"Search me. I listened to the program and it wasn't anything. Seemed to be some kind of prospector, or desert rat."

Sergeant Coons looked inquiringly at Lash. The latter examined his finger nails.

"What about it, Lash?" Coons asked testily.

"That's right."

"Where's the percentage?" Coons snapped. "What'd he pay two hundred dollars for?"

"Why does a man pay a dollar a pound for caviar when beans are just as filling and a lot cheaper."

Coons glowered. "The minute I came

in here and saw you, Lash, I wished I hadn't come. A job isn't bad enough I have to draw you along with it. What're you doing here anyway?"

"Client," said Lash. "Confidential."

Coons groaned. "That routine again. Who's the client?"

Lash remained silent.

"This is murder, Lash. If you won't talk for me, you'll talk for the D. A."

"Have him come and see me some time. You come, too . . . some time."

Coons waved his hand helplessly, then suddenly stepped to Lash's side and caught hold of his coat pocket. "Let me see the rod, Lash," he snarled, trying to thrust his hand into the pocket.

Lash knocked away the sergeant's hand. "Don't ever try to search me without a warrant, Coons."

"Let me see the gun!"

Lash took it out and handed it to Coons. The latter quickly slipped out the magazine and sniffed the muzzle. He frowned and looked at Eddie Slocum.

Eddie grinned and flipped the tails of his coat to show that he carried no heavy objects.

Coons returned the gun to Lash. "All right, you can go, but I still think the D. A.'s going to ask you to come to his office."

"Good night, Sergeant." Lash walked to the door, then turned. "Good night, Mr. Lupton."

He went out, with Eddie following. They climbed into the car and Eddie turned it around with difficulty. He let it coast down the incline toward Ventura Boulevard.

When they reached the main thorough-fare, Lash said: "Now drive like the devil to Laurel Canyon. The house ought to be around Magnolia."

"Whose?"

"Dunlap's. I'd like to see him before he hears about Hastings."

Eddie Slocum turned right on Ventura and sped swiftly to Laurel Canyon, a half mile away. There he turned left and let the car out to nearly seventy.

Crossing Magnolia he slackened speed and began to search for house numbers. It was a slow process for the houses were few and far between and the numbers on them difficult to find. But after five minutes or so they reached a rambling stucco house with a concrete wall built around it.

An old flivver stood at the curb.

Eddie Slocum stopped the car behind the flivver and switched out the lights. "This is it and it looks like they've got company, the way the place is all lit up."

Lash got out of the coupé and approached the flivver. He rubbed a hand on one of the dented fenders. "Looks like they're from the wide open spaces."

"You mean the desert?" Slocum asked.

Lash nodded and headed for the wrought-iron gate in front of the house. He opened it and stepped through. Eddie followed.

Lash pressed the door buzzer and after a moment the door was opened by Betty Dunlap. She gasped when she saw Lash. "You . . . !"

"Yes," said Lash.

Betty Dunlap pushed open the screen door and stepped out to the porch. "Why did you come here?" she asked in a whisper.

"I wanted to ask you some questions," Lash said in a voice that was louder than necessary. "I didn't get that Lansford Hastings business straight . . . "

"Please!" exclaimed Betty Dunlap. "I'll telephone you tomorrow . . . "

But it was too late. A voice called from inside the house: "Who is it, Betty?"

"No one, father," Betty Dunlap replied.

"What do you mean — no one?" the voice inside the house exclaimed. "I thought I heard the name of Lansford Hastings . . . "

A heavy step sounded inside the house and a lean, gray-haired man appeared behind Betty Dunlap. "Hello," he said. "What is it?"

"I'm Simon Lash," Lash said. "Can I come in?"

"Simon Lash! Yes, come in. As a matter of fact I called your office this evening."

Betty Dunlap groaned and opened the screen door. Lash and Slocum entered an attractive living room. A man with a skin like old leather was sprawled in a big armchair. He had white hair that came almost to his shoulders and he wore an ill-fitting suit of black broadcloth. He was quite old.

Jim Dunlap faced Simon Lash but did not invite him to take a seat. "Now, what's all this nonsense about Betty employing you, Mr. Lash?"

Lash's eyes smoldered at Jim Dunlap. "Nonsense, Mr. Dunlap?"

"Yes, of course. She had no call to go running to a detective. Certainly not for a misplaced child's toy . . . "

"Misplaced, Mr. Dunlap?"

"The box has been found, Mr. Lash," said Betty Dunlap quietly.

"Ah! Lansford Hastings returned it?"

The leather-faced old man exploded. "Lansford Hastings!"

"Yeah," said Lash, "the Flying Dutchman of the desert. The original Lansing Hastings himself."

The old man spat. "Lansford Hastings, my eye! He's been dead for seventy-five years."

"The first time," said Lash. "He died again — this evening!"

For a moment there was deathly silence in the room, then Betty Dunlap cried out: "Oh, no!"

"Oh yes," said Lash. "This time he was murdered . . . "

70

"Serves him right," said the old man, viciously.

Jim Dunlap scowled. "Now look, Lash — "

"You look, Mr. Dunlap," Lash snapped. "The police are going to be here in a little while and I suggest you all start thinking about your alibis. Where were you, say, a half hour ago?"

"Right here, but — "

"And you, Miss Dunlap? Were you at the broadcast?"

"No, I — "

"Yes?"

"I arrived home fif — "

"Two hours ago," cut in Jim Dunlap. "You were here when Cousin Isaac arrived."

Lash's eyes darted to the old man. "Cousin Isaac?"

Dunlap frowned. "Yes, this is Isaac Eckert."

"Number one, two, or three?"

Isaac Eckert opened his mouth which was almost toothless. "Say, who is this fella?" he asked.

"A private detective," Dunlap explained wearily. "Betty foolishly employed him to find the — the buffalo box which she thought had been lost . . . "

"You mean the box I brought — "

"Cousin Isaac!" cried Betty.

"Eh?"

"Go ahead, mister," said Lash. "The box *you* brought."

"What about it?"

Jim Dunlap took a quick step toward Lash. "Now, see here, you're only a private detective. You have no official status and I think this has gone quite far enough. I must ask you to leave, at once."

Lash turned inquiringly to Betty Dunlap. She nodded. "I'm sorry, but it won't be necessary — "

"I'm fired?"

"That's right. You may keep the retainer."

Lash turned abruptly. "Okay, Eddie."

Eddie Slocum was already opening the door. Lash walked stiffly behind him to the coupé. As he was climbing in, a police siren wailed in the distance.

"Sergeant Coons," exclaimed Slocum.

"It's all his," Lash said.

7

EDDIE SLOCUM came into the library where Lash was sprawled on the couch reading a copy of *The Reign of Soapy Smith*.

"A client, chief," he said.

"I'm not in the mood," Lash replied, keeping his eyes on the book. "Send him away."

"It's a her, not a him."

"All right, send *her* away."

"Maybe you'd better look at these pictures first."

Lash lowered the book and looked at the fan of five one-hundred-dollar bills. "Do we need it?"

Slocum whistled. "No, we don't need it. But the landlady does. She was asking for the rent yesterday."

Lash groaned. "Again? Well, what's she look like?"

Slocum rolled his eyes and smacked his lips. "Mmm."

"I hate good-looking women clients,"

said Lash. "They think they can pay off with smiles . . . "

"These bills ain't smiles, chief."

"All right, all right."

Lash put down his book and got up. He looked at his carpet slippers, then shrugging, proceeded to his office.

The client wore a blue silk dress, a silver fox neckpiece and a hat with a black veil. As Lash entered the room she lifted up the veil and revealed a face that was honey and peaches. Only the eyes were off-key. They were blue with a greenish tint.

Lash nodded and seated himself in his swivel chair. "I saw your money," he said, bluntly. "What's your trouble?"

"Trouble?" the woman asked. "I don't understand . . . ?"

"If you weren't in trouble you wouldn't be here."

"Why I merely want you to make an identification for me."

"For five hundred dollars?"

"For five hundred dollars."

"All right, it's your money. Who do you want identified?"

"My husband, Richard Evanston."

"Where is he?"

"That's part of the identification . . . Perhaps I put that wrong. I *think* I know where he is, but I'm not sure."

"Where do you think he is?"

"In the morgue."

Lash looked sharply at the woman. "The Los Angeles morgue?"

"Yes."

"You can go there yourself."

"I can't. I — I couldn't bear it."

"If you have a photograph, you can hand it to a morgue attendant and he'll make the identification for you. It won't cost you five hundred dollars."

Mrs. Evanston looked thoughtfully at Lash for a moment. Then she said: "I have a photograph of my husband here in my purse." She unsnapped a blue suede purse, took out a three-by-five photograph and leaning forward slid it across Lash's desk.

Lash looked at the photograph. It showed a man in his middle thirties, a broad-faced man with rather full lips and bold nose.

"You've never seen him?" Mrs. Evanston asked.

Lash frowned. "No. I never forget a face . . . yet, he vaguely resembles someone I've seen."

"Who?" Mrs. Evanston asked eagerly.

"I don't know." Lash looked up suddenly. "Your name is Evanston?"

"Anne Evanston?"

"And your husband's name is Richard Evanston?"

"Of course. That's what I said . . . "

"Then I'm wrong. I'm quite sure I've never known anyone named Evanston."

"Perhaps that wasn't the name under which you knew him. I . . . you see, that's one of the reasons I . . . I don't want to make the identification myself. Dick may have been using another name."

"What name?"

Anne Evanston hesitated. "Lansford Hastings."

Lash turned the photograph face down and slid it back across the desk. "Sorry. I won't be able to handle the matter."

"What? Why . . . why not?"

"Because I don't like to be made a fool of twice in one week. And because I've had policemen climbing all over me for the last two days."

76

"But you did see Lansford — my husband. You're the only one who can identify him."

"*You* can identify him."

"No, I can't."

"Neither can I. Anyway — that photograph isn't the man I knew as Lansford Hastings."

"You're not sure. You admitted he looked familiar."

"Lansford Hastings was a much older man. He looked like a desert rat."

"Dick was an outdoor man. He — might have disguised himself."

"With a jackass?"

"I beg your pardon!"

Lash laughed harshly. "Lansford Hastings came here, riding a jackass."

Color flooded Anne Evanston's face. "I'm almost sure now that it was Dick. He — had a streak of exhibitionism. Please . . . at least look at the photograph again."

Lash started to get up, then shrugged and reached for the picture once more. He studied it for a long moment. "No, the face reminds me vaguely of someone I've seen, but not Lansford Hastings."

Mrs. Evanston exclaimed in disappointment: "I read the description in the newspapers. It seemed such an obvious disguise and knowing Dick's mania for theatricals . . . "

"Your husband was an actor?"

"Only an amateur. He is . . . was . . . an advertising man. The Evanston Advertising Agency of Columbus, Ohio."

"You've just come from Ohio?"

"Yes. I came by airplane. I left the moment I read about his — Lansford Hastings' death."

Lash leaned back in his chair. "The name Lansford Hastings meant something to you?"

"To Richard."

"In what respect?"

"Why, he was a descendant of — "

Lash held up his hand. "I'll take the case."

Anne Evanston seemed suddenly startled. "You mean . . . you'll make the identification."

"I'll take the case. All of it."

"But I only want you to make an identification."

"No, you don't. You want more than

78

that. Now, start at the beginning."

"But that's all there's to it. I think my husband was mur — killed — here the day before yesterday."

"Perhaps. But you have the advantage of me; you know from the newspapers that I found the body. That's why you came here. Now, suppose you tell me why the man who called himself Hastings — which may or may not have been your husband — should have come here to see me. What relation was he to . . . Isaac Eckert?"

Anne Evanston gasped. "Why . . . he was a descendant. Isaac Eckert was his great-grand-father."

"How?"

"I don't understand."

"My hobby is frontier history."

"So I understand, but you certainly don't know the genealogy of every pioneer character."

"No? Well, listen to this: Isaac Eckert died in January, 1847. He left three small children, Isaac, George and Elizabeth. Now, from which of these was your husband descended?"

"None."

"Then how can he be related to Isaac Eckert?"

Anne Evanston laughed. "Mr. Lash, you may know your genealogy, but you don't know the facts of life. Isaac Eckert had two sons and a daughter. But didn't he also have a wife?"

Lash winced. "Ah, yes. Her name was Ellen, wasn't it?"

"Ellen Ford, who at the time of her marriage to Isaac Eckert was a widow with a daughter by her first husband. The daughter's name was Lucinda. She did not emigrate to California with her mother because at that time she was already married; although only seventeen years of age. She married a man named Courtney."

"Odd records made no mention of her," Lash remarked.

"That may be because she died about the same time as her mother. She died, in fact, giving birth to a child, Ellen Courtney, who married a man named Evanston who was my husband's grandfather."

"I see," said Lash. "But since your husband's great-grandmother was merely a stepdaughter of Isaac Eckert, what's his interest in the Eckerts? How can he expect to profit . . . financially?"

"I didn't say he expected to profit."

Lash wrinkled his face. "Oh, come now. Isaac Eckert was supposed to have fifty thousand dollars in gold when he died."

"Where did he get it?"

"I never checked into that. Several of the emigrants were well-heeled. Retired farmers and businessmen . . . "

"Did it ever occur to you that the money may have been Ellen Eckert's?"

"Was it?"

"Some of it was. Ellen Ford had a great deal more money than Isaac Eckert when they were married. Now use your pencil and do a little figuring. With both Isaac and his wife dead how would the inheritance be divided?"

"Ah," said Lash. "Now we're getting to the point. I don't know what the inheritance laws were at that time."

"Much the same as today."

"Then I imagine the money went to the children, say four shares, or twelve thousand five hundred apiece."

"I thought you'd figure that way," Anne Evanston said. "But you're wrong. Suppose Isaac died before his wife? Ellen automatically inherits the widow's third, doesn't she? Or roughly sixteen thousand seven hundred. That leaves only around thirty-three thousand to divide among the children — "

"No," said Lash. "Because she, too, died. She wouldn't discriminate against the child of her first husband."

"Probably not, but suppose Ellen Ford died first? Isaac *might* discriminate against his step-daughter, in favor of his natural children."

Lash's eyes narrowed. "Yes, he might. And the inheritance might be altered entirely if either of the parents left a will, leaving everything to the survivor. If Isaac died first he might have left everything to his wife, who might in turn have left a will leaving everything to the daughter of her first marriage. It's an interesting point."

"Isn't it? Do you understand now why my husband was interested?"

"Yes, I do. And you still want me to identify the body of Lansford Hastings

. . . and that's all you want?"

Anne Evanston got to her feet. "That's all. When shall I call you?"

"Where are you staying? I'll phone you . . . "

"I'd rather telephone you. You see, I haven't checked into a hotel as yet. Say around three this afternoon?"

Lash nodded and pushed back his swivel chair. "I ought to know by that time."

He opened the door for Mrs. Evanston and followed her to the stairs leading down to the first floor. As he passed the library door he signaled to Eddie Slocum and the latter moved backwards out of sight. Lash kept Mrs. Evanston a moment at the head of the stairs, so Slocum would have time to leave the apartment by the rear door and get out upon the street in order to follow Mrs. Evanston.

When she had finally gone Lash returned to the library and found his shoes. He put them on and got his coat and hat from a closet. He caught sight of himself in the mirror and realized that he needed a shave. But he shrugged and left the apartment.

On the street he walked down to Sunset Boulevard and caught a taxicab. "County morgue," he said, as he stepped in.

84

8

THE morgue attendant was very bored by it all. "It's no money out of my pocket if the county buries 'em," he said. "I go by the rules, that's all. They say you gotta give a name if you want to see a stiff and here's the book. Put your autograph on it and you can see 'im."

Lash wrote 'John W. Booth' in the book, then followed the attendant into a dark room. The man opened a door that reminded Lash of a refrigerator door and pulled out a slab on which lay a sheet-covered body.

"Help yourself," he said, laconically.

Lash took hold of the edge of the sheet and peeled it back gingerly. He exclaimed in consternation. The cold, dead features of the man on the slab bore no resemblance whatever to the face on the photograph in his pocket. Nor did the dead man look anything like the Lansford Hastings that Lash recalled.

"You're sure this is the right body?" he asked the attendant.

"Lansford Hastings, Slab No. 14," replied the attendant. "This is it — and him. You don't know him? I didn't think you would. We ain't had an identification all week. Times are getting tough."

Lash left the morgue and went to a drugstore. Looking up the number in a telephone directory he called the sheriff's office and asked for Sergeant Coons.

When he got the sergeant he said: "Look, Sergeant, you've been bothering me about this Lansford Hastings — "

"Oh, you're ready to confess?" Coons cut in sarcastically.

"No. Why didn't you tell me that he had false whiskers?"

"How do you know?"

"I just left the morgue."

"I thought you weren't interested in the case any more?"

"I'm not, but my morbid curiosity got the best of me."

The noise that came across the wire to Lash sounded as if Sergeant Coons were blowing his nose. Lash slammed the receiver on the hook.

He dropped another nickel into the slot and dialed the number of his apartment. Eddie Slocum answered instantly.

"Chief?"

"Yes. Did you follow her?"

"Uh-huh, right to the Lincoln Hotel."

"Did she know she was being followed?"

"I don't think so."

"She was already registered at the hotel."

"Three days."

"All right," said Lash. "Get out the car and meet me at the Lincoln Hotel. I may be up in her room so wait for me downstairs."

Lash left the drugstore and found a taxicab in its stand just outside the store. He stepped in and ten minutes later paid off the meter charge at the Lincoln Hotel.

George, the doorman, shook his head when he recognized Lash. "He was here, but he left a half hour ago."

"Eddie Slocum? You know who I'm interested in then; Mrs. Evanston."

"Yes, sir," said the doorman.

"All right, what room's she got?"

"For free?"

Lash grimaced and took a dollar from his pocket. Then he changed his mind and fished out a half dollar. George took the coin and squeezed it. "Fifty cents, huh? I guess it's worth about that, since the clerk is a sourpuss and wouldn't give you the information."

"One of the bellboys would do it for a quarter," Lash reminded.

"They're pikers. All right, she had Room 1116."

Lash started for the door then turned back. "Had?"

"Yep, she checked out ten minutes ago."

Lash swore. "Give me back my money."

George handed back the half dollar. "Okay, I was going to charge you two bucks for the rest of it, but now it's costing five . . . and the bellboys don't know."

Lash shot a quick glance toward the taxi stand nearby. "You overheard her tell the cabdriver."

The doorman grinned derisively. "It was a private car and you better grab it quick 'cause I might raise the price to ten dollars."

Lash swore under his breath but produced a five-dollar bill. "All right, you amateur blackmailer."

"The license number is 4 R 46 – 17. A green Cadillac."

"Baggage?"

"Two fitted cases. Uh, they had airplane stickers on them."

Eddie Slocum drew up to the curb with the coupé. Lash walked to it. "That friend of yours down at the Motor Vehicle Bureau, Eddie . . . "

"Henry Pitzer?"

"Yes. License Number 4 R 46 – 17; find out the name and address of the owner."

Slocum slid out from behind the wheel and hurried into the hotel. Lash climbed into the car and slumped down in the seat. George, the doorman, came over.

"I saw your friend with the jackass again."

Lash nodded. "You won't see him again."

"Why not?"

"Because he died two days ago."

George shook his head. "I guess we're talking about different people. I saw him this morning."

"What?"

"He was going right past this hotel; same long-legged fellow. His feet were dragging the street on both sides of the jackass."

"You were mistaken; it couldn't have been the same man."

"So I'm seeing things. That's three days in a row, every day at eleven fifteen."

"Yesterday, too?"

"Uh-huh; the day before yesterday the first time, yesterday the second and today the third."

"And he was going west each time? A man with a dirty red beard, on a flea-bitten burro?"

" . . . And he looks like a prospector."

Eddie Slocum came trotting out of the hotel, his manner one of constrained excitement. Lash gave him a warning look and Eddie ran around the car and got in behind the wheel.

"All right, Eddie."

Slocum stepped on the starter and

90

zoomed the car away in second gear. "Sheridan Eckert!" he cried then.

Lash swore.

"You know what I think, chief? The little lady tells fibs."

"Lies, Eddie. And somebody else is lying to us. Did you get a look at the dead man in Luke Lupton's house?"

"Yeah sure; why?"

"It was Lansford Hastings?"

"We don't know his name for sure, do we?"

"No, but we know it was the same desert rat who called on us. We know that, don't we?"

"Yeah sure."

"Well, we're wrong. One, I went down to the morgue and the stiff didn't have a beard, or even gray hair . . . "

"Well, she said he might have been disguised."

"Number two, George, the doorman, saw the desert rat riding by the hotel on his burro. He saw him this morning and again, yesterday."

Slocum gasped. "But he was dead! The papers said so and . . . "

"Yes?"

"Maybe Coons is playing a rib on us."

"Coons wouldn't know a rib if one came up and bit him. A man was murdered in Luke Lupton's house; you can be sure of that. But we can't be sure of anything else . . . Drive out to Sheridan Eckert's place."

"His home? Wouldn't he be at his office this time of the afternoon?"

"Probably; try there first."

Twenty minutes later, Slocum parked the car near an eight-story office building on Wilshire Boulevard.

Lash got out. "Stay here and keep an eye on the entrance. Just in case."

Lash entered the building and consulted the directory. He learned that Sheridan Eckert's office was in Suite 710 – 12 and rode up to the seventh floor in the elevator.

A ground-glass door gave him the legend that Sheridan Eckert was a member of the law firm of Marx, Dooley & Eckert. He pushed open the door and found himself in a tiny anteroom, over which a gorgeous blonde presided.

"Yes, sir?" she said to Lash.

"Mr. Eckert."

"Did you have an appointment with him?"

Lash scowled. "Tell him it's about Mrs. Evanston . . . "

"Mrs. Evanston," said the receptionist, "Why . . . " She caught herself. "Will you wait a moment, please?" She got up and went to a private office. Lash followed her noiselessly and, as she opened the door, brushed past her.

Anne Evanston exclaimed in consternation when she saw Lash. Sheridan Eckert pushed back his swivel chair and sprang to his feet. "See here, what's the idea . . . ?"

"I asked him to wait, Mr. Eckert," cried the receptionist.

"I'm sorry," Lash said, "I was so eager to tell the good news I couldn't wait. Mrs. Evanston, it wasn't your husband."

Her reaction was surprising to say the least. Instead of joy, horror spread across her face. "But who . . . ?"

"I don't know, but it's not your husband."

"What are you talking about?" Eckert demanded.

"Oh, hasn't Mrs. Evanston told you?" Lash asked innocently. "She employed me to go down to the morgue to identify — "

"Please!" Anne Evanston interrupted.

Eckert suddenly pointed a lean forefinger at Lash. "I've placed you now. You're the private detective who questioned me the other evening."

"That's right. Mrs. Evanston saw my name in the papers in connection with the affair — and came to me. She flew here from Columbus."

Anne Evanston exhaled heavily. "Very well, Cousin Sheridan, I see where I must tell you everything."

"Wait," Eckert said harshly. "As I understand the situation, you employed this man to identify the body of . . . the man who was killed the other night. You were afraid it might be Richard. Well, he's performed that task now."

"I'm fired?" Lash asked, looking at Anne Evanston.

Her forehead creased. She started to shake her head, when Sheridan Eckert said, decisively: "Of course. We haven't any need for a detective. If it wasn't

Richard — well, it wasn't."

Lash continued to look at Anne Evanston. She finally nodded. "I said that was all I wanted. Thank you."

"All right," said Lash and, turning abruptly, walked out of the office.

Down on the street he walked to the car. "We're fired again, Eddie."

"It's getting to be a habit. I didn't like the case anyway."

"I said we were fired, but we're not quitting. From here on, we work for ourselves. You stay here and follow Mrs. Evanston. I think she's going to be suspicious from now on."

9

EDDIE SLOCUM got out of the car and Lash climbed in. He made a quick U turn on Wilshire and drove cityward for several miles, deep into the heart of Beverly Hills. Near Rodeo he parked the car and entered a two-story building. He climbed a flight of stairs and opened a door on which was lettered: STEVENS DETECTIVE SERVICE.

The reception room was large and contained red leather couches and armchairs and a redhaired girl. "I want to see Milo," Lash said.

"Your name?"

"Simon Lash."

The girl's eyes widened. "Simon Lash, why you don't . . . "

"If I'd known *you* were here," Lash said pointedly, "I would have got a shave."

"Oh, it's not necessary," the redhead replied, sweetly. "I love *virile* men."

"And a haircut," Lash added.

The redhead made a connection on the switchboard and announced Simon Lash. The reply was favorable and she said: "Right down the hall, Mr. Lash."

Lash walked down a wide hall between rows of offices until he came to an oak-paneled door. He pushed it open and Milo Stevens bounced up from a chair.

"Simon Lash!" He rushed around his desk and thrust out a big hand. He was a fat, flabby-faced man of about fifty. Lash tried to avoid the tendered hand, but Stevens would not be denied and pumped Lash's hand with fervor.

"I'm glad you dropped in, Simon. I've got a half hour and I was just sitting here thinking I'd like to play a rubber of gin rummy. How about it?"

"What's gin rummy?"

Milo Stevens stared at Lash. "Are you kidding? Why, everybody's playing it."

"I don't."

"No, I guess you wouldn't," said Stevens. "You keep your nose in books. I suppose you're on the trail of a new first edition."

"The first editions I collect aren't new.

This is a business call, Milo. I want you to do a job for me."

"You want *me* to do a job for *you*? You kidding?"

"No. I have to find something and I need an organization like yours to find it quickly."

"How many men would you need?"

"Five or six. Maybe more."

"That many? Well, I've got the men all right, Simon, but naturally, I'd have to charge you . . . "

"How much?"

"Depends on how long it takes to find — "

"I can only give you a day. A half dozen men ought to be enough."

"At twenty-five dollars each — "

"That's for your sucker customers, Milo. Ten a day per man."

"Hey!" exclaimed Stevens. "You're confusing me with that blackmailer, Henry Otis. He's got men you can hire for ten bucks a day, but not highclass operators like my boys."

"Fifteen."

"Make it a hundred even for six boys."

"It isn't worth it, but all right."

"It's a deal. Now, what do you want them to find?"

"A jackass."

"A what?"

"A burro. It's been riding down Hollywood Boulevard every morning for the last three days. It's been passing the Lincoln Hotel, at around eleven-fifteen. A man who looks like a movie prospector has been riding it, but you don't have to find the man. If you do, all right, but I'm mainly interested in finding the burro."

Stevens backed away from Lash and studied the latter's face. "I saw in the paper that you found a dead prospector the other night . . . "

"That's right. That's another lead for your men."

"But the man's dead. You just said — "

"Did I? I made a mistake; it's the burro I'm interested in. And you shouldn't have any trouble finding it. As I said, it's been coming down Hollywood Boulevard every day for at least the last three days and your men ought to be able to backtrack it."

"What do they do with it when they find it?"

"Nothing. Just let me know where it is."

"Consider the job done."

Lash hesitated.

"Anything else, Simon?" Stevens asked.

"No, I guess not."

"We're not too busy right now. If the case is a good one, I might cut you in on one of my own some time. As a matter of fact, my old offer of coming into the business still stands."

Lash shook his head. "It's too strenuous."

Stevens jeered. "I'll bet you're working for peanuts."

"Not peanuts. A book." Lash grinned and left Stevens' office.

In the car he started the motor, but did not shift into gear. After a moment he shut off the motor and climbing out of the car went to a drugstore. Going inside he looked up an address in the telephone directory, then returning to the car started it and turned into Rodeo Drive.

He drove swiftly along the palm-shaded street to Sunset Boulevard and there turned east. He traversed the Sunset Strip well within the posted speed limits and reaching West Hollyood stopped before a tall apartment house that dwarfed the neighboring two-story stucco buildings.

He went in and approached the desk. A spectacled clerk looked at him inquiringly.

"Mr. Harold Wade."

"Who's calling?"

"Simon Lash."

The clerk inserted a plug into the switchboard and said, after a moment, "A Mr. Simon Lash calling to see Mr. Wade . . . Yes sir."

The clerk kept the headpiece to his ear and looked up at Lash. "What is it about, Mr. Lash? Mr. Wade doesn't seem to know you."

"Tell him I'm the man who was at the studio the other night, listening to the playback of his last week's program."

The clerk relayed the information, listened for a moment, then said. "Very well, sir." Then, to Lash: "Mr. Wade was just about to go out. He'll be down in just a moment."

The moment stretched to five minutes and when Harold Wade finally stepped out of the elevator, the blank expression on his face did not make Lash feel any better.

"You don't remember me, Wade?" he asked, savagely.

Wade frowned. "Your face is familiar, but . . ."

"I'm the private detective to whom you sent Betty Dunlap," Lash snarled. "And I was at the studio the other night."

"Of course!" cried Wade. "You'll pardon me; I meet so many people, you know . . ."

"Then I don't suppose you remember Lansford Hastings?"

"I'm afraid I don't."

"The desert rat who was on your program last week."

"What about him?"

"He said his name was Lansford Hastings."

"Oh yes, of course, he was the man with the singing pigeons."

Lash gritted his teeth. "Cut it out, Wade."

"I beg your pardon?"

"You're not that rattlebrained."

Wade drew himself up stiffly. "I say,

you're a rather aggressive person. I don't know's I care for your attitude at all."

"I'll draw you a picture, Wade. Luke Lupton is the name of the man who has the singing owls — owls, not pigeons. He was supposed to be on your program, but when he didn't show up you picked up this Lansford Hastings in front of the studio."

"What of it?"

"Nothing of it — yet. Lansford Hastings pretended to be a desert rat. So then you sent Betty Dunlap to me . . . "

"I sent her to you? You're mistaken . . . "

"We'll let that pass. She said you sent her . . . "

"But I didn't. I never even heard of you until the other night. She told me about you."

"All right. Anyway, she came to me and asked me to find a box for her; she described it; a small box with buffaloes carved in relief on the outside. Lansford Hastings had such a box. *He* came to me first, before Betty — "

"Whoa!" exclaimed Harold Wade. "You say Lansford Hastings stole Betty's buffalo box . . . ?"

"I didn't say he stole the box," Lash snapped. "I said he had such a box when he came to my office. He wanted me to find the owner. Then the same afternoon Betty Dunlap came to me — "

"She didn't come to you; she ran into you in a bookstore."

"How do you remember that?" Lash snarled, "if you're so rattlebrained about everything else."

"That's twice you've said that," Wade said. "I don't have to take it from anyone."

"Then why don't you do something about it?" Lash sneered.

Wade took a step back. He was five feet ten and probably outweighed Lash by at least ten pounds. But he hesitated and it was well that he did for Lash would have beaten him into insensibility.

"*Well?*" Lash asked.

Wade muttered something under his breath and rushed out of the apartment-hotel lobby. Lash followed leisurely and saw the radio man walking hurriedly down Sunset Boulevard.

He got into his car and passed Wade. He crossed Laurel Canyon a couple of blocks beyond, but at the next block whipped the coupé to the left and drove back to Laurel. He turned into the canyon road and sent the car screeching up the two dozen hairpin turns, over the mountain and down on the other side.

He slackened speed as he neared Ventura, but beyond the boulevard let the car out again until he reached the house of Jim Dunlap, beyond Magnolia.

The ancient flivver was still parked at the curb. Lash walked up to the front door and pressed the doorbell impatiently.

The door was opened by Isaac Eckert. "We ain't buyin' nothin', young fella," the old man said.

"Did I offer to sell you anything?" Lash retorted. "I want to see Jim Dunlap."

"Y'can't; he's busy in his laboratory."

"Then Miss Dunlap?"

"She ain't home."

Lash suddenly brushed past Isaac Eckert. "Then you'll have to do. Which Isaac Eckert are you, two, three, or four?"

The old man turned on Lash and closed the door behind him. "Say, I thought I'd seen you somewheres. You're the young squirt was here t'other night. The one that was shootin' off about Lansford Hastings."

"I'm still shooting off about him."

"What for? He's dead, ain't he? And Jim told you off about the girl's stuff, didn't he?"

"I've got a new client," Lash said. "Another relative."

"Who?"

Lash shook his head. "I can't tell that."

"Sheridan?"

"Is he the only other relative, outside of this house?"

The old man's bright eyes studied Lash for a moment. Then he suddenly nodded. "See here, young fella, I was talkin' to Betty yest'day. She said you're a readin' fella, that y'know a lot about the Donners and Eckerts. Just what do you know?"

"Why," said Lash, "I know that if you're not a fraud you must be Isaac Eckert III. That would make you eighty years old . . . "

"Eighty-one," snapped Eckert. "And

106

I'm good for another twenty years. What do you think of that?"

"I'll tell you in twenty years if you're still around. Mr. Eckert, I'm going to tell you a secret. The man who called himself Lansford Hastings was an imposter."

Eckert snorted. "Who you tryin' to kid? Of course he was a phoney. Lansford Hastings was a grown man before my pa was born."

"This could have been the original Hastings' son — or grandson."

"Naw, Hastings died in South America. He had a scheme to settle Confederate soldiers down there, but like most of his schemes it fizzled out. I thought you knew your hist'ry."

Lash shrugged. "I only know what I read. I know that your grandfather had fifty thousand dollars in gold and it's never been found."

"Not yet it ain't," declared Isaac Eckert, "but I'm a-gittin' close. That's why I'm here now. Jim Dunlap's one of them scientific fellas and he's fixin' up a machine . . . hey, wait a minute! What's the idee tryin' to pump me?"

"I wasn't pumping you, Mr. Eckert."

"The devil you wasn't. You was tryin' to worm outta me about that there machine Jim's been a-workin' on. Well, you ain't a-goin' to get it outta me. Nossir, I'm onto your game and you won't get a thing outta me."

"I'm not interested in the gold," Lash said. "It wouldn't do me any good even if I found it since I'm not a relative."

"But you're workin' for my nephy Sheridan and he's nothin' but a low-down crook. I don't mind if I do say it. I've worked fifty years for that money and when I get it I'm a-goin' to keep it. If there's any left I'm leavin' it to Jim Dunlap on account of the machine he's invented for me . . . "

"Cousin Isaac!" Jim Dunlap said from a doorway in the rear.

10

LASH said evenly: "How do you do, Mr. Dunlap?"

"What do you want?" Dunlap asked, curtly.

"He's been a-tryin' to pump me, Jim," Isaac Eckert cried. "Watch out for him; he's a spy for Sher'dan."

"Pick up the telephone," Lash said. "Call Sheridan Eckert and mention my name. Then stuff your ears with cotton."

"Look, Mr. Lash," said Jim Dunlap. "I know all about you. You're supposed to be a very astute detective. But what's in this for you? My daughter discharged you. There's nothing you can gain by continuing your investigation."

"He says Sher'dan hired him," exclaimed Old Eckert.

"I didn't say that," Lash denied.

"You did so."

"I said I had a client . . . another relative."

Jim Dunlap came farther into the

room. "What do you mean? There are no other Eckerts. None that are related to us."

"No?"

Dunlap scowled. "What are you driving at? Cousin Isaac's son . . . ?"

"Ah, he has one?"

"He's dead."

"I was under the impression that Cousin Isaac was dead, too."

Old Isaac cackled. "Do I look dead? Heh-heh!"

"Cousin Isaac lost touch with the family years ago. He left home when he was a boy and was a sailor for some years. When he finally came ashore he took up prospecting — "

"Fifty years of it, too!" the old man boasted. "Fifty years of eatin' beans and bacon, and I'm as fit today as any man of sixty-five. I'm good for twenty years more. Only I'm gettin' kind of tired of beans, that's why I — "

"Cousin Isaac!" Jim Dunlap said sharply.

"Eh?"

"I'll do the talking. Mr. Lash, you've covered the ground. There isn't anything else."

"Oh, but there is. A man was murdered the other night. A man who had a hand-carved buffalo box."

"Anybody can have a wooden box."

"This box is about three inches deep, four wide and six long. The outside is covered with relief carvings of buffaloes, each figure about a half inch in size . . . "

"Betty described her box to you," Dunlap said.

"No," Lash said.

"Yes!"

Lash drew a deep breath and exhaled heavily. "A man was still murdered."

"The police have bothered us enough about that. *You* led them here. And you're the man who found the body."

"So I did. By the way — I went down today to identify the body, and I was surprised to discover that Lansford Hastings was actually quite a young man. The beard was false . . . "

Dunlap's eyes narrowed. "The man was an imposter, of course."

"But he had a box and knew all about the Eckerts . . . "

"*You* know all about us," Dunlap pointed out. "There are fifty books in the library that can tell anyone more about my great-grandfather than I knew myself."

"True," said Lash. "But books can be wrong sometimes. For example, not one of the books has ever told who died first — your grandmother or your grandfather . . . "

Jim Dunlap's nostrils were suddenly distended. "What do you mean by that?" he asked, thickly.

"When your mother was carried out by the rescue party, your grandfather and grandmother were left behind. They were pretty far gone, and by the time the next rescue party came almost a month later, they were both dead. The general assumption is that when a man and woman die simultaneously — no evidence to the contrary — the woman predeceases the man."

"I'm beginning to get your point," Dunlap said, an ominous note in his tone.

Lash ignored the interruption. "Yet every student of the Donner tragedy noted one salient fact — it was so obvious they could not avoid it — that the women stood up better under starvation than the men. When the first party left Donner Lake, it consisted of twelve men and five women. Of that number four women and one man got through. For inheritance purposes, the law says today that if a husband and wife are both killed in an automobile accident, the wife is considered to have died first. But, in view of the known facts regarding the entire Donner episode, I contend that your grandfather predeceased your grandmother."

"I thought you were a detective, Lash," said Dunlap. "Not a lawyer."

"I was a lawyer before I became a detective."

"How interesting? And you're acting in both capacities now? Your client wouldn't be Richard Evanston, by any chance?"

"No," said Lash. "Richard Evanston isn't my client." He nodded and without another word took his departure.

Outside he climbed into the coupé and starting the motor made a wide U turn. As he was straightening the car to head west, an automobile horn honked and a yellow convertible made a U turn behind him.

Lash drew up to the curb a block from the Dunlap home. Betty Dunlap brought the yellow car to a stop behind Lash's car and climbing out ran quickly up to where Lash remained behind the wheel.

"Mr. Lash," she exclaimed. "I've been wanting to talk to you."

"You discharged me the other evening."

"I know, but I had to under the circumstances. I — I want to employ you again."

"I'm sorry," said Lash, "but that may not be possible."

"Why not?"

"Because a detective, like an attorney, cannot have two clients whose interests are adverse."

Betty Dunlap recoiled. "What do you mean; you've . . . ?"

"I have another client."

"Who?"

"I can't tell you that."

"But perhaps his interests will not conflict with mine."

"That depends on what you want me to do."

Betty Dunlap's white teeth worried her lower lip. "All I want you to do is investigate my Cousin Isaac."

Lash looked at her sharply. "What do you want to know about him?"

"Everything there is to know. You see, the family hasn't been in touch with him for a good many years, and then the other evening he appeared out of nowhere — "

"I see. You suspect that he may not actually be your cousin?"

"No. I don't suspect *that*. He knows too much about the family. It's just that there's . . . *something* about him."

"He doesn't ring true?"

Betty Dunlap frowned. "Perhaps that's it. He lays too much emphasis on his relationship."

"But he brought back your box?"

"Oh, no. What makes you say that?"

"The box was lost; so was Cousin Isaac. Cousin Isaac shows up, so does the box."

Betty exclaimed, "That's it, Mr. Lash, the thing I've been groping for. The *coincidence*. The box was mislaid. But I *was* seeking it. I hadn't thought of it in years; I hadn't been particularly conscious of the family legend for a long time; and then it all came at once — the desert rat on Harold's radio program, my search for the box, and Cousin Isaac's appearance."

"All right," said Lash. "I'll take the case."

"It doesn't conflict with the interests of the client you already have?"

"No. But you'll have to tell me the truth. About everything."

"What do you want to know?"

"You might begin at the beginning. Your revived interest in the family's history; Wade's radio program brought that on?"

"In a way, yes. The man who called himself Lansford Hastings mentioned Donner Pass and Donner Lake in his talk. His own name stuck in my mind, and the next day when I was browsing in the attic storeroom, I came across that book. It reminded me of the box I used to play with when I was a girl. I searched for it and couldn't find it."

"Where did you finally find it?"

"In the storeroom."

116

"Where you'd already searched?"

"Yes. In Grandmother's trunk."

"You overlooked the trunk in your first search?"

"No, that's where I found the book."

"Yet the box is a sizable object."

Betty's forehead creased. "I know; that's the odd part of it. I took everything out of the trunk and put it back. I don't see how I could have missed anything as large as the box. Yet . . . I must have."

"Why must you have?"

"Because when I looked again the other day the box was there, wrapped in an old shawl."

"Exactly when did you find the box? After your Cousin Isaac showed up?"

"Yes. Just a moment." Betty walked around the car, and opening the door slipped in beside Lash. "That's what first made me suspicious about Cousin Isaac. I remembered having taken the shawl out of the trunk when I first searched it. I'm sure that I even shook it."

Lash nodded. "Well, tell me, who else has access to this storeroom?"

"No one."

"What do you mean by no one?"

"Just that. Our housekeeper sleeps out."

"But your father has access, doesn't he?"

"Of course. But it's because of him that we keep the storeroom locked. I told you, didn't I, that father is an inventor? He keeps a lot of his old papers in the storeroom. Old blueprints and such. He has the only key to the storeroom and keeps it on his key ring."

"What kind of lock is it?"

"A Yale. As I said, the housekeeper doesn't even have access to the room."

"How do you get in if your father has the only key?"

"Well, he lends me the key whenever I need to get into the room. I return it immediately after I'm through."

"Always? You never forgot to return the key?"

"Not recently. Once, several months ago, I forgot and carried it in my purse for two or three days."

Lash turned in his seat so he could look better at Betty. "The housekeeper is the only servant you have and you say she goes home at night?"

"That's right."

"But she works every day."

"Yes."

"Well, where is she today? I've just come from the house, and your cousin let me in."

"Why, I imagine she's doing the marketing. She takes an hour or more every afternoon, and this is just about the time."

Lash nodded thoughtfully. "Where is your father's laboratory?"

"In the rear of the house. There's a building there that used to be a garage, which father has turned into a laboratory. The new garage is smaller and built on to the laboratory."

"That's about fifty feet behind the house."

"Yes. You're thinking of burglars?"

"I'm trying to consider all possibilities. If your father is working in his laboratory and the housekeeper is doing the marketing and you're out, a person could easily enough enter the house and make a search."

"Yes, but it would have to be during the day, because there's a burglar alarm that is put on at night."

"Burglars have been known to work during the day. What sort of burglar alarm is it, by the way?"

"Dad's own invention. If he is home alone in the evening and decides to work in his laboratory, he throws a switch and if anyone tries to enter the house, it will ring a bell in his laboratory."

"Even if the intruder has a key to the house?"

"Especially if he has a key. The touch of metal upon the lock breaks a circuit."

"What about when you come to the house?"

"Why, I throw off the switch before I unlock the door."

"From the outside?"

"Yes, it's a concealed switch."

Lash shook his head. "So anyone who happened to be coming home with you would know about the concealed switch?"

"The only one who's ever come home with me is Harold Wade."

"That's enough."

Betty blinked in annoyance. "What do you mean by that?"

"A thing's no longer a secret if one outside person knows it."

"Harold Wade is my fiancé."

"You denied that the other day."

"I saw no reason to tell you then."

"But he knows about the secret switch?"

"He hasn't commented about it, but he's probably seen me operating it. But if you think Harold's the one who took the box, you're mistaken."

"I didn't say he was the one. I merely pointed out that another person could have known about the burglar alarm switch. He, in turn, could have told someone else and that someone else . . . "

"No. Harold wouldn't tell anyone."

"All right, that still leaves the afternoons. Anyone could have walked into the house and got into the storeroom."

"But the lock was never forced."

Lash snickered. "Let me just walk past that door once and the next time I come to your house I'll have a key for the Yale lock. Did you ever hear of a wax impression? Or a master key?"

Betty Dunlap sighed wearily. "Very

well, that's your case. Someone could have got into the room then and someone could have taken the buffalo box and returned it . . . but why?"

"You'd know that better than I. What was in the box?"

"Nothing."

"Then what's its value?"

"It's an heirloom; naturally, I want it. Besides, it may be of historical importance — like the Lansford Hastings book you seemed to set such store by."

"I see. Yet you were quite willing to give me the book."

"The book wasn't a personal object. The box is. It was carved up by my great-grandfather. He must have spent days and days on it, when he was — well, starving."

"That's true. Well, look, Miss Dunlap, could you let me see the box sometime?"

"Why, it's just a wooden box . . . "

"The man who called himself Lansford Hastings had a box like that; I wanted to see if it was the same box?"

"How would you know; you didn't get to keep the box, did you?"

"No, but I have a good memory. I'd

like to see your box."

Betty Dunlap frowned. "When . . . ?"

"As soon as possible. Could you bring it to my office?"

"Today?"

"This evening."

Betty hesitated. "Well, I have a date, but I guess I could run up with it . . . say around seven?"

"That'll be fine. If I'm not there give the box to my assistant, Eddie Slocum."

"But that would mean leaving it."

"It won't be harmed."

"All right." She started to open the door, but Lash reached out and touched her arm. "Just a moment. You haven't given me anything about Cousin Isaac to go on. Where does he say he's been living all these years?"

"The desert. He hasn't mentioned any specific place. Just that he's been prospecting all over California and Nevada . . . "

"And around Donner Pass?"

"I imagine."

"What's this invention your father is making for him?"

123

Betty gasped. "What do you know about that?"

Lash grinned wryly. "It's a secret, so Cousin Isaac mentioned it in every other breath. Some sort of divining rod for finding treasure, isn't it?"

"He told you that?"

"Not in so many words. But it's obvious enough. There's been talk about fifty thousand dollars in gold, and your father is perfecting some sort of divining rod that will locate this treasure."

Betty shook her head in annoyance. "*I* think the whole idea is rather farfetched, and I imagine father does too, but Cousin Isaac is so persistent that I guess he gave in to him. Father likes Cousin Isaac."

"You don't?"

"I don't."

Lash nodded. "I'll probably see you this evening, then. Just one thing more — did you ever hear of Richard Evanston?"

"Who?" exclaimed Betty Dunlap.

"Richard Evanston."

"I never heard of him," Betty Dunlap said, but both her tone and expression gave the lie to her statement. Lash didn't press the question.

As Betty Dunlap climbed out of the car, he shifted into low and started swiftly back to Hollywood.

11

EDDIE SLOCUM met Simon Lash at the head of the stairs as the latter climbed up to his apartment. "Did you hire Milo Stevens, chief?"

"Yes; has he telephoned?"

"Twice since I've been back."

"What's he got?"

"He says the jackass passed the Lincoln Hotel three times in the last three days."

"I knew that before I went to him."

"It also passed a filling station on Franklin and Highland."

"That was the last call?"

"Yes."

Lash grunted. "Looks like it came from the valley. Now, about your own job?"

Eddie Slocum grimaced. "Mrs. Evanston came out about five minutes after you left. She went to a department store on Wilshire and Fairfax. I followed her up to the third floor where she entered the ladies' washroom. I waited about three minutes, then decided I'd better see if there was another exit from the washroom. There was."

"She knew you were following her?"

"She considerately took a bus down Wilshire. I followed in a taxi. She's a smart gal. Never looked back once."

"All these people are smart, Eddie," Lash said. "We're not working for Mrs. Evanston any more. But we've got an old client back . . . "

The telephone rang, and Lash walked quickly to his desk and scooped it up. "Yes?"

"Simon?" asked the voice of Milo Stevens. "One of my men just called in. The jackass passed the drive-in at Ventura and Laurel Canyon."

"Coming from what direction?"

"Ventura . . . "

"Good! Don't call again until you've found it, or get to Longridge."

"Why Longridge?"

"Just because."

"All right, Simon. How do you like the service I'm giving you?"

"It's simply marvelous," said Lash hanging up the receiver. He turned to

Eddie Slocum. "Do you remember that fellow who used to stand on the corner of Hollywood and Highland with the big telescope?"

"Yeah sure," replied Slocum. "The astrologer."

"Astronomer, not astrologer. He charged ten cents a peek at the stars. Is he still operating?"

"He was last week."

"But he doesn't come out until dark. Mmm, that's two-three hours. You wait here until after Betty Dunlap's come and gone . . . "

"She's coming here?"

"At seven. She's bringing the buffalo box. I might not be back before then. Even if I am, I don't want to see her. I want her to leave the box. So after she's gone, you hike down to Highland and get the big telescope."

"What?" cried Eddie.

"Rent it. After all, how much can the man make at ten cents a look? I'll want it for at least two days. Offer him twenty dollars."

"You're taking up astrology?"

"Astronomy, I said. And I'm not. But

128

that's about as powerful a telescope as I'll be able to get."

"Yeah, but you're not serious about looking at the stars?"

"Oh, I'm not going to use the telescope, Eddie. You are."

"Me? What for?"

"Yep. You're going to set it up at the corner of Laurel and Magnolia. That's about a thousand feet from the Dunlap house. You ought to be able to see the flyspecks on the wall with the glass at that distance."

"Oh," said Slocum. "What's wrong with the fly-specks?"

"Don't be funny, Eddie. You're to look at the windows. Particularly the laboratory at the rear of the house. Since it's back from the street so far, I've a hunch Dunlap won't be particular about pulling down the shades."

"And what about the people who'll be passing while I'm doing the spying? And the cops?"

"They won't bother you. Naturally, you'll keep the sign up."

"The ten-cents-a-peek sign? But what if someone wants to peek?"

"You'll just have to let them peek. But naturally you'll tilt up the telescope before you do."

"Suppose they ask me questions about the stars? I don't know Venus from Mars."

"You don't have to. Maybe you'd better focus the telescope on the moon and if anyone wants to look, tell them it's made of cheese. They've heard that, anyway, so you won't disappoint them."

Lash left the apartment and getting into the coupé drove down to Eisenschiml's bookstore on Wilcox. The bookdealer greeted him with waving arms.

"Ah, here you are, Mr. Lash. I suppose you've come to pay me that commission?"

"What commission?"

"The one you did me out of on the Lansford Hastings book."

"All right, how much is it?"

Eisenschiml cleared his throat. "Twenty-five percent . . . "

"Twenty-five dollars, eh? Pretty stiff . . . "

"Twenty-five dollars nothing. A hun'erd and a quarter. You were talking about five hundred dollars?"

130

"We were *talking*. You know very well the book wasn't worth five hundred."

"It certain'y was, Lash. You took it for that much . . . "

"I'll tell you what," said Lash. "I'll pay you the hundred and twenty-five dollars; then I'll sell you the book — for two hundred and fifty."

Eisenschiml's eyes drew together as he calculated mentally. Then he shook his head. "No, I don't want the book."

"Why not? You buy and sell Americana, don't you? You've bought plenty of books from me — and I've bought enough from you."

"Yeah, sure, but that's bad business. I couldn't get — I mean there isn't much market for California stuff right now. I might have to keep the book in stock for a long time, and to tell you the truth I'm overstocked and short of cash."

"I'm glad to hear that. I'll keep the book then and pay you, mmm, fifteen dollars commission."

"Hey, what're you talking about now?"

"I'm getting down to cases; the book's worth fifty or sixty dollars and you know it."

Eisenschiml groaned. "Gimme the twenty-five dollars you offered at first and let's forget the whole deal, huh?"

Lash took the money out of his pocket and dropped it on the counter. Then he said: "Now, I'd like to get a book on magic."

"Magic? I haven't got any books on magic."

"You're sure? I thought I'd noticed some paperbound books awhile ago."

"Oh, those!" Eisenschiml came around the counter and walked to a big table on which were strewn several hundred 'bargain' books. He pawed over the books for a moment, then came up with a small paper-bound volume. "Is this what you meant? *Twenty Simple Card Tricks*."

"That must be the book. But it's only card tricks?"

"I dunno, I never read it. It's yours for fifteen cents."

Lash took the book and riffled the pages. He shook his head. "I'm afraid not. I think I want something more advanced."

"You're taking up magic? Then why don't you go over to Maxon's Magic

Mart? He's got all sorts of gimmicks . . . "

"I think that's just the kind of place I'm looking for. Where is it?"

"On Hollywood, right near Ivar. It's on the second floor. Tell Maxon I sent you."

"I will." Lash left the store and drove down Hollywood to Ivar. He turned into the latter street and parked the coupé in a parking lot. Then he walked back to Hollywood and searched for the magic shop. He found it after a moment or two.

Although it was on the second floor, it was fitted up with counters like a regular store. Three or four men were watching another man perform card tricks. Behind the counter, a bored, bald-headed man was reading a copy of a pamphlet with the intriguing title *The Phoenix.*

"Mr. Maxon?" Lash asked. "Eisenschiml sent me here."

"Yeah, how's his racket?"

"He's just had a good day. Look, Mr. Maxon, I'm an amateur magician. I understand you sell, uh, gimmicks for magicians . . . "

"The best line west of the Rockies,

that's all. I got a swell new trick here I'd like to show you." Maxon picked up a pack of cards, shuffled quickly, then fanned the cards out for Lash. "Take a card. Look at it. Now put it on top of the pack. Now watch."

Maxon put the entire pack of cards back into the pasteboard box. Then with Lash watching closely, he set the box into a contraption which looked somewhat like a miniature scaffold. Then he took a metal rod and tapped the contraption.

There was a flutter and snap, and the card Lash had selected appeared at the top of the scaffold, held there by a spring clip.

"Not bad," he said. "How does it work?"

Maxon smiled. "Naturally, I'll show you if you buy it. Only twelve fifty."

Lash frowned. "It's a good trick, but what I'm really looking for is something entirely different. Mmm, don't you have some sort of box that has a false bottom . . . ?"

"A Japanese box?" Maxon made a clucking sound with his tongue against the roof of his mouth, then walked back into a small room behind the counter. He returned after a moment, carrying a lacquered box about three by four by six inches.

"Boys!" he called to the group who were watching the card trick. "Let me show you the Japanese box. This one's a honey; I'd almost forgotten I had it."

The group promptly lined up against the glass showcase.

Maxon chuckled and raised the lid of the lacquered box. Then he handed it to Lash. "Look it over."

Lash examined the box closely, even tapping the sides and bottom. It seemed solid enough and it was certainly empty. He turned it to Maxon. "It looks all right."

"It is all right," said Maxon. He held up a tiny metal key so all along the showcase could see. Then he closed the box and inserting the key into the keyhole turned it. He withdrew the key and handed it to Lash. "You examined the box, so you know it's empty. Now, unlock the box and look again."

Lash inserted the key in the lock and turned it. He raised the lid of the box and was astonished when a double handful of filmy silk popped up.

The other men along the showcase showed their surprise with suitable comments. Lash took out the silk cloth, squeezing it into a small wad. It was quite resilient, and could be wadded into a small bundle, but that didn't alter the fact that the silk must have come from somewhere and it certainly hadn't been in the box when he had examined it a moment ago.

"Put it back in the box," Maxon said. "And lock it up."

Lash complied with the request. Then Maxon handed the box and key to another man. "You open it."

The man did and the silk popped out again.

Maxon made another clucking sound. "Tsk. Tsk. Here, let *me* lock it." He did and handed the box and key to still another man.

When the man opened the box this time, it was completely empty and the astonishment of the audience was complete. Lash nodded thoughtfully. "If

I buy the box you'll show me how it works?"

"Of course. But not before these gentlemen. The trick's too good."

"It *is* a trick?"

"Eh?"

"I mean, it's a good trick."

"Just about the best in the business. I'll bet there aren't two of these boxes in this country. Plenty of Japanese boxes, yeah, but none that work like this one."

"How much is it?"

Maxon looked thoughtfully at Lash. "That's the trouble. I paid such a big price for it, I'd have to have seventy-five dollars."

Lash whistled softly. "That's too much!"

"Sure, but when will another one like it come from Japan? As a matter of fact the man who made this box is dead. There may never be another one like it. I tell you frankly, *I* couldn't make one."

"I might go twenty dollars," Lash said.

Maxon shook his head. "I couldn't consider that. I paid more for it. I'll tell you what, I'll auction it off to the highest bidder, right now. Any of you gentlemen want to make an offer?"

"I'll pay thirty for it," one of the men said.

"I'll pay thirty-five," another said.

Lash groaned. "Fifty dollars."

"Fifty-five."

"Sixty," said Lash and swore under his breath.

He got the box for seventy-two fifty and wondered how many of the other bidders had been Maxon's stooges. The magic-shop man, however, went through with the act by taking Lash into the rear room and explaining the secret of the box in a hoarse whisper so that none of the men in the other room could hear.

The explanation of the secret took less than thirty seconds to tell, and Lash exclaimed in chagrin at the simplicity of it.

"Ain't it a beaut?" Maxon exulted.

"Yes," Lash agreed.

He left the shop with the box under his arm. Retrieving his car at the parking lot, he drove up Ivar, across Hollywood Boulevard, toward Cahuenga Pass.

12

IT was getting dark as he rolled through Studio City and turned into Longridge a few minutes later. But it was still light enough to note that the doors of the garage attached to Luke Lupton's house were closed.

The house, however, was dark. Nevertheless, Lash rang the doorbell and heard chimes bong inside. After waiting a sufficiently long period, he set off the chimes once more. There was still no response, and he was turning away from the door when a man came suddenly around the corner of the garage.

"Mr. Lupton ain't home," he said.

"You live here?" Lash asked.

"Well, no," the man said. Then, "Say, aren't you Simon Lash?"

Lash looked sharply at the man. "That's my name; why?"

The man came closer and grinned sheepishly. "I work for Milo Stevens."

Lash exclaimed. "What are you doing here?"

"It's your job, isn't it? The jackass . . . "

"It's here?"

"Not now, but this is where it was. We traced it up the street, then to here. The property runs all the way through those trees in back, up over the hill. There's a horse barn on the other side, although I don't think Lupton's had a horse for some time. But he sure as the devil had a jackass."

"You checked with the neighbors?"

The man nodded. "He had it all right, but it's gone now. And so's Lupton. Leastwise he hasn't been home since this morning."

"What about his owls?"

"Owls?"

Lash made an impatient gesture. "You don't know about them. He had four singing owls. I wonder if they're in the house."

"I can find out — after it's dark."

"No. Let it go. Mmm, but I wish you'd stay around and watch the house. You're here alone?"

"Nick Joppa's down at the corner of

Ventura and Longridge. He's in the green Ford. If you'll stop and tell him that I'm staying here, he can call in to the office. I'm sure it'll be all right, though. Milo said to stick on the job until we got results."

"I'll talk to Joppa and call Milo myself. Keep out of sight, but the minute Lupton comes home, get down to the corner and telephone the office."

"Okay, Mr. Lash."

Lash turned his coupé and drove back to Ventura, where he found a lean, dark man seated in a Ford smoking a cigarette. "Your name Joppa?" Lash asked, after he had parked his car behind the other's and gone forward.

"What's it to you?"

"My name's Simon Lash; your partner told me to tell you to call the office. He's staying up there to keep an eye on the place."

"Yeah? Well, you don't look like Simon Lash."

"And you don't look like the jackass you're hunting," Lash retorted. "Your ears are too long."

He went back to his own car and

141

drove swiftly to Hollywood. At Highland he stopped and went into a drugstore, where he called the office.

"Eddie, has Miss Dunlap called yet?"

"Yes," said Eddie.

"She's there now?"

"Uh-huh. I'm sorry, Mr. Jenkins, but Mr. Lash won't be back for an hour or so."

"All right," said Lash. "Make her leave the box and get rid of her. I'm at Highland and I want to come home."

He hung up and left the drugstore. A short distance away, the man with the big telescope was adjusting his instrument for the evening's stargazing.

Lash went up to him and held out a dime. "Let me take a look."

"The Big Dipper's very bright tonight," the man said. "I'll focus it for you . . ."

"No," said Lash. "Turn it around. I'm curious to see just how powerful one of these things is and I'd like to see something tangible. Like the hotel over there."

The astronomer gave Lash a wise look. "Okay, Mister, I'll give you your dime's worth." He swung the telescope around so that it faced the Lincoln Hotel a couple of blocks away. He put his eye to it and did a little jiggling with a couple of turnscrews. "I ought to charge you a quarter for this peek," he said.

Lash put his eye to the instrument and a hotel bedroom leaped at him. The shade was only half drawn, and a woman in an early stage of dress left very little to the imagination.

Lash straightened. "Swell! How much do you make in an evening's peeking?"

"At ten cents a look? In forty-four years I'll pay for the instrument."

"Then this is your lucky day. I want to rent the telescope for two days."

"Huh? Why — "

"I'll give you twenty dollars."

"You couldn't make that thirty dollars, could you? I want to buy a saxophone."

"How much is the glass worth?"

The astronomer shrugged. "How much is a white elephant worth?"

Lash took three ten dollar bills from his pocket. He added his business card and showed his driver's license. "You can call for it the day after tomorrow."

"A detective, eh? I get it. It's a deal."

The man helped Lash put the telescope in the rumble seat of Lash's coupé, then watched him drive off. Lash drove leisurely to the apartment on Harper and nodded when he saw that the curb was clear in front of the building.

He left the telescope in the car and ran quickly up the stairs. "Did you get the box, Eddie?"

"She didn't want to leave it, but I told her she could pick it up on her way home."

"Maybe," said Lash. "Has Milo Stevens called?"

"Four times. He says he's found the home of the jackass."

"I know about that. All right, I picked up the telescope for you. It's in the rumble seat. You'd better get going."

"Yes, but what am I trying to see?"

"Whatever's to be seen; I took a look through the glass. You can almost read a newspaper at a half mile. I think Dunlap's working on an invention. I hope you can get a fair description of it; but don't miss anything. Particularly his callers, if any."

Slocum nodded and getting his hat left the apartment. Lash turned to the wooden buffalo box which was on his desk, but before he could touch it, the phone rang.

"Mr. Lash?" asked a feminine voice. "This is Anne Evanston."

"Ah yes, my former client."

"That's what I'm calling about. You know you put me on rather a spot this afternoon, breaking in on Sheridan Eckert like that. There wasn't anything I could do but say what I did."

"What did you say?"

"Why, you know very well. I said I wouldn't require your services any longer. But I do want you to go on. I want to know who the man was who was killed and . . . " Anne Evanston paused for so long that Lash asked impatiently.

"Yes?"

"I want you to find my husband."

"Richard Evanston?"

"Of course."

Lash scowled at the telephone. "Look, Mrs. Evanston, I accepted your original assignment, and I performed it. But I'm afraid I can't do anything else for you."

"But why not? You're in the business, aren't you . . . ?"

"I told you when you first came to me that I expected you to be honest with me . . ."

"But I was!"

"You said you'd just flown in from Ohio, yet you'd been registered at the Lincoln Hotel for the last three days."

"I see," said Anne Evanston in a strangely modified voice. "You've been checking up on me. I hardly know what to say now."

"Why not say good-bye?"

"Very well then — good-bye."

Lash hung up and had scarcely let go of the phone when it rang again. It was Milo Stevens this time.

"Lash, were you just out on Longridge?"

"Yes, I talked to a couple of your men there."

"You told Winship to watch the house. That'll cost you extra, Simon."

"What for?"

"You only engaged this agency to find the jackass. The stakeout wasn't included . . ."

"They didn't find the jackass, did they?"

"They found the place where it had been."

"The deal was that you find the animal."

Milo Stevens exclaimed peevishly. "Damn it, Simon, you know you only wanted to find the owner. We did and — "

"Save it for your suckers, Milo. I said I'd pay for a twenty-four hour job, and your men haven't been on it that long. Let them watch the Longridge place until morning, then we'll call it quits."

Stevens started another protest, but Lash slammed the receiver on the hook. Then he went around his desk and sat down heavily in the swivel chair. He leaned forward and moved the buffalo box beside the lacquered one he had purchased in the magic shop. The Japanese box was the smaller of the two.

Lash turned the buffalo box around and exclaimed. It had no lock. There was a crack indicating where the lid rested on the body of the box, and one side was

147

hinged intricately.

He tried to pry up the lid with his hands but found it impossible. Yet there had to be a lock, and he examined the relief carvings. It was obviously the work of an expert and had undoubtedly taken a great deal of time. There were no less than fifty buffaloes and in addition carvings of trees and other objects. In the center of the lid was an irregular circle. Lash stared at it for some moments, then suddenly rose and went to his library. He searched the shelves and took down a rather weathered book. He carried it back to his office and began skimming through the pages.

Near the center of the book he same to an illustration. The moment he saw it he exclaimed. It was a drawing of Donner Lake and the surrounding territory. The irregular outline of the lake matched the circle on the lid of the buffalo box. Tiny raised squares matched the roughly sketched cabins of the Donner Party. Lash took a pencil from the desk and located the Eckert cabin, which was the closest to the lake. He located its counterpart on the box lid. A file of eight miniature buffaloes circled the cabin and went to a tiny bay at the southeastern edge of the map.

Another row of buffaloes — four in number — pointed toward the hinged side of the box. Lash turned the box and found two rows of five buffaloes each crossing in the form of an X. On the bottom of the box a row of buffaloes seemingly marched between two trees.

On the front of the box, where there should have been a lock, were two large buffaloes, one on each side of the box, and between them three much smaller animals.

Lash looked at the five buffaloes for a moment and idly pressed the large one at the left. It seemed to give under his thumb, and he pressed the other large carving. It, too, seemed to give.

Inhaling softly, he pressed, in turn, each of the small buffaloes. As the last one gave way under the pressure, the lid of the box snapped open.

The box was empty.

Lash tapped the sides, bottom, and lid. All seemed solid.

Lash looked at the lacquered Japanese

box and shook his head. He went over the box once more, pressing every carving on it, but nothing happened.

He closed the box and picked up the book that contained the map. He leafed through it, reading a paragraph or two here and there. After ten minutes or so a paragraph leaped out from a page:

It read: '*Jonathan Walton sang the popular songs of the day before the campfire; Isaac Eckert entertained the emigrants with feats of magic . . .*'

Lash tapped the buffalo box once more and muttered under his breath. A hatchet would solve the secret of it in a few seconds, but he could not use force, because it wasn't his box. And he did not believe Betty Dunlap would sanction the destruction of the box, no matter what its secret.

Engrossed in the puzzle, Lash heard a bell ring and reached automatically for the phone. He had the receiver off the hook before he realized that it was the doorbell and not the telephone that had rung.

He exclaimed angrily but got up and went to the head of the stairs. He switched on the stair light and pressed a button, which released the door catch.

The door was opened and Anne Evanston looked up at him. "Good evening, Mr. Lash," she said and started climbing the stairs.

"I thought you'd said good-bye," Lash called down.

"I did," she retorted, "but I've exercised a woman's prerogative. I've changed my mind."

She came up, and Lash retreated to his office. Anne Evanston followed him. Lash nodded to the red leather armchair, but Mrs. Evanston remained on her feet, her eyes fixed on the buffalo box on Lash's desk.

He winced. "Won't you have a seat?"

"Where'd you get that box?" Anne Evanston asked, tautly.

Lash picked up the Japanese box. "This? I picked it up in a magic shop. I'm somewhat of an amateur magician . . . "

"I meant the other box."

"Oh, that's a magic box, too."

"Would you let me see it?"

Lash hesitated a moment, then shrugged.

"Of course." He picked it up and handed it to Mrs. Evanston. She turned it over in her hands.

Lash, watching closely, heard a click and saw something move in the box. He took a quick step forward and then cried out and lunged for Anne Evanston's hand.

She tried to jerk it away, but he caught her wrist and twisting it caused her to drop something. She kicked at the object, but Lash, pushing her back, stooped and scooped up a small, leather notebook.

13

THE leather was stiff and cracked, the pages between the covers brittle and yellow with age.

"Well!" he said. "Thanks for finding this for me."

"Give it to me," Anne Evanston cried. "You have no right to it."

"Neither have you."

"I have more right than you."

"I wonder. By the way, how did you know how to open the box?"

She laughed scornfully. "Wouldn't you like to know?"

"Yes, I would."

Her blazing eyes suddenly narrowed. "I'll make a deal with you. Give me the book and I'll tell you."

Lash laughed raucously.

Anne Evanston took a step toward him. "Sight unseen," she said, "I'll give you a thousand dollars for that book."

"Sight unseen, it's worth fifty thousand."

"You're crazy; it's merely a diary of no interest to anyone but a relative of Isaac Eckert; I mean, Ellen Ford Eckert, my husband's great-grand-mother."

"True," said Lash, "about it's being a diary. But it might be more than that; it might be the key to a treasure of fifty thousand dollars in gold."

"You really believe there's a treasure?"

"I know several people who think so; including James and Betty Dunlap, Sheridan Eckert — and Isaac Eckert."

"Isaac Eckert?"

"Number three. He's come back to the clan."

"He's an imposter. Isaac Eckert has been dead for more than fifty years. I thought you knew the history of the Eckert family."

"I do; there was an Isaac Eckert who wandered off fifty or sixty years ago. His death was not recorded."

Anne Evanston tossed her head. "Would it interest you to know that I have a box just like that one?"

"With the buffalo carvings?"

"With buffaloes."

"That's impossible. Isaac Eckert carved

this while he was snowbound at Donner Lake."

"He made one just like it before he left Ohio. He gave it to his stepdaughter, my husband's grandmother."

Lash reached for the buffalo box in Anne Evanston's hands. She surrendered it readily enough, and he noted that it was once more empty, and the inside appeared as before.

"You may have a box like this; I imagine that's how you learned its secret."

"That's right. It has a false panel — naturally."

"Naturally. But how does it work?"

She made no reply. Lash put the buffalo box on his desk and picked up the lacquered one. "Here's an interesting box. It, also, has a double panel, but its operation is ridiculously simple, yet quite baffling if you don't know the secret."

"I'm not interested in trick boxes," Anne Evanston said.

"Only in what they contain?"

Anne Evanston drew in a deep breath. "Mr. Lash, I'll talk plainly to you."

"Go ahead."

"I'll begin with my husband. I've told you his relationship to the Eckerts. He's as much of an heir to whatever Isaac Eckert left as anyone else. Well, he got the treasure-hunting bug a while ago. I wasn't very keen on having him run around the desert, and we had words. He walked out on me."

"Sometimes women walk out on men," Lash said.

"You're not married, are you?"

Lash shook his head. "I worry; that's what makes me look so haggard."

Anne Evanston laughed harshly. "You'd make a fine husband for — for a female Bluebeard."

"Thank you, Mrs. Evanston. And now . . . ."

"Ten thousand dollars!"

"You have ten thousand dollars?"

"I can have the money here by tomorrow afternoon."

"Don't you think ten thousand dollars in the hand is worth fifty thousand in the snow?"

"I'm willing to gamble."

"I'm sorry," said Lash, "it isn't up

to me to sell this book. It belongs to a client."

"You're still working for the Dunlap girl?"

Lash shrugged. "You discharged me."

"I'll rehire you; that's why I came up here."

"It's no use. Your interests conflict with those of another client."

"But you had her as a client when you accepted my retainer."

"No, I didn't."

Anne Evanston adjusted her silver fox fur. Her eyes were flashing. She was a very attractive woman. "Very well, Mr. Lash, at least we understand each other."

"No hard feelings?"

Her lips curled and without another word she turned and walked out of the office. Lash listened to her heels clicking on the stairs before he followed. He watched her step through the door and waited until it closed before returning to his office.

Then he went swiftly to his chair and opened the little leather booklet. His first glance caused him to exclaim. The handwriting was definitely feminine and the first entry established the authorship.

It read:

November 10. We have been here a week and it has been snowing continuously. Isaac says the snow is eight feet deep. The children are becoming restless under the confinement but we have enough food and Isaac intends to hunt as soon as the snow stops.

As yet no hint of the horror. Lash skipped several pages and read again:

November 26. I reached the bottom of the flour barrel today. What the future holds in store for us only God can tell. We have a little meat left but after it's gone I don't know what we'll do. The others are as low on food as we, some even worse. Isaac has tried to hunt but the snow is too deep and light. Game seems scarce. The children cry.

Ellen Eckert did not keep her diary too regularly for the next entry was dated December I and a few days were skipped after that. But beginning with the middle of December there was an almost daily entry, even though sometimes short.

For December 15 the diary read: *We*

are eating the hides. I boil them for hours and make a thick soup. The taste is horrible and Isaac has difficulty keeping it on his stomach, but the children don't seem to mind.

Tragedy struck on the eighteenth of December. The diary said: *This is the end. Isaac cut his foot with the axe. It is a terrible wound and he cannot possibly stand on his foot. The good Lord have mercy.*

The record from this point on continued to a rising crest of tragedy. Ellen Eckert chopped wood; she tried hunting without result. She begged for food from some of the more fortunate neighbors but none would give her any.

A party of seventeen left the camp in a desperate attempt to scale the mountains and reach Sutter's Fort. Ellen Eckert never learned their fate. Simon Lash, almost a hundred years later, knew that only five of the seventeen reached Sutter's Fort. During the trip they ate human flesh.

Simon Lash put down the book and stared at the buffalo box. Isaac Eckert had worked on it during those last, black days. He had been laid up, unable to walk. The hours had been long.

Lash turned another page in the diary but before he could read, the phone at his elbow rang. He picked it up.

"Yes?"

"Milo Stevens, Simon. Joppa phoned in. There's something queer about the Longridge place, and I don't like it. Winship has disappeared. He was watching the house, but he and Joppa had an arrangement where they'd get together every half hour. Joppa can't find Winship."

Lash sniffed. "Tell him to look behind the house. There's a hill there and some woods. Winship's gone to sleep."

"I don't believe it, Simon. Winship's one of my best men."

"There's always a first time. Send out a couple more men."

"I have, and Joppa's searching the grounds now. If something's happened to Winship, you're going to hear about it, Simon."

"I'll bet," said Lash. He hung up.

"Hello," said a voice.

Lash whirled. A man was standing in the doorway of the office. He wore a

160

slicker that was turned up and half concealed his face, but not quite enough.

The man was Luke Lupton, whose home Stevens' men were searching even now. Lash nodded.

"Hello, Lupton. How's the owls?"

He swung around in the swivel chair and reached casually for the top drawer of the desk. Lupton's voice stopped him.

"Hold it, Lash!"

Lash stopped. Lupton's hands were in his pockets, but somehow Lash had a feeling that the right hand, at least, was not empty.

"What's on your mind, Lupton?" he asked.

"Nothing special. Only I heard you'd been at my place, so I thought I'd drop over here and see what it was you wanted."

"When was I at your place, Lupton?"

"This evening. I've just come from there. Mmm, there was a prowler in back of the house with whom I had some difficulty."

"You killed him?"

"Oh no, but he did give me a little tussle."

"Go ahead, Lupton."

"Yes, of course. I see you have Lansford Hastings' box."

Lash tapped the buffalo box and left his arm on the desk, so that his elbow covered the little leather-covered diary. "Yes," he said, "unfortunately, it was empty. I supposed you killed him for the box."

Lupton laughed harshly. "*I?* Then how did *you* get the box?"

"He gave it to me. He wanted me to find the owner."

"Come again, Lash. Hastings had the box when he called on me that evening. He had it when I went off to the studio. When I came back Hastings was dead — and the box was gone. I figure the murderer took it with him. And if you'll think very hard, Simon Lash, you'll remember that I found *you* with Hastings. The police let you drive off with the box in your car. I didn't say anything about it — but I want the box now."

"Your argument is sound, Lupton. Here, take the box." Lash whipped it up and hurled it at the intruder.

Thunder rocked the room, and a bullet splintered the top of Lash's desk. Lash gasped and came up from his chair. Lupton met him halfway. Lash had a flash of an automatic smashing down at his head. He tried to throw himself sideways but was too late.

Lightning exploded in his brain.

14

"THAT's a pretty bad bruise," the doctor said. "A little harder and you'd have had a fracture. Take it easy for a couple of days."

"Sure," said Simon Lash. "How much is it?"

"Five dollars."

"Pay him, Eddie."

Eddie Slocum paid the doctor and he came and smiled down at Lash once more. "Well, good-bye, Mr. Lash. Take the sedative and get a good night's sleep. You'll feel a lot better in the morning."

He went out and Betty Dunlap came and looked down at Lash. "The box is gone," she said.

"Of course," he replied. "Why do you suppose I got conked?"

Her sharp white teeth bit at her lower lip. Eddie Slocum came back from showing the doctor to the door. "Take it easy, chief," he cautioned.

Lash sat up on the leather couch and

winced from the pain that shot through his head. "Which one of you came first?" he asked.

"I found Miss Dunlap ringing the doorbell," Slocum said.

"I'd been ringing it for ten minutes," Betty Dunlap said. "I could see the light upstairs and knew that someone must be home and I wanted the box."

"Wade wasn't with you?" Lash asked.

"No, but . . . who was it?"

"A man named Lupton . . . "

"Lupton?" cried Betty Dunlap. "The man at whose home Lansford Hastings was killed?"

"That's right."

"But why would he want the box?"

Lash started to shake his head but the twinge of pain stopped him. "Why was Hastings killed at his house?"

"You mean Lupton . . . ?"

"I don't know. I didn't think so. We left the studio within two minutes of his own departure and Eddie drove about as fast as you can drive over Ventura without getting arrested. I don't think Lupton could have beaten us to his house."

"We were there five minutes before he showed up," Slocum said.

"I know, but if he'd had the time he could have come up from the rear, killed Hastings, then circled around and come up from the front. But as I said, there wasn't enough time. Wade's program was just over when we came out of the other sound room."

"Yes, but Harold's program is a half hour one."

Lash inhaled sharply. "You mean Lupton might have been on early in the program and left before it was all over?"

"Yes."

"I'll be damned," Lash muttered. "I didn't know they let them leave the studio during a program."

"They don't like anyone to leave, but actually no one would stop anyone."

"Telephone Wade, Miss Dunlap. Ask him if he can remember when Lupton was on the program and whether or not he left the studio early."

Betty Dunlap stepped to the desk and dialed a number. After a moment she said: "Miss Dunlap calling Mr. Wade.

What . . . ? He hasn't been in all evening? Thank you. No, there's no message."

She put down the receiver, a thoughtful expression in her eyes. "He isn't at home."

"Weren't you out with him this evening?" Lash asked.

"No."

"But you said you had a date."

"I went to a preview with a girl-friend, Rita Schwenneker. Harold had a rehearsal this evening."

Lash scowled. He looked at Eddie Slocum and the latter put his tongue in his cheek and winked. Lash nodded thoughtfully.

"Well, there isn't anything else we can do tonight, Miss Dunlap. You have your car here?"

"Yes, but — well, what about the box? Father will be furious if he learns that I brought it here and it's disappeared . . . "

"Disappeared?"

"Of course. I mean . . . well, you said it was stolen . . . "

"I *said*. Don't you believe me?"

Betty replied in the affirmative but there was a fraction of a second's hesitation. Lash said, irascibly:

"Where's that sedative, Eddie. My head is splitting."

"Good night, Mr. Lash. I — I'll telephone you in the morning."

"Do that. And don't worry about the box. I'll get it back for you. That's a promise."

"Thank you."

Slocum went down to the door with her. When he returned to the office, Lash was back at his desk.

"Aren't you going to bed, chief?" Slocum asked.

"No!" snapped Lash. "Now, spill it. Why'd you quit so early?"

"They went to bed."

"How do you know?"

Slocum laughed. "Didn't I have the telescope? Hell, Dunlap pulled down the shade to within an inch of the bottom, but the glass showed his bare knees as he was putting on his pyjamas . . ."

"Well, what'd you learn?"

"I don't know. He and the old geezer had a row; at least it looked like it and then about ten minutes later the old boy came tearing out, carrying a sack. He passed me on the street — "

"Did he spot you?"

"I don't think so. I was on the other side of the street. Anyway, by the time he came up, I had the telescope turned up and was examining Jupiter Pluvius or some such star."

"What time was that?"

"Nine-forty. I looked at my watch. I got out to the corner a few minutes after eight and by that time both Dunlap and old Isaac were out in the laboratory. You were right about the shades. They had them up."

Lash held up a hand. "Let's get this straight now. You got out there at about eight-five or ten. At nine-forty, Isaac left the house and about ten minutes before that he checked out of the laboratory."

"That's right. Dunlap stayed in the lab until a quarter after ten, when he went to the house and put out the lights — after undressing. Then I quit. I got back here at five minutes to eleven and found Betty Dunlap at the door."

Lash nodded. "Could you see what they were doing in the laboratory?"

"They were fooling around with a box

169

that looked like a suitcase radio set. At least it had a handle by which they carried it around and it had headphones, which first one would put on, then the other . . ."

"The divining rod!" exclaimed Lash.

"Eh?"

"Dunlap's been trying to invent some contraption with which to find the buried treasure."

Slocum exclaimed: "I didn't think he was that goofy."

"I don't think he is. He strikes me as a pretty shrewd bird. But the thing isn't impossible. There are instruments by which you can detect the presence of metals in the ground . . . "

"Whoa," said Eddie Slocum. "You mean that Rube Goldberg invention of Dunlap's is supposed to show them where the gold is buried?"

"That's the general idea. Isaac Eckert practically told me so when I was out there the last time."

"But I thought Dunlap was a smart inventor. Doesn't he know he can get a much simpler outfit for that by just going down to the water company?"

"What do you mean, Eddie?"

Slocum snorted. "A couple of weeks ago there was a crew from the water company working across the street. They wanted to locate the water pipes in the ground, so what'd they do? They took a simple little gadget and just walked back and forth across the lawn. When they passed the water pipe there was a needle on the gadget that turned down. I saw the thing; it looked just like a compass."

Lash swore. "And a bunch of laborers were operating it?"

"Yeah sure, a couple of the guys couldn't even talk English. If a simple gadget like that can locate a buried water pipe, couldn't it locate a pot of gold?"

"You're sure of that thing, Eddie?"

"Yeah, I thought it was kinda cute and I asked them to let me work it. The foreman said every gas and water company in the country had gadgets like that. You'd think Dunlap being an inventor and all would know about it."

Lash's eyes narrowed thoughtfully. "You'd think so, yes . . . "

The telephone rang and Lash started

to pick it up, then caught himself and nodded to Eddie. "If it's Milo Stevens tell him I'm out at a night club or something."

Slocum took the phone and instantly covered up the mouthpiece. "It's him all right and he sounds burned."

"Get rid of him."

"Yes, Mr. Stevens," Slocum said into the telephone. "I'm sorry Mr. Lash isn't home. No, he isn't. Yes . . . What . . . ?" He covered the phone again. "He says it's important. He's found out something for you."

Lash groaned and reached for the phone. "Hello, Milo, I was just coming in . . . "

"From the bedroom, eh?" Stevens snapped. "Well, listen, we found Winship. He was knocked stiff and I had to send him to the hospital. You'll get the bill for that."

"I will not," Lash retorted. "Winship's a detective and he takes a chance getting a tap on the head. I got one tonight and I never even left the office. The same guy gave it to me."

"Lupton? He came to your office . . . ?"

172

"Yes, and he admitted sapping Winship."

"And you say he sapped you? Good . . . "

"I was out for an hour, if that makes you feel any happier."

"It does. And maybe now you'll be in the right mood to believe what I'm going to tell you . . . "

"What is it?"

Milo Stevens laughed harshly. "You'll pay Winship's hospital bill?"

"You know I'd have paid it without your asking. I just didn't like the idea of your browbeating me into it. All right, spill it."

"His bill will be two hundred and fifty dollars. I've got a man listening on the extension. As a witness. You agree to pay it?"

"Look, Stevens," Lash snarled. "I told you I don't like being hi-jacked. Keep your information . . . "

"It won't keep. If you don't act on it right away, it's no good. You'll pay for it?"

"How do I know it's worth two hundred and fifty dollars?"

"Maybe it isn't. You ought to know better than me. But if it isn't, you won't have to pay. Okay?"

"Okay."

"Lupton's a phony. He bought the house three weeks ago, making only a small down-payment. He bought the singing owls from a guy out in Calabasas who makes a specialty of training animals. He's had a fellow living with him for most of the time he's been in the house. The guy who was killed. The cops got his name as Lansford Hastings, but that was a phony. His real name was . . . hang on . . . Eckert."

"Eckert?" Lash cried. "How do you know?"

"I can't tell you that. Maybe somebody broke into the house and searched it. But that'd be burglary so I wouldn't know about it. Anyway the guy's name was Fremont Eckert and Lupton's real name is Evanston . . ."

Lash yelled in astonishment. "Evanston! Not Richard Evanston?"

"Yeah, how'd you know?"

"I didn't."

"Furthermore," Milo Stevens continued,

174

"the guy's got a wife back in Ohio. There was a letter from her — "

"You've got the letter?"

Stevens coughed. "How would I have the letter, Simon . . . ?"

"Cut it out, Milo. Read the letter."

"What I've told you is worth the two fifty?"

"Yes, I'll pay it."

"And you're interested in the letter another hundred dollars worth . . . ?"

"You robber!" Lash roared. "Read the letter!"

"Okay, here goes:

'Dear Dick:

That I'm burned is putting it mildly. I talked to Handley about it and he contends that I've grounds for divorce and that's going to cost you heavy alimony, old boy. I've still got those nice snaps of you and the redhead, you know. But I'm going to hold off for a few days and maybe you'll come back to your senses. That game's too risky, as I've told you time and time again. If you sit tight nothing's going to happen. The statutes of limitation protect you. Now be a good boy and come home to mama, or else gives it trouble right here at home. And you don't have to run off to California to look for it. *Come on home.*

Ever,

Anne'"

"That letter was in an envelope, Milo?" Lash asked.

"Uh-huh. Return address, too. Anne Evanston, Evanston Hill, Columbus, Ohio. Does it help you any, Simon?"

"A little. Enough so you can call off the boys from the Longridge house. I don't think Mr. Lupton will be going home this evening."

"And you'll mail the check in the morning. Four fifty, altogether."

Lash laughed. "This'll kill you, Millo. I told you that Lupton conked me, but I forgot to tell you that he hurt my right hand, too. I can't write . . . if you know what I mean . . ."

"Simon, you . . . !" Stevens roared.

Lash hung up. The phone rang again

a moment later and Lash took off the receiver and placed it against the mouthpiece. He held it for a moment, then put it back on the hook.

"Fun's fun, Eddie," he said. "But now comes the work. Is the car gassed?"

"Yeah, but — say, the doc said you had to take it easy for a couple of days."

"I know how I feel better than the doc does. In two days I'd be too late. I've got to go now."

"Go? Where . . . ?"

Lash shrugged. "Same place Lupton's gone to; Donner Lake."

"Jeez," Slocum gasped. "That's a couple hundred miles from here."

"Twice that; that's why I've got to get started. Lupton'll be traveling fast. I'll have to travel faster to beat him."

Slocum's forehead creased. "Well, if we've got to go, all right . . . "

"Not you, Eddie. You're staying here."

"But you can't drive that far, after the banging — "

"I haven't got time to argue, Eddie. You're staying right here. The Dunlap girl's going to be bothering you in the morning. Don't tell her where I am. Just stall her. And I have a hunch Mrs. Evanston is going to come around again — she was here this evening, just a half hour before Lupton got in. I have an idea she's the one fixed the door latch down below . . . "

"You think so? I'll give her something to remember me by . . . "

"No. She's much too smart for you, Eddie. Keep your mouth closed. Say no to everything even if she asks you about the weather. And the first thing in the morning order some groceries so you won't have to leave the place. I'll probably be telephoning you and I'll want you right here. How much money is there in the safe?"

"Only about two hundred."

"Get it."

Slocum trotted off to another room and Lash got his hat and a light topcoat from a closet. He was taking a .32 caliber automatic from the desk drawer when Slocum came in with the money.

"What's the black box, chief?"

"Oh that. Guess I'll take it along. Might come in handy." Lash picked it up. "All right, Eddie, stay near that telephone."

"I will. Watch yourself."

Lash nodded and took his departure. As he climbed into the coupé in front of the apartment house he switched on the lights and noted by the dashboard clock that it was five minutes to one. Well, there wouldn't be much traffic on the roads at this time.

He opened the glove compartment and took out a road map of Californa. After consulting it a moment he put the map back and started the car.

15

SIMON LASH took the hairpin turns of Laurel Canyon at maximum speed, but turning into Ventura he kept down to the speed limit of forty-five miles per hour. At Van Nuys he turned right to San Fernando Road, where he picked up Highway 6. He kept his foot lightly on the throttle until he had gone through the city of San Fernando, but once beyond he began letting it out. He was doing seventy climbing the easy mountain grades.

He used the brakes freely rolling down into Antelope Valley, but once he reached the floor of the valley he let out the coupé. The road was good and straight and there was practically no traffic. The stepped-up motor purred at eighty and even when it reached ninety ran smoothly.

The lights of Palmdale showed in the distance and rushed to meet Lash. He slowed to sixty going through the little village, but once beyond settled down to the serious business of driving. From here on there was no speed limit and driving conditions, even at night, were ideal. The desert town of Mojave was but a wide spot in the road. Lash kept his foot pressed heavily on the accelerator and the speedometer needle crept up to ninety-eight. He held it there. The coupé could do a maximum of 108, but there was no reason to crowd it to the limit. Lash was traveling faster than any car likely to be on the road that night.

He stopped at Mojave and had the tank refilled with gasoline and drank a coca cola. He lost less than five minutes.

He drove the next two hundred miles in slightly under three hours. At the town of Bishop he stopped once more for gasoline. He got out of the car and discovered that it had grown somewhat chilly. He spoke to the filling station attendant about it.

The man chuckled. "You're up in the mountains, Mister. It gets cold here, but nothing like it does where you're going. And snow . . . brrr!"

"There's snow in the mountains?"

"Snow? Where you from? Oh — Los Angeles. You get rain there, it snows in the mountains. You get up around Tahoe and you'll see snow and pray that it ain't snowing when you're driving."

"Don't they keep the roads open pretty well?"

"They got the best snow crew in the country around there and wait'll you see them big rotary snowplows in action. But like I said it really snows there. They lost the road twice last winter."

"What do you mean — lost the road?"

"That's what they call it. They try to keep the main road open at all times, but once in awhile a snowslide blocks the road. If they can't cut through it in three-four hours they call that losing the road. They don't like that."

"Well, it isn't snowing up there today, is it?"

"No, but it's been threatening. I got it on the radio that it's raining pretty hard at Sacramento . . . Where you going, Reno?"

"Yes."

"Well, the road's open all the way and if you keep moving you ought to be ahead of the snow. 'Bout four hours to get there."

It was ten minutes after five when Lash pulled out of the station and the sky in the east was getting gray. He was now on Highway 395 and the topography of the country was rougher so he could not make as good time as he had been making, but he managed to make short runs at better than eighty and seldom throttled below seventy even on the curves.

For the last hour he had been expecting to overtake a Los Angeles car, but none materialized. He did pass a car or two, but they were small cars driven by local residents, as a quick glance in passing revealed.

Dawn came slowly and after awhile the sun came up over the eastern horizon, but it remained only a few minutes, being obscured by clouds. He studied the clouds in the north and west and shook his head. They were black and low-hanging.

He was driving through the big tree country now and while the road was perfectly clear there was snow on the ground among the trees. The depth of it increased as he drove along. Shortly before seven o'clock in the morning he crossed the Nevada state line and a half hour later rolled into the smallest state capital in the country, Carson City. He stopped at a restaurant for a cup of coffee and doughnuts, then returned to his car and drove the thirty-odd miles to Reno in less than a half hour.

He crossed the Truckee River and parked at the curb in the next block. He climbed out of the car and felt a drop of rain on his face. The rain was cold and the raw wind cut through Lash's light topcoat.

He looked to the west and shook his head. A few doors up the street he saw a clothing store and went to it. A man was just unlocking the door and Lash followed him into the store.

"Yes, sir, what can I do for you?" the man asked.

"How's the skiing at Lake Tahoe?"

"Oh, splendid. They've got four feet of snow right now and it looks like they'll have a couple more feet today. You're interested in some skiing togs?"

"Yes."

"Then you've come to the right place. I can outfit you right down to the skis. Now, here are some shirts that are all the rage . . . "

Lash made his selections quickly, a heavy plaid flannel shirt, breeches, a windbreaker, wool socks and high-top shoes and a knitted cap. He completed the ensemble by purchasing a fleece-lined knee-length coat. The outfit came to ninety dollars. Lash paid the bill then went into a dressing room and put on the clothes.

"You forgot the most important of all," the clothing store man told him when he came out of the dressing room. "The skis."

"Oh, but I can't ski!"

"But you intend to learn . . . "

"No, I haven't time. I'm going treasure-hunting. Ever hear of the Donner gold?"

The man gasped. "I beg your pardon?"

"The Donner Party who starved to death just west of Lake Tahoe. Didn't you ever hear of them?"

"Oh, that! Of course. And seems to me I've heard about the gold, although not much in recent years. When I was a kid hereabouts there used to be a party every now and then would try to find that gold. But gosh, they never tried it in winter."

Lash winked. "That's where they were wrong; the gold was buried in winter, so they should have looked for it in winter."

The clothing man rubbed his chin. "You're serious about that?"

"I've just spent ninety dollars with you."

"Yes, mm, well look, would you be interested in buying a map? An authentic map . . . "

"Made by Rand McNally?"

"No-no; this was drawn by one of the Donner Party. There's a man in this town who's related to a member of the Donner Party. The map was given to him by his grandfather . . . "

"If it's a good map why hasn't he ever gone after the treasure?"

"Well, you know these desert rats . . . "

"He's a desert rat?"

"Yeah, an old geezer by the name of Ike Eckert . . . "

"Ike Eckert lives in Reno?"

186

"Do you know him?"

"I've heard of him. What's he like?"

"Oh, he's quite old, although pretty well preserved. About eighty, I imagine. He was here when my father moved here, twenty-five years ago."

"How does he make a living?"

"Prospecting. At least he used to do that. People would grubstake him and he'd go off for weeks at a time with his burro. The last few years the tourists have supported him. They have a little place out here — "

"They?"

"Oh yes, he has a son. Fremont Eckert. He and his father have had this place for a good many years. They call it Donner's Camp. They've got a couple of cabins and a gasoline pump and a place that you might call a tavern if you were feeling charitable."

"Where is the place?"

"Right out of town about two miles. On Highway 40. Right-hand side of the road as you go west." The clothing man chuckled. "I was just kidding about that map business, you know. Old Ike's sold a dozen of the maps. I hear he used to clip suckers fifty to a hundred dollars apiece in the old days. Forget it."

"Sure. Now can you tell me where your local water works are located?"

"What? The water works . . . ?"

"Yes."

"The office is in the courthouse, but . . . "

"Thank you," said Lash. He picked up the bundle containing his old clothing and left the store. He returned to the car and deposited the bundle in the car and was chagrined to discover that the big telescope that Eddie Slocum had used the evening before was still in the opened rumble seat.

He located the courthouse without difficulty, but since it was only ten minutes to nine he had to wait until the county employees came to the respective places of employment. A girl opened the water office at five minutes after nine.

Lash went in and asked to see the chief engineer.

"Sorry," the girl said, "but he's down in Carson City today. What did you wish to see him about?"

"About water."

"What about water?"

"There's a break in the main at my place and I wanted to have it fixed."

"Oh, you won't need the chief engineer for that. Just give me the address and I'll see that someone comes out."

"Whom would you send?"

"Some repair men."

"Where will I find them? You see, it's a kind of difficult leak and I'd like to explain it. If they're on a job, I don't mind running out."

"They are out; they had an emergency call late yesterday afternoon and I don't believe they finished the job. Let's see . . . "

She picked up some papers that were held together by a spring clip and leafed through them. "Ah yes, they're on a job at the Washoe Zephyr Club."

"Where's that?"

"Right at the edge of the town, on Highway 40. Don't you know where it is?"

"Yes, on Highway 40. Thank you."

Lash left the courthouse and returned to his car. He got in and drove quickly through 'the biggest little city in the world.'

He had no trouble finding the Washoe Zephyr Club. It was a huge, California-style building with red and blue neon lights that were lighted even now. A truck was parked in front of the place and some men were digging a hole.

Lash got out of his car and approached the group. "Who's the foreman here, boys?"

A hard-faced man with a dead cigar in his mouth scowled at him: "What're you trying to sell — magazine subscriptions?"

"Why no," said Lash. "I'm selling pictures. I'd like to show you one . . . "

"Beat it, buddy," the foreman snapped.

"This is a picture of Alexander Hamilton," Lash continued. "Take a peek at it." He held up his palm in which he had a folded ten dollar blil. "What do you think of it?"

The foreman shot a quick glance at his workmen, then came closer to Lash. "That's a nice picture," he said. "What do you want for it?"

Lash gestured with his head and the foreman followed him to the far side of the work truck, where they were out of sight of the workers.

Lash handed the man the ten dollar bill. "You have an instrument in your truck; a sort of compass affair that you carry around and use to locate buried water pipes."

"Yeah sure, what of it?"

"I want to borrow it."

"What? Why I can't give it to you. It belongs to the city . . . "

"You're the foreman, aren't you?"

"Yeah sure, but gee whiz, I can't lend city property . . . "

Lash took another ten dollar bill from his pocket. "If you lost it you wouldn't get fired, would you?"

"No, but . . . "

"But what?"

"Why would you want such a thing?"

"A game," Lash said. "I've got some city folks out to my place and we want to play Treasure Hunt. Someone will bury an iron box and . . . well, you catch on?"

"Sure, this thing will help you find it in no time. But . . . "

Lash took a third ten dollar bill from

his pocket. "Until tomorrow?"

"You'll return it?"

"Oh, yes. Where'll I find you?"

"Right here. This is a three days' job we've got. And for Pete's sake, don't break it."

"I'll treat it gently."

The foreman went to the rear of the truck and reaching in brought out a boxlike affair with a handle. He handed it to Lash. "And don't tell anyone where you got it."

"I won't. Now, can you tell me where Ike Eckert's place is?"

"Right up the road, about a mile. On this side. He just went by a few minutes ago."

Lash took the instrument to his car and started off, driving slowly. The buildings along the roadside had thinned out, and he had no trouble finding 'Donner's Camp,' a half dozen miserable shacks, built around a gasoline pump and 'store.'

Lash slowed his car but did not stop. Rain was beginning to pelt his windshield and it seemed to be solidifying. A mile beyond Eckert's place, the rain was definitely turning into snow.

Lash was tempted to return to Reno and await more auspicious weather, but he knew that he would be too impatient remaining idle and he doubted whether he could risk sitting it out at this juncture. Isaac Eckert was home and the old boy had lived in this country all his life. A little snow or rain would scarcely deter him.

He drove on, climbing gradually, and the snow thickened and was soon falling so heavily that Lash was compelled to slacken his speed. The snow was still melting as it touched the pavement, but the resultant slush was slippery. On the straightaways Lash kept his speed up to fifty but on the mountain grades was compelled to slow down to thirty and sometimes less. By the time he reached the California state line, fifteen miles southwest of Reno, he had to cut his speed by one half.

A few minutes later he came up with the first snowplow. The snow was six inches deep on the pavement by this time, soft but no longer slush.

The windshield wiper had difficulty in keeping the snow from the windshield.

Occasionally the road ran through a sheltered cut and in these spots snow had drifted to an alarming depth. Lash had to take the coupé through one or two of the drifts in low gear and even then the wheels spun madly.

He passed a car that was barely crawling along in low gear, then hit the ruts of a big truck and followed in comparative ease for a mile or so when he caught up with the truck. It was laboring heavily up a grade and Lash had difficulty keeping his stepped-up motor down to such a slow pace.

On a fairly clear stretch of pavement he passed the truck and regretted it a few moments later when he hit a drift more than a foot deep. He assaulted the drift in low, got stuck, and backing away sent the car forward in accelerated low gear. The force drove him through the drift and then suddenly he hit a clear patch of pavement. He raced along at almost fifty miles an hour for two miles, when he caught up with a huge rotary snowplow.

The machine was throwing clouds of snow to both sides of the pavement, but it proceeded at a speed of about a half mile per hour. Lash followed behind the big rotary plow for five minutes, when they met another coming toward them. When it passed, Lash scooted out into the clear left-hand lane and after a few minutes burst into the sprawling village of Truckee. As nearly as he could determine, this was the end of the trail. He pulled into a filling station, had gas put into the tank, and spoke to the attendant.

"Where'll I find Donner Lake?"

"T'other side of town," replied the gasoline attendant, "but you won't find it, not on a day like this."

"Why not?"

"Road's closed, or will be in a little while. I'm surprised you made it into town. This storm's a beaut."

"Isn't the lake right by the town?"

"Uh-uh, it's almost three miles. What're you lookin' for?"

"Donner Lake."

"What for? You can't skate on it, and you can't ski until the snow stops. Be worth your life to go out there now."

Lash paid for the gas and drove a block

up the street where he parked the coupé with difficulty at the curb. He climbed out of the car and went into a store.

He bought a pair of snow shoes and a long-handled steel shovel. He deposited the purchases in the car, then went to a hotel before which he had parked. A half-dozen guests wearing skiing costumes sat in the lobby. Skis were strewn all around.

He approached the desk and said to the clerk, "What're the chances of hiring a guide for a short trip?"

"The chances are swell," the clerk replied, "after the snow stops."

"When do you figure that'll be?"

The clerk shrugged. "I got a telephone report a few minutes ago that it isn't coming down as heavy now around Emigrant Gap. But it might start up again. You won't want to try anything until tomorrow, though. And maybe not then."

"I want to go out today — now," Lash persisted. "I'll pay double rates for a guide."

"You could offer ten times the regular rate and you couldn't get a guide to go out in this. Not off the main road and I understand that's about gone."

"This is only a short trip, out to Donner Lake. You're quite sure I couldn't get a guide?"

The clerk looked at Lash, frowning. "You'll go out even if you don't get a guide?"

"Yes."

"I thought so. Well, look, go across the street to that dive that calls itself The Traveler's Rest. Ask if Sam Higby's in the place. He's crazy, and if he's drunk enough, he might take you on. But don't say I didn't warn you."

"You warned me," said Lash. "Thanks."

He left the hotel and crossed to The Traveler's Rest, which turned out to be a combination restaurant, tavern and poolroom.

Lash stepped up to the bar and ordered a glass of rye. He drank the stuff and shuddered.

At a pool table nearby, a huge redheaded man leaned across the table and, missing a shot, tore a six-inch rip in the green cloth.

The bartender swore roundly and

rushed from behind the bar to the table. "I warned you about that, Sam. You're going to pay for that cloth."

"Sure," said the pool player. "How much?"

"A dollar an inch. That's the regular charge."

"A dollar an inch, eh? Well . . . " Sam walked around to the side of the table and reaching deliberately for a torn edge of the cloth gave it a yank that tore it down the table for more than two feet. "There," he said to the bartender, "now I owe you about thirty dollars."

The bartender screamed and rushed back to the bar. He stooped out of sight and came up with a baseball bat.

Lash scooped up the bottle of whisky that still stood before him and hurled it at the bartender. It missed by several inches, but shattered against the wall.

This second act of vandalism deflected the bartender from his rush upon the pool player. He turned toward Lash and stared at him openmouthed.

"What the . . . ?" he began.

"Put down the bat," Lash snapped. "If

you want to fight, fight him with your fists."

"I'll fight," the bartender snarled. "I'll fight you . . . "

He raised the baseball bat over his shoulder and stepped toward Lash. For the moment he had completely forgotten the pool player named Sam. But the latter hadn't forgotten. He stepped up behind the bartender and smashed him a terrific blow on the side of the head.

The bartender staggered, and the baseball bat fell from his hands. Sam took two quick steps, one to the side and another forward. He lashed out with his left, hitting the bartender in the stomach. As he bent forward, Sam hit him on the chin, and that was all for the bartender. He went down to the floor and lay there motionless.

"Nice work," Lash said.

"You, too," Sam returned the compliment.

"Your name wouldn't be Sam Higby, would it?" Lash asked.

"It would be; why?"

"I've been told you're a good guide."

"You ain't been told wrong. I'm the

best in this territory."

"Good enough to go out to Donner Lake in this weather?"

"You're going out there — now?" Sam Higby asked.

Lash nodded. "Right now."

"You're crazy, mister!"

"That's what the man said about you."

Sam Higby's tongue came out and licked his lips. Then his eyes fell on the unconscious bartender. "Okay, mister, let's go."

"You've got snowshoes?"

"I'll meet you in front of the hotel in two minutes."

Lash nodded and headed for the door. Sam Higby followed him, but darted into a house next to the tavern. Lash crossed to the car and got out the magnetic water pipe locater, his snowshoes, and the shovel. As an afterthought he took his automatic from the glove compartment and dropped it into the pocket of the sheepskin-lined coat.

16

AS he stepped away from the car, Sam Higby came along, carrying a pair of snowshoes. "I'm ready," he said laconically.

"Shall we drive as far as we can?"

Higby looked at Lash's coupé and shook his head. "You wouldn't get out of town."

The snow seemed to be coming down even heavier. Visibility was cut to less than fifty feet. Higby and Lash trotted down the center of the street, which was also U. S. Highway #40.

As they cleared the village, Higby, who was in in the lead, let Lash come up. "You want the Lake or the monument?"

"Both."

Higby nodded. "What's the dingus?"

"A treasure finder."

"Eh?" Higby stopped and stared into Lash's face. Then he began to swear.

Lash cut him off. "You can go back if you like."

"I never went back from anything," Sam Higby retorted. "But I'm going to be awful damn sore if I freeze to death humoring a lunatic. I've taken out fifty treasure-hunting nuts, but you're the first that came around on a day like this."

"The weather was something like this when they buried the gold," Lash said. "It ought to be the best time to find it."

Higby spat angrily. "Guys been diggin' up that ground for the last ninety years. What makes you think *you* can find it?"

"I've got a map."

"I've seen sixteen maps. I can run over to Reno and get you one from a guy whose grandfather was one of the Donner Party."

"You mean Isaac Eckert?"

"You know him?"

"Yes. And you?"

"When I was a kid, Old Ike would camp here all summer and dig. He never found the gold."

"Do you know his son, Fremont Eckert?"

"Yeah, sure, but I haven't seen him in quite a spell. The old man had him out here one summer. Must be twenty-five years ago now. Fremont was about my age then, fifteen or sixteen. I've seen him since then, but not in the last eight or ten years . . . That shovel ain't going to be much good. If you get down to the ground you'll find it frozen. You shouldda brought a pick. Or better yet, some dynamite."

"I'll try the shovel."

"All right, I'll humor you. Let me carry the shovel."

Lash surrendered it to the big guide, and the latter plunged ahead into the almost blinding snow. They passed a rotary plow coming toward them, and one of the crew leaned out of the window at the side and yelled at them, but the wind tore away his words so Lash couldn't hear.

The walking was fairly easy when they traveled in the path cleared by the plow, although the snow was three inches deep within a half mile after passing the plow.

They were two miles out of Truckee, and the countryside was a vast whiteness, when Higby fell back and gestured to the left. "That's the Graves cabin over there."

Lash looked but could see nothing. "Do we turn off here?"

"In a minute."

They continued for another three hundred yards or so when Higby stopped and stuck the shovel into the snow. He stooped and began putting on his snowshoes. Lash followed his example but was slower. By the time he got them adjusted, Higby had plunged into the deep snow at the side of the road. He went fifty feet and turning saw Lash floundering at the edge of the road.

"What's the matter?" he called.

"Nothing," Lash replied. "I've just got to get the hang of these things."

"Holy Hannah!" Higby cried. "Don't tell me you never wore snowshoes before?"

"I live in Hollywood," Lash retorted. "The snow doesn't get quite as deep there."

Higby swore. "I shouldda known. Well, come on, stay behind and walk just like I do. That's the best way to get along. Now, just where the devil do you want to go? . . . There's the Pioneer Monument."

Lash wiped the moisture from his eyes and looked at the huge stone block which contained the heroic bronze figures of a man, a woman and a child.

"I've seen a picture of this," he said. "The Breens' cabin was here."

"That's right. And over there against that big boulder was the Murphy shack. Beyond it over there is the lake."

Higby led the way to the big boulder, and Lash looked around. The highway was out of sight. The scene was one of desolate whiteness. A slight shiver ran through him.

"Those stumps," he said to Higby, "they were the trees?"

"Yeah. The snow was twenty feet deep. They chopped the trees off at snow level. If it keeps on snowing like this for a couple more days, you won't be able to see the stumps. Where to now?"

"Just a minute." Lash regarded the surroundings thoughtfully for a moment. The snow was coming down so heavily the visibility was not more than fifty or sixty feet, and it was difficult for him to

205

reconstruct the scene as it was imprinted in his mind from ardent study of all available material on the Donner Party.

But after a few moments he nodded and headed toward two tall stumps. Higby came up and plodded along beside him. They passed between the stumps and walked down a slope to the edge of Donner Lake, frozen and covered with two feet of snow. At the edge of the lake he turned and looked back at the two big stumps, then moved to the left about thirty feet. He sighted again and moved a few feet more.

"This," he said, "is where the Eckert cabin originally stood."

"Uh-uh," said Higby. "You're wrong. It was away over there, two hundred feet."

"No," said Lash. "This is the spot."

"How do you know?"

"I said I'd seen a map."

"Let's see it."

"I haven't got it."

"Then how do you know you're right?"

"Follow me and I'll show you. But don't talk."

Higby looked at him sharply, but fell

in behind Lash. The latter stepped off briskly along the shore of the lake, counting his steps. When he had counted eighty-four, he stopped and made a half right turn. He walked seven paces away from the lake and made another right angle turn, which brought him facing the two tall stumps through which he had passed a short time before.

He frowned but began pacing off sixty-four paces. He wound up within three feet of one of the two stumps. He stepped up to it, and facing east leaned his back against the aged, rotting wood.

Higby standing by watched him curiously. "I read a book once," he said. "It was called *The Gold Bug*. You remind me of it. All you need is a skull."

Lash ignored him. He stepped off fourteen paces from the stump and stopped. "We dig here."

"How do you know?" Higby asked. "Does the dingus say so?"

Lash winced. He had completely forgotten the magnetic compass. He looked down at it. The needle was quivering slightly. He held the instrument motionless for a moment and the needle became steady.

"It don't work," said Higby.

"Clear the snow and it'll work," Lash said.

"Okay, pal," said Higby, grinning. "Step aside."

Lash moved back a few feet, and the big guide scooped up a shovel full of snow and tossed it away. The stuff was fairly wet and packed, and Higby made rapid progress. In three minutes he touched earth, and in five minutes more had cleared a circle about five feet in diameter.

Lash stepped forward, and getting down into the hole rested the compass on the ground. The needle remained in a horizontal position.

"I get it," Higby chuckled. "It works like a magnet. The gold is supposed to turn down the needle."

"I must be off a little," Lash said, irritably. He climbed out of the hole and walked back to the tree stump. He put his back to it again and faced the lake. He found himself looking directly at the hole in the snow.

He muttered under his breath and stepped away from the tree three feet, the spot where he had wound up in his pace-counting a few minutes ago. He faced the lake once more.

"Move it over three feet," he said to the guide.

"No sooner said than done," Higby said, and began shoveling a trench southward.

Lash moved back to the stump and leaned against it. He watched Higby shovel for a few minutes, then called to him. "I'll spell you, Higby."

"What for?" Higby asked. "I haven't even worked up a sweat . . . Say . . . !"

Higby threw aside the shovel and springing out of the trench rushed toward him. Lash started to step aside, but Higby yelled,

"Stand still! Jeez, lookit that needle!"

Startled, Lash brought up the compass to look at it, and the needle jerked up and pointed toward the stump. Uttering a low cry, Lash put the box up against the wood. The needle promptly moved upwards.

"In the tree," Higby said thickly.

"Of course," Lash cried. "The last direction was fourteen . . . It didn't mean fourteen paces from the tree. It meant fourteen feet from the top . . . from where they'd chopped off the tree."

He reached up to the height of his head and placed his palm against the wood.

"No," said Higby, "the stump's twenty feet, and we're two feet above the ground now. Fourteen feet from the top would make it . . . four feet." He brought his hand up slightly above his waist and from that level touched the tree. He began circling the tree slowly. Lash reached out to the same level and started in the other direction. But it was Higby who cried out.

Lash quickly stepped around the thick trunk and saw Higby clawing at the rotten wood. Pieces came away in his hand, and suddenly a complete panel about two by seven inches broke out. Higby thrust his hand into the opening.

"Gawd!" he exclaimed.

He clawed frantically at the slot and after a moment brought out a rusted tube of metal. It was about an inch and a half thick and six inches long. Lash jerked it from Higby's hand and poked at one end, which seemed to have been plugged with wood. He was unable to clear out the wood, and Higby took a pocket knife from his pocket and opening the small blade handed the knife to Lash. With its aid Lash was able to remove the wood.

Then he looked into the tube and whistled softly. He up-ended the tube and tapped it on his open palm. A cylinder of yellowed paper came out.

He stuck the rusted tube in his pocket and gingerly unrolled the paper. It was brittle and rust-stained, but perfectly legible. With Higby looking over his shoulder and holding one hand over it to prevent melting snowflakes from blurring the writing, Lash read:

February, 2, 1847

"To my dear children: —

My days are numbered. The relief party has been gone for more than a month. Sutter's Fort is only a hundred miles and if anyone had got through, help should have reached us before this. I fear they all perished and since I am going shortly I must write this, my last will and testament. To my wife Ellen, I leave everything of earthly possessions in the full knowledge that she will provide for you to the utmost of her strength. Already she is giving you her few morsels of food. Remember that, children, if you survive. Forget this horror, but remember your mother's devotion. Farewell.

Isaac Eckert"

Isaac Eckert's statement covered a little more than half of the page. Below it, in another hand — one familiar to Simon Lash — were Ellen Eckert's last written words:

February 28, 1847

"Seven California men came on February 10. They took the children and have hopes of getting through, although they say it will be difficult. I could not go, because Isaac was at death's door and the men would not wait. Children, your father passed away on February 15 and I fear I have no more than a day or two myself. There is no food and none of the others can give me any. They are . . . I cannot write it. My children, Isaac, George, Elizabeth, and Ellen, I want you all to share equally in everything I leave. Your father feared for the gold from the start and put it in a water cask and chopped a hold in the ice in the lake, thirty feet from the cabin. The weight of the gold will keep the cask down. In the spring it can be retrieved. I have not strength to write more. Good-bye, my children, I love you all. Your mother,

Ellen Eckert"

Lash let go of one end of the paper, and it rolled itself up into a tight cylinder. He cleared his throat and looked at big Sam Higby. The guide's face was white.

"Well," he said, "we know where the gold is. Under fifty feet of water. It'll be there until spring."

"A diver can go down for it."

"Maybe, but there's a silt bottom here.

213

Take quite a spell of looking if the keg's shifted, as it probably has. You finished here now?"

"Yes."

"Then let's get back to town. I want to get drunk."

"I may join you in that, Sam."

"You earned it, pal . . . You going to cut the Eckerts in on the gold?"

"They get it all," said Lash.

"But you found it. You're entitled . . . "

" . . . only to my fee. I'm working for one of the Eckerts . . . "

"What are you, a lawyer?"

"No, a detective. My name's Simon Lash . . . "

"Lash? Say, aren't you the fellow who solved a case for Sheriff Rucker down at Ocelot Springs, a couple of months ago? I go hunting with Rucker every year. He was up here two-three weeks ago and talked about you. Yeah, you fit his description." Higby suddenly laughed. "I remember one thing he said about you, that you were the most even-tempered man he knew — always mad."

Lash made no reply. He was already snowshoeing through the snow toward the highway. At least six inches of snow had fallen in the short time they had been at the lake. When they reached the main road they discovered a line of cars stalled on the right hand side.

Higby hailed a harassed-looking highway patrolman. "Is the road lost, Mac?"

"And how!" replied the patrolman. "If the snow doesn't stop, it'll be lost for a week. A big slide at the pass."

17

LASH and Higby passed the stalled cars and followed several people who had deserted their cars and were plodding back to the village of Truckee. The snow in the lane that had been plowed by the rotary snowplow was over a foot deep. Higby used his snowshoes, but Lash took off his own. It was difficult going without them, but not as difficult as with the encumbrances.

As they neared a group of hikers, Lash closed up on Higby. "I suppose there's no use asking you to keep to yourself what we found?"

"Hardly any use," Higby replied cheerfully. "After this I've got to get drunk, and I tell everything I know when I'm drunk. But don't worry, no one's going out there to dig up the treasure."

Lash wasn't worried about the gold. He was thinking about a murderer.

He said nothing further to Higby until they reached the edge of Truckee. Then he moved up to the big guide and tried to press a twenty dollar bill on him.

"This is from me," he said. "And I'll talk to the Eckerts and see if they won't give you something additional."

"From them I'll take it," Higby declared. "But for you I did it free. You saved me maybe a busted skull over at The Traveler's Rest. I suppose you'll be sticking around town awhile?"

"No, I'm leaving for Reno right away."

"Guess again," said Higby. "Where's your car?"

They were within fifty feet of the hotel, and Lash exclaimed in chagrin. A pusher plow had come along the street since he had parked the car, and a five-foot wall of snow had almost buried the coupé.

Higby laughed. "You couldn't have got through to Reno, anyway. Maybe tomorrow they'll have the road open. I may see you around."

"All right," said Lash. He went to the hotel and entering approached the desk.

"I'd like a room and bath," he said to the clerk.

The man shook his head. "You can have the bath all right, but we haven't got a vacant room in the place. The storm caught a lot of people here."

"But the roads are blocked. Where'll I stay until it's over?"

"It's possible," said the clerk, "that I can persuade one of the guests to share a room with you . . ."

"I'll be glad to do that," said a voice behind Lash.

Lash turned and looked at Isaac Eckert. The old man grinned at him. "Going snowshoeing, Mr. Lash?"

"Ah!" said the clerk, "you gentlemen are acquainted? Splendid! Then your problem is solved."

Lash shrugged. "I rather thought you'd be here."

"I got in fifteen minutes ago, and it's lucky for you I did. Because I got the last room in the house, and if I hadn't, someone else would've and you'd had to sleep on the floor down here. What say we go up to *our* room? We can have a nice talky-talk."

"I have to make a telephone call first."

"Telephone? I figured you were a stranger around here."

"I am, practically." Lash smiled thinly

and stepping past Eckert went to a telephone booth. He entered and closed the door. As he took down the receiver he looked through the glass door and saw Eckert glowering at him.

"Long distance," he said to the operator. "I want to put in a reversed charge call to Hollywood, California. Mill Spring 3644 . . . "

He repeated the information to the long distance operator, then waited as the various connections were made. Then he heard Eddie Slocum's voice.

"Chief? Gosh, I'm glad you called. Things have been popping!"

"What?"

"Well, first of all, the Evanston doll was here this morning. Bright and early. She offered ten thousand dollars for the buffalo box . . . "

"Which we haven't got. Did you think she knew that?"

"I dunno, chief. Only I was thinking it's a lot easier to offer a pile of dough for something you know the other guy hasn't got than to offer a small amount for something you figure you'll actually have to take. She didn't seem too disappointed when she didn't get the box. She was mostly worried about your not being there . . . "

"You didn't let on where I'd gone?"

"No-no, of course not. But she's sure checking up on you, because a half hour ago she telephoned to ask if you'd gotten in yet. I told her I was expecting you any minute."

"Good, Eddie. Now, what else?"

"Sergeant Coons. I think there was a warrant in his pocket. And he sounded like it. He found out you were down at the morgue making that identification, and he was burned up about your having hired Milo Stevens' men to stake out the Lupton house."

"Stevens snitched?"

"It sounds like it, doesn't it?"

"Then he can whistle for his dough. Well, look, Eddie. I'm up here at Donner Lake in a town called Truckee. Now, listen, get Columbus, Ohio, on the telephone. I don't know any agencies there, but you can look them up in the Guaranteed Detective Agencies List. I want to know everything about the Evanstons — particularly their ancestry

— and I want to know it fast. Telephone me the minute you get anything, but if I'm not here don't worry, I'll telephone you. I might be able to get through, and if I can, I'll start back. After you put in the Columbus call, ring up the Donnelley Agency. Have them put men on the Eckerts; that includes Betty and Jim Dunlap as well as Sheridan Eckert. Got all that?"

"Yes. Call Columbus, Ohio, on the Evanstons, and get the Donnelley Agency on the Eckerts. Right."

Lash hung up and stepped out of the booth. Isaac Eckert bore down on him, a suspicious gleam in his rheumy old eyes. "Say, was you telephoning long distance?"

"Yes. Any objections?"

"None. But it won't do anyone any good, on account of they won't be able to get here before tomorrow or the day after, and by then it'll be too late. My dingus works in the snow."

"Oh," said Lash, "you brought your treasure hunting box with you?"

"Damn right I did. And it's going to work, too."

"Where've you got it, in your room?"

"Wouldn't you like to know?"

Lash grinned frostily. Then he held up the little water pipe locater. "Take a look at this, Ike. Tell me what it is."

Isaac Eckert looked blankly at the simple instrument. He shrugged. "How should I know?"

"Why, I thought maybe you'd seen one around somewhere. It's a rather common article. Sanitary engineers use it to locate water pipes under the ground. It works on the magnetic compass principle. Metal attracts the compass needle . . . "

Consternation spread across Old Isaac's face. "You mean that there thing works like *my* machine?"

"Much simpler, probably. And you could have gone to your local water department in Reno and borrowed it. That's where I got it."

Eckert reeled. "Gawd! Jim Dunlap . . . Jim knew, you suppose?"

"I'm afraid he did."

Isaac Eckert looked for a moment as if he would burst into tears. Then suddenly he pulled himself together. "But you don't know where to look. I was over that ground fifty years ago when parts of the cabins was still standing."

"What about the snow?"

"The snow? Bah! I've been in deeper snow than this. I've . . . " Eckert suddenly broke off and rushed for the stairs. For a man of his age he was quite spry.

Lash strolled to the desk. "Have you got a small piece of wrapping paper — and a piece of string?"

The clerk got it for him, and Lash took the rusted cylinder and wrapped it up in the paper. He tied it with the string and was using the hotel pen to address it when Isaac Eckert came tearing down the stairs, carrying a large box, from which a set of headphones dangled. He also had a pair of snow-shoes. He shot Lash a malignant glance, then rushed out of the hotel.

Lash finished addressing his small parcel, then asked for the direction to the post office. He was told that it was three doors up the street, and taking the parcel there, he had it weighed and mailed.

The snow was still coming down, but the sky seemed a little grayer in the west.

As he approached his car in front of the hotel, a shovelful of snow was thrown at his feet.

"I forgot to return your shovel," Sam Higby said, grinning.

"What're you doing?" Lash exclaimed.

"Digging out your car. The road's still open to Reno and it looks like the snow's going to stop in a little while. It's already stopped at Emigrant Gap."

"What about Donner Pass?"

"Oh, they'll lick that. By the time you get the car out, you'll be able to get through. But your best bet's by way of Reno. A half hour and you'll be out of the snow belt."

"Good!" Lash exclaimed. "Now, if you'll tell me where I can find another shovel . . ."

"Right here. I brought one along . . ."

Lash grabbed it up and pitched into the snow. As fast as Higby cleared it away from the car, Lash scooped it out into the middle of the street.

In ten minutes the snow was all cleared from behind the car. Lash got in and started the motor. Then he climbed out of the car.

"This time you've got to take the money, Sam." He held out two twenty-dollar bills. But Higby still shook his head. "I got a confession to make — the reason I dug your car out. I want to go along to Reno with you."

"Oh," said Lash. "But I was planning to go west from here. However . . . "

"That's even better," exclaimed Higby. "Matter of fact, the bartender across the street's sworn out a warrant for me. The town marshal's out by the snowplows, but as soon as he comes back he's going to arrest me. I'd like to be out of town by then . . . "

"Put the shovels in back," Lash said, "and climb in."

Higby obeyed promptly, and Lash backed away from the curb and putting the car in low gear gunned it through the loose snow he had thrown into the street. The front wheels couldn't quite make it through, so Lash backed the car and sent it into the snow once more. The car shot through this time.

Lash shifted into second gear and then into high. The stepped-up motor responded nobly, and they raced out of

Truckee. A short distance out of town they hit a drift and were compelled to make three assaults on it before they won through.

They had no further difficulty then until they came to the line of cars that had been deserted by their drivers when the rotary plows had been seemingly stopped. Lash turned out to pass the cars and had a bad five minutes in a drift. Higby had to get out and work with the shovel before the car got through.

They came up to the Pioneer Monument and Lash thought he saw a figure in the snow near the lake. Then he hit a spot in the road that was almost clear and raced for a quarter of a mile until he caught up with a pusher plow. They had to crawl behind it for fifteen minutes, when they met another pusher plow coming toward them.

The clear lane on the left side of the road enabled Lash to pass the plow ahead, and the lane was clear all the way to Donner Pass, where two rotary plows, one traveling behind the other, were fighting a slide.

They lost a half hour at this point.

At the end of that time a rotary broke through from the east and then there were ten clear miles to Cisco. At the latter point the snow had stopped, but a pair of rotaries were clearing out some drifts. After twenty minutes the lead plow let off a blast with a whistle and the road was clear.

Eight miles beyond, at Emigrant Gap, the snow was turning into slush, and it was downhill all the way.

"Too bad the Donner Party didn't have a couple of those rotary plows," Higby remarked.

Lash nodded and, stopping the car, took a road map out of the glove compartment. He studied it for a moment. "How far west did you want to go, Sam?"

"Oh, anywhere. I just want to stay away from Truckee for a couple of weeks. By that time it'll have blown over."

"Have you ever been in Placerville?"

"Oh sure. I did a little panning three-four-five years ago. Wasn't worth while. That stuff was pretty well worked over in the old days, and the luckiest of them aren't able to make more than two dollars a day now. You going there?"

"Yes. I figure on taking Highway 49 at Auburn. If you'd rather go on to Sacramento, however, you can grab a bus at Auburn. Or a train."

"I'll go to Placerville." He grinned. "Know what the old name of that place used to be?"

"Hangtown."

Higby was surprised. "You're pretty well posted on your history."

The snow on the countryside thinned rapidly as they drove down into the valley country. By the time they got to Colfax there were bare patches here and there, and at Auburn it looked merely as if a heavy rain had recently soaked the ground. At this point Lash left Highway 40 and turned on to Highway 49.

Now Lash treated Sam Higby to some speed. It was twenty-seven miles to Placerville, much of it winding road. Lash made the trip in twenty-four minutes. Higby didn't speak during the entire time. He sat with his feet braced against the sloping floor-boards and never took his eyes off the road. When Lash finally slackened speed in Placerville, the heavy exhalation of Higby's breath clouded the windshield.

"I always figured flying must be something like this. I don't think I'd like flying."

"I was traveling slow," Lash said. "This car can do one hundred and eight . . . There's the court-house."

Higby blinked uneasily. "What'd you want to go in there for?"

"I want to see some old records. You can wait out in the car if you like."

"Guess I will."

Lash parked the car and proceeded to the courthouse. There he went through the usual procedure a citizen encounters in a public building. He was shunted from department to department and from person to person, but at last he wound up in the basement, facing a gray-haired, doddering old man.

"Eighteen fifty-six?" the old man repeated. "Gosh, I didn't start working here until '78."

"I didn't expect you to remember personally," Lash said. "I merely want to see the records of 1856. I want to see if a man named Eckert died here that year."

"Eckert? Name's familiar."

"Of course. This man's father was one of the Donner Party . . . "

"Ike Eckert? Say, I 'member now. You won't have to look at the records. He died all right. You know this place used to be called Hangtown. Folks didn't like the old name, 'cause it didn't sound right. But they sure hanged a lot of boys in the old days. Ten-twelve years ago I was talkin' with a newspaper fella, who wrote a piece about it, and I dug up a list of the fellas that was hung. Kept the list in my desk for a long time and got to know the names pretty well. Ike Eckert was Number 33."

"You're sure of that?" Lash cried.

"Course I'm sure. I remember his name on account of the newspaper piece the fella wrote. He had quite a piece about Ike in it. Somethin' about his havin' been saved from starvin' when he was a baby and then grew up to bein' hanged."

"What newspaper was it?"

"The old *Argus*. It ain't bein' printed

no more. Dan Waggoner bought it out and merged it with his *Independent* . . . "

"Where's the office of *The Independent*?"

"'Cross the Square. On top of the new super market."

Lash made an abrupt departure. Leaving the courthouse, he crossed to his car and was surprised to find that Higby was gone. The ignition key was still in the lock, however. Lash took it and went off to find the newspaper office.

He found it over the grocery store as directed and explained his request to a girl, who took him into a musty room and showed him a shelf of bound file copies, one for each year.

"I think you'll find it for nineteen twenty-nine," the girl said and left him in the room.

Lash found the volume and took it down from the shelf. Placing it on a table he began at the beginning. An hour and a half later he found the article in a November issue and cursed himself for not having started at the rear of the volume.

The article occupied most of a page and was entitled alliteratively: THEY HUNG THEM HIGH IN HANGTOWN.

Two paragraphs were devoted to Isaac Eckert. They read:

Most ironical death by hanging in Hangtown was the lynching of Isaac Eckert. Eckert, a member of the famous Donner Party, had been saved from starvation thirteen years previously. As a boy he had eaten human flesh; as a man he was known as the roughest, toughest miner in Hangtown. He jumped more than a half-dozen claims by the simple process of merely serving notice upon a miner that he desired the particular claim. Once or twice miners resisted, and Isaac, who disdained revolvers, carved them up a little with a huge bowie knife. Isaac was not popular in Hangtown.

A woman was his downfall. The Mexican actress, Leona Gallegos, who had been bowling them over in San Francisco, came to Hangtown for a limited engagement. She brought with her a man named Huntley, who was reputed to be her manager. Isaac saw the olive-skinned Leona and was immediately enamored of her. He jumped Huntley's claim as promptly as he had jumped placer claims. In the process he decorated Huntley with a little knifework. But Huntley, unlike the miners whose claims had been jumped, returned to Hangtown after a couple of months. He found his former client married to Eckert and immediately tried to make her a widow, but, alas, his aim was poor and Isaac Eckert finished the job he had started several months previously. Claim-jumping was one thing, but murder was another, and Hangtown had had enough murders, so Isaac Eckert was taken out and hanged. Leona pleaded for his life, but the mob was angry and somewhat inclined to hang her along with her spouse. Only her condition saved her.

Lash started to close the bound volume of the old newspapers, but caught himself and opened it once more. Then he took a pencil from his pocket and, using it as a knife, cut the paragraphs out of the paper. He put the slip into his pocket and closed the book.

In the outer office he thanked the girl, who had shown him to the file-copy room, and took his departure.

18

SAM HIGBY was slouched in the car, playing softly on a harmonica.

"I see you took the key," he remarked as Lash came up.

"Yes, I thought you'd lit out."

"I got hungry and had a bite to eat. Find what you want?"

"Yes, but now I'm hungry. Mmm, no wonder, it's almost four o'clock."

"You want a real feed and some information?"

"Information?"

"You're looking up dope on the Eckerts, aren't you? One of them lived here once."

"How do *you* know?"

"I didn't until a little while ago. I had a bite in a coffee pot around the corner. Fella I used to know in Truckee runs it and I got to gassing with him. He says there's a place up the canyon that one of the Eckerts had in the old days. It's a sort of tavern now, but Andy

235

claims the food's pretty good. It's called Eckert's Inn after the old-timer, who was supposed to be a famous bird around here."

"Do you know how to get there?"

"Yeah, sure. It's only a couple of miles out of town. Good road."

Lash got into the car and backed away from the curb. "Turn right around the block," Higby directed.

Lash made the turn but at the next corner turned left.

"No, no," Higby exclaimed. "Straight ahead."

"I've changed my mind," said Lash. "Eckert doesn't live there any more, so why should I go out?"

"Because," said Higby. He took a revolver from his pocket and laid it on his knees so that the muzzle pointed at Lash. "Make the next right turn."

Lash sighed wearily. "So you couldn't resist cutting in?"

"That's right. But you remember I wouldn't take any money from you."

"That wouldn't have been right," Lash said sarcastically. "Don't take money from a man for a service, but stick a gun in his ribs."

"The money you offered was chicken feed. Turn right here, then stop the car and gimme the will."

Lash made the turn. "I'll stop the car, but I haven't got any will."

"You know what I mean; the piece of paper in the sawed-off gun barrel that we found by the lake."

"Oh, that," said Lash. "Why I haven't got it any more."

Higby swore and jerked up his revolver. "What do you mean, you haven't got it?"

"Because Isaac Eckert came to Truckee."

"I saw him. Who do you suppose I'm working with?"

"Oh," said Lash. "So you didn't really eat awhile ago. You made a telephone call to Truckee."

"Of course. And Ike says you didn't give him anything but a lot of crap. I could tell from the proposition he made to me."

Lash steered the car to the side of the road, but Higby prodded him with the gun. "Keep driving; at the next corner, the gravel road, turn left."

The graveled road led into a tortuous canyon. Lash could seldom see more than fifty feet ahead. The graveled road went uphill. After about two miles it was cut by a little-used dirt road that ran up into a side canyon.

Prodded by Higby, Lash turned up the side canyon. After a half mile, Higby said: "This is it."

Almost concealed by shrubbery was a building that had probably been considered pretentious many years ago. It was two stories high and had a veranda running along the front that was covered by a wooden awning. A weathered sign over the awning revealed that the place had once been called: *Gold Gulch Hotel*.

Lash stopped the car in front of the old hotel. Higby opened the door on his side and climbing down held the door open. "All right, Lash, out on this side."

Lash slipped across the seat and climbed out of the coupé, as a man stepped out to the veranda of the old hotel. He was middle-aged and the filthiest-looking man Lash had ever

238

seen. His clothing was dirty and ragged, and his face looked as if it hadn't been washed since the last time he had shaved, which was at least a month ago.

He said, "Hey . . . !" then exclaimed and stepped down from the veranda. "Sam Higby, of all the consarn fools; what're you doing here?"

"Hello, Amos," said Higby easily. "I thought I'd stop in and pay you a visit. After all, you're practically my second cousin, aren't you?"

"Yeah, but what's the gun for? You ain't . . . ?"

"He is," said Lash. "And you're a fool if you help him."

"You're damn right, mister," declared Higby's cousin, Amos. "Sam, I ain't responsible for what you do away from here, but I'm a-tellin' you now, take yourself and that gun away from here. I don't want any trouble with the law. Not any more I don't."

Sam Higby chuckled. "You still remember the six months you did in the clink? Well, what'd you get it for? Selling a dollar's worth of moonshine. I'm giving you a chance to make a hundred dollars . . . "

"A hundred dollars! Say — let's see the money."

"It's coming. That's why I want to wait here."

"Who's bringing the money?"

"The man who's going to give it to you. He'll be here in two or three hours. Maybe we won't even have to stay after that."

"No? Well, what're we standing out here for? Come on in the hotel."

Higby nodded to Lash. "Go ahead."

Lash shrugged and walked into the 'hotel.' The interior could have been used for a Hollywood haunted house set. Cobwebs hung everywhere, and there was a thick layer of dust except for paths that had been worn clean by Amos. What furniture there was in the 'lobby' was broken and sagging.

"Siddown," Amos said, pointing to a sofa whose springs were touching the floor.

"Got a loaded gun, Amos?" Higby asked.

Amos went behind the partition that

240

had once been the desk and laid a double-barreled shotgun across the top. The muzzles were pointed at Lash. "And there ain't bird shot in this," he said.

"Fine, Amos," said Higby. "Watch him for a couple of minutes while I see if there's something in the car."

The moment Higby had stepped out of the hotel, Lash said: "I'll give you two hundred dollars, Amos."

Amos exclaimed, "For what?"

"For that gun."

"But Sam's my cousin. I couldn't do nothin' like that."

"You're going to get into serious trouble over this. Kidnaping is a Federal offense these days."

"I didn't kidnap you."

"You're an accessory after the fact."

"What's that?"

"You're helping him; your guilt is equal to his."

"How could that be? I ain't done nothin'. I didn't even know Sam was bringin' anyone here. I ain't seen him in four-five years. And anyway, how do I know you won't turn the gun on me . . . "

"I won't," Lash said. "I want to get out of here, that's all."

Amos hesitated a moment, then shook his head. "Can't do it, mister. You'd shoot Sam and after all he's . . . "

Sam Higby came back into the hotel, his face dark with anger.

"Get up, Lash!"

Lash rose from the sagging couch, and Higby stepping behind him searched him thoroughly. When it proved fruitless he stepped away. "What'd you do with it?"

"Apparently I left it in Truckee."

"You didn't get a room at the hotel. They were full up."

"Eckert offered to share his room with me."

"It's not in his room; he said so."

Lash shrugged and sat down on the couch. "How much is Old Ike paying you for this?"

Higby shot a quick glance at his cousin Amos. "More than you'd pay."

"How do you know? I told you that I was representing one of the Eckerts . . . "

"Which one?"

"Not Isaac."

"It isn't Fremont; Ike says he's dead.

242

How much will he pay?"

"I'd have to consult."

Higby laughed scornfully. "And you'll write me a letter? Thanks, I think I'll play this hand."

"You can't. You haven't got a hand."

"The hell I haven't. I saw you get that will and you'll come through with it."

"No, I won't."

Higby walked over to Lash and looked down at him thoughtfully. Then suddenly he feinted a kick at Lash's head. Lash ducked to the right and collided with Higby's fist. The blow sent him sprawling over the couch and started his ears to ringing.

"Where is it?" Higby cried. "That'll show you that I'm not fooling. You'll talk or I'll bust every bone in your body. And don't think I can't do it."

The big mountain man was working himself into a fine frenzy. He pocketed his revolver and reaching down caught Lash by the front of his fleece-lined overcoat. He jerked him off the couch.

Before he could roll over, Higby kicked him in the ribs with his hobnailed boots.

Lash gasped in agony and rolled off the couch to the floor. Too late he saw Higby's foot coming for his head. Fire exploded in his brain and he lapsed into unconsciousness.

19

LASH had almost recovered consciousness when the bucket of water was dumped on his face. Some of it got into his mouth and nostrils and got him to coughing. When he recovered he looked up into the brutal face of Sam Higby and beside it the seamed and leathery features of old Isaac Eckert.

He shook his head to clear away the buzzing and climbed to his knees. There a spell of dizziness seized him and he half fell, half climbed onto the couch.

"So you thought you was smart," Ike Eckert said, "sending me out to the snow when you were already there and got the thing."

"The gold's under the ice," Lash said. "Higby can tell you that."

"Yeah," said Eckert, "but that ain't all. I want the rest of it."

"You can't spend fifty thousand dollars in the time you've got left."

"The hell I can't," Eckert snapped. "I've lived on short rations all my life, and all the time I said to myself, 'Some day I'm going to strike it rich and then I'm going to go to Chicago and New York and buy me a bunch of women and champagne and fancy duds and have a good time.'"

Lash felt of his aching ribs and decided that at least one of them was fractured. "You waited rather long for women," he said sarcastically.

"I'm only eighty," Eckert retorted. "I'll live to be a hundred. Right now I could lick the tar out of you myself."

"That won't be necessary, Ike," Sam Higby said. "I'll handle the licking. This fella can't take much, but I'm kinda hoping he holds out a little while. I haven't had much fun lately. How about it, Lash?"

Across the room Amos, Higby's cousin, whined: "Cut it out, Sam. You can't hit him no more, you'll kill him."

"I'll kill him if he doesn't talk," Higby snarled. "We're playing for big money and I'm not going to let a little killing stand between me and a bankroll."

246

"They don't hang them any more in Hangtown," Lash said. "They execute them in a gas chamber. They tie them in a chair and . . . "

Higby swore and reached for Lash once more. The latter fell forward, just eluding Higby's reach, but Higby whirled agilely and smashed at the back of Lash's head.

The blow was a heavy one and sent Lash staggering clear across the room, where he fell almost under the muzzzles of Amos' shotgun.

"Five hundred, Amos," he said.

The twin muzzles of the gun came down. Lash grabbed them and pulled the rest of the gun down to him. Higby screamed hoarsely.

"Amos, you . . . "

"Look out!" cried old Ike Eckert.

Lash brought the shotgun up with great deliberation. He waited until Higby had the revolver halfway out of his pocket. Then he pulled the rear trigger.

At the last moment he deflected the gun a little so that Higby took most of the charge in his legs. The big man hit the floor and pounded the boards with his fists, the while he screamed and screamed in agony. His revolver had flown from his hand and landed near Ike Eckert.

The old man looked down at the gun and started to stoop for it, but stopped when he saw the shotgun pointed at him.

"Go ahead," Lash invited. "I won't feel bad about killing a man who's outlived his span anyway."

Eckert's mouth was open and he began swallowing noisily. "You're a hard man, Simon Lash."

"So're you, Eckert. You killed your own son."

"I never did," Eckert whined. "I didn't have anythin' to do with that. You're the one killed him. The police practic'ly said so."

Lash looked at him sharply. Then he shifted his gaze to Sam Higby. The wounded man had stopped pounding the floor and was climbing to a sitting position. His face was twisted in pain and tears were streaming down his face.

"You've shot off my legs," he moaned. "I'm bleeding to death. Take me to a doctor."

"It's only bird shot," Lash said. "You stopped a lot of shot, but not many penetrated your skin through your boots and clothes. You're hardly bleeding. Although I don't think you'll enjoy walking for awhile ... You've got a telephone here, Amos?"

Higby's cousin nodded. "Yeah, but — "

"What?"

"You ain't goin' to leave them here with me?"

"I was counting on doing just that."

"But you can't. Not after — "

"After what? You couldn't help that I took your gun away from you ... "

"Took my gun away ... yeah. Yeah sure. You took me by surprise."

Lash stooped and picked up Higby's revolver and discovered to his chagrin that it was his own gun. Higby had apparently taken it out of the glove compartment of the coupé while Lash had been in the Placerville courthouse.

He stuck the gun in his pocket and stepped around Isaac Eckert. Amos came around from behind the counter. "Wait a minute!"

Lash continued to the door. He was

opening it when Amos bleated and rushed after him. Lash stopped in the doorway and broke the gun. Removing the second twelve-gauge shell, he tossed the gun to the floor.

"I want the money," Amos said desperately.

"What money?" Lash sneered. "You just admitted that I took the gun away from you."

"That don't go," Amos yelled. "You said five hundred dollars . . . "

"If I had five hundred dollars I certainly wouldn't give it to you," Lash said harshly. "You were willing to help Higby for a hundred dollars."

He let the door slam in Amos's face, then went quickly to the coupé. He started the motor, backed and turned in front of the hotel, then started off down the canyon road. He did not even look back.

It was getting dark when he reached Placerville. He drove the coupé to a hotel and locking the ignition got out and entered the hotel. He noted by a wall clock that it was almost six-thirty.

He found a telephone booth and

entering put in a reverse charge call to his apartment in Hollywood.

Eddie Slocum's voice sighed in relief as it came on. "Where are you, chief? I been trying all day to get you in Truckee."

"I'm in Placerville now. What've you got?"

"Plenty. I think the Evanstons are phonies . . . "

"What do you mean?" Lash cried. "There aren't any Evanstons in Columbus?"

"No, no, it isn't that. There's a man named Richard Evanston there all right, but he can't be our man on account of he's one of the richest men in the city. A millionaire."

"Did you get his description?"

"Yeah, that could fit. For his wife, too. But they're in Florida now. They go there every winter . . . "

"What business is Richard Evanston in?"

"Real estate. He built a whole subdivision in Columbus. Made a pile of money, the agency says, although he was supposed to have started out with plenty. His father was well-heeled, but Richard's doubled the money. The fifty thousand bucks he could get out here would be cigarette money for him."

"Perhaps," said Lash. "Has Anne Evanston called again?"

"Twice more, before noon. Then she gave up. Hasn't called since. Sergeant Coons has a man staked out across the street, though . . . "

"I hope it rains. What about the Eckerts?"

"Nothing."

"What do you mean — nothing?"

"Sheridan spent the day at his office. Jim Dunlap never left his house."

"But is he there?"

"I don't know. The agency says he is. I asked them how they knew and they said they telephoned and the girl told them her father was busy in his laboratory and couldn't come to the telephone."

"Which doesn't mean a thing." Lash groaned. "That's what you get for trusting an outside detective agency. What else . . . ?"

"Nothing," said Slocum. "Except that the jackass went past the apartment . . . "

"You're kidding!" Lash gasped.

"No. It was around twelve o'clock. I

was sitting by the window, looking out. It looked like the same donkey . . . and the same rider . . . "

"Lansford Hastings? That's impossible."

"Why? You said yourself that he's been riding past the hotel ever since he was killed."

"The damn fool," Lash swore. "How long does he think he can get away with that?"

"Who?"

"The man who's riding the donkey. The job on which Milo Stevens fell down."

"I thought he traced it to Lupton's place."

"But did he produce the jackass? Well, never mind. I'll be home in the morning . . . "

"How can you be? You drove all last night; you can't drive again tonight."

Lash hung up without comment and returned to his car. He studied his road map for a few minutes, then shaking his head started out of Placerville on Highway #49. He drove twenty-three miles to Highway #8 and turned right on it to Stockton. At the latter city he had dinner in a roadstand, finishing with two cups of coffee. He bought a box of No-Sleep tablets and swallowed two.

Then he started out on the long, straight stretch down Highway #99. It was eight thirty.

The drive was a nightmare to Simon Lash. He had been driving for practically twenty-four hours and had not slept for at least fifteen hours before setting out. The terrific beating he had taken at the Gold Gulch Hotel, more than anything else, kept him from getting too groggy. No bones had been broken but his entire body ached, at times so excruciatingly that he had to clench his teeth to keep from gasping.

After some hours the pain subsided into numbness and now Lash found the desire for sleep almost overwhelming. The No-Sleep tablets helped for only an hour or so at a time. Lash kept swallowing more of them. At Fresno he stopped his car and leaning over the wheel dozed for fifteen minutes. A cup of coffee and two tablets from a new box of No-Sleeps enabled him to continue.

Near Bakersfield his eyes closed for

a fraction of a second and he ran off the slab to the road shoulder, which fortunately was graveled at the spot. The near-accident shocked him to wakefulness and in Bakersfield he stopped for gas and took a brisk walk of a block or two.

Returning to the car he settled down with grim determination for the last, long run.

20

SHORTLY before four-thirty in the morning he turned into Ventura Boulevard in North Hollywood, having traveled 1100 miles just a little over thirty hours. He drove into the court of a hotel and awakening the night attendant rented a cabin.

He went in and latching the door threw himself on the bed, without undressing. He was sound asleep inside of sixty seconds.

A banging on the door awakened him. "Say, mister, it's noon. I got to clean up."

Lash opened his eyes and stared at the ceiling as he collected his thoughts. Then he groaned and got up. Leaving the cabin he got into his car and drove into Hollywood. But he did not go to his apartment on Harper.

Instead he parked his car on Ivar and went to a small, fourth-rate hotel where he rented a room for which he paid in advance. He went up to it and the moment the bellboy had gone, put in a telephone call to Eddie Slocum.

"I'm back, Eddie," he said. "Is Coons still watching the apartment?"

"Two men now. Betty Dunlap called. She's pretty sore about the buffalo box."

"Did you tell her I lost it?"

"No, I stalled. Told her you were out working but I didn't know where you were. I didn't, the way you moved around."

"Are you getting reports from the agency?"

"Yes, but I don't know how good they are. Jim Dunlap never left the house yesterday, but they said that the lights were on in his laboratory until after twelve last night. Since the girl stayed at home all evening that might not mean anything. She could have put the lights on and off. Sheridan Eckert spent all day at his office on Wilshire."

"And you haven't heard a thing from the Evanstons?"

"Nothing since she stopped checking up on you yesterday."

Lash frowned at the telephone. "Look,

Eddie, do you think you could get out of the place without being followed?"

"I'll be followed all right," Slocum said, "but the question is, can I ditch them? I think I can. Where'll I find you?"

"At the El Mirage Hotel on Ivar. Room 408. Come right up to the room, but make sure you're not followed. I think Coons would like to haul me down to Headquarters and I'm not in the mood for that."

Lash hung up on Slocum, then consulted the telephone directory for the number of the Donnelley Detective Agency. When he found it he called the number and asked for Jim Donnelley.

When the agency head came on Lash lit into him. "What kind of a detective do you call yourself? I give you a job and you handle it like an old maid school teacher."

"Wait a minute, Lash!" Donnelley cried. "We've been giving hourly reports to your assistant, Slocum. Our men have never left the job for a minute. What more do you want?"

"Results!" Lash snapped. "I tell you to

watch a house and because a man doesn't come out, you say he's at home all the time. How do you know he's at home? Anyone can put on a light and turn it off again."

"You mean Dunlap?"

"Of course."

"But he was home all the time, Lash. My man checked up on that."

"How? He telephoned and Dunlap's daughter said papa was working in his laboratory. You see the light on there and you assume he's really working — "

"We assumed nothing, Lash. My man looked into the window and saw Dunlap."

"How do you know it was Dunlap?"

"That we don't know, never having seen Dunlap before and not being provided with a photo of him. What more do you expect?"

"Plenty more. I'll give you another chance — "

"You don't have to, Lash," the detective agency man snapped. "If that's your attitude I don't think we care for your business . . . "

"You mean because it's too tough?"

"I can do anything you can do, Lash," Donnelley snarled.

"Yeah? Well, let's see how quick you handle this job. I want to find Richard Evanston and his wife, Anne Evanston. The woman's about thirty, brunette and a knockout. Her husband's crowding forty. They're registered at some hotel or other, but they may not be together. It's possible they're using the names of Evanston, but you might try Lupton or Eckert or even Smith."

"You'll pay for the job?"

"If you can find at least one of them before six this evening."

"It's a deal, Lash," Donnelley said coldly. "And I think I'll make you eat your words."

"If you can produce, I'll eat them," said Lash. "Without salt."

He slammed the receiver on the hook and took a quick turn about the room. Pausing at the window a moment his eyes caught sight of the tall building in which the broadcasting studio was located. He stared at the building for a long moment, then a crooked grin broke his face.

Abruptly he left his room and going

downstairs walked across the street to the parking lot where he had left the coupé. The big telescope was still in the rumble seat, somewhat the worse for its eleven hundred mile trip. It had been covered with snow in the mountain country, which had melted and rusted the metal of the instrument. But it did not impair its usefulness and Lash knew that a little oil would clean off the rust.

He carried the heavy instrument and tripod back to the hotel where the clerk made caustic comment: "Going to see what the stars have to say?"

Lash shooed away a couple of bellboys who wanted to carry the instrument for him. He got it to his room safely and set it up by the window. Pointing it toward the building a block away he put his eye to the eyepiece.

The result was astonishing. The building seemed to dart toward him and come to a halt a couple of feet from his eyes. Lash located a turnscrew at the side of the telescope and with it moved the telescope tube, so that he looked directly into a window of the building.

A man was seated in a chair, his back

to the window, reading a newspaper. So well did the powerful telescope magnify that Lash could actually read the big headline on the newspaper.

He uttered an exclamation and raised his head. Scrutinizing the building a block away he discovered that it had eight stories and that six showed above a neighboring two-story roof. He could see all of the windows of one entire side above this level.

He counted the windows and discovered that there were eighteen per floor.

He adjusted the telescope so that it pointed to the first window from the left on the eighth floor. Unashamed he looked at the occupants of the office, a girl applying lipstick and another plucking her eyebrows with a tweezer.

Lash shifted to the next window and found a vacant office. He continued along the level of the eighth floor, in one or two instances moving the telescope hastily.

He worked along the seventh floor and was half way through the sixth when there was a soft knocking on the door.

Lash moved away from the telescope. "Who is it?"

"Slocum," was the reply and Eddie came into the room. "Hi, chief."

"You're sure you weren't followed?" Lash asked immediately.

"Only one of them followed me," Slocum replied. "I went to Musso Frank's Restaurant and ordered a steak, medium rare. When the waiter brought it I took one mouthful and went to the washroom. It's on the first floor, you know, and I climbed out of the window and ducked through to Franklin Avenue. I walked down Franklin all the way to Gower, then came back on Sunset. I think the cop's still over at Musso Frank's."

Lash nodded. "I guess it's okay."

Slocum took a cylindrical parcel from his pocket. "The mailman brought this just as I was leaving. I saw the postmark was Truckee, so I thought you'd want to see it."

"Swell!" Lash exclaimed "This is the thing that all the Eckerts have been scrambling for."

"That? It only weighs about half a pound. What's in it?"

263

"A length of steel sawed from a shotgun barrel. It contains the last words written by the original Mrs. Isaac Eckert. It tells where the fifty thousand in gold is stashed . . . ."

"Did you get it?"

"It's under about fifty feet of water — ten of ice and about that of snow. Nobody's going to get it until spring . . . if they ever get it at all. But look, I ran into Old Ike Eckert up there. You said that he and Jim Dunlap had a fight the other night and that Ike left in a mad. I think you were wrong, because Ike had the machine Dunlap invented for him — the metal finder." Lash laughed shortly. "That reminds me I never did return the water pipe locater to the boys in Reno. Serves them right, they had no business lending it to a perfect stranger."

"It worked?"

"A lot better than Dunlap's Rube Goldberg contraption. If you ask me, Dunlap was playing a game on the old boy. An inventor like him must have known about the electromagnetic water pipe finder."

"You'd think so . . . Why the telescope here, chief?"

"I got bored," Lash said sarcastically, "so I thought I'd take up being a Peeping Tom."

Slocum chuckled. "See anything interesting?"

"Too much. There ought to be a law requiring business firms to keep their window shades down. Some guy not as honest as myself might think up this gag sometime and use it to build up a swell blackmailing business. Look, Eddie, that's the broadcasting building where Harold Wade has his office. I want you to run over there and find out from the building directory or maybe an elevator operator where Wade's office is."

"Are we interested in Wade?"

Lash shrugged. "He's got an office in that building and I'm here with a telescope and he knows most of the people connected with this affair. There's one chance in about three that his office will be in sight of this room. If I win, I've got a stunt figured out that might work."

Eddie Slocum shook his head and

went off. Lash spent the ten minutes that Slocum was gone in spying on the broadcasting building. He got down to the third floor but had still not located Wade. Then Eddie returned.

"You win. He's in Room 421, which faces the rear."

"I just passed the fourth floor," Lash exclaimed. "I didn't see him."

"He's been in a rehearsal studio; I asked. He's due out at three o'clock; that's in a few minutes."

Lash nodded thoughtfully. "All right then, let's get started. Telephone the Dunlaps. Tell them it's urgent that they call on Harold Wade at once."

Slocum whistled. "But suppose they don't do it? Uh, the girl is quite likely to call him back."

"So much the better. Wade will be as puzzled as she and will stick around. In fact, we might inject a note of mystery into the thing. Say you've heard from me and that I'm going to tell them about a matter of life and death."

Slocum regarded Lash curiously. "Are you going over there?"

"No, I just want to watch their

reactions as they discuss the matter. Too bad I can't read lips but I believe I can learn quite a bit from their expressions and gestures. Call Sheridan Eckert, too." He sighed. "If we only had Ike Eckert here and could locate the Evanstons I think I could wash up this business."

"With the telescope?"

"With the telescope."

Slocum had been looking up the numbers and now he put in a call to Santa Monica. He got Sheridan Eckert with some difficulty.

"Mr. Eckert?" he said, "This is Eddie Slocum. I'm Simon Lash's assistant. He's just telephoned from Donner Lake, upstate, and he's asked me to tell you to go right down to the office of Harold Wade and learn something of vital importance."

Sheridan Eckert laughed cynically. "Nothing Simon Lash could tell you would be of any importance to me."

Slocum covered the mouthpiece and said to Lash: "Eckert says he's not interested."

Lash stepped quickly to the phone and put his ear against the receiver, so he could hear as well as Slocum. Then he said to Eddie: "Tell him I've found the last will and testament of Ellen Ford Eckert."

Slocum repeated the information. There was a pause, then Sheridan Eckert said: "The will's invalid. Buried money comes in the Treasure Trove category; it belongs to whoever finds it."

Lash, who had been listening at the receiver, signaled for Slocum to cover the mouthpiece. "Ask him about real estate."

"What about real estate?" Slocum repeated.

There was a pause, then Sheridan Eckert asked: "How much real estate?"

Lash took the telephone from Eddie Slocum and laughed into the mouthpiece. Then he put the receiver onto the hook.

"That'll get him."

"How do you know?"

"He's a lawyer. The affair presents interesting possibilities — to a lawyer. Now call the Dunlaps."

21

SLOCUM asked for the number and got Betty Dunlap. "Miss Dunlap," he said, "I've just had word from Mr. Lash. He says it's important that you get down to Harold Wade's office at once."

"Harold?" exclaimed Betty Dunlap. "What's he got to do with this. And where is Mr. Lash?"

"He was up at Donner Lake," Slocum replied. "He . . . " Slocum looked inquiringly at Lash and the latter nodded. "He found something important up there — "

"What?" Betty Dunlap cried, excitedly.

"Your great-grandmother's will."

"He did! But why — why should I meet him at Harold's office?"

"I dunno, except that that's what he said. Uh, he wants your father to be there, too. Right away."

Betty began to protest but Slocum, acting upon Lash's signal, hung up.

Lash's face screwed up in thought for a moment, then he took the telephone and called the office of Milo Stevens. He got through to Milo promptly after he gave his name. Then he let go.

"Listen, you chiseling blackmailer," he told Stevens. "What was the idea of — "

"Lash," cut in Milo Stevens, "where the devil are you . . . ?"

"That's none of your business. You snitched once to the cops on me and I'm not going to give you another opportunity. I just wanted to tell you that a couple of campfire girls did a better job for me than your entire detective agency. They found that jackass that you couldn't — "

"We found it, too," Milo Stevens snarled.

"You did like hell. It came up and brayed at your detectives and they couldn't find it."

"You're crazy, Lash. I could've told you day before yesterday where the jackass was, but you insisted on my man watching the house and I assumed naturally — "

270

"You assumed — pfft!" Lash said and broke the connection. After a moment he called the office of the Donnelley Agency.

"Donnelley, one more little job. Rush a couple of men out to Longridge Avenue in Van Nuys. Have them chase all the way up into the canyon and see if they can find a jackass that's staked out there somewhere. I have an idea that it'll be tied to a tree or something."

"What the devil do you want with a jackass, Lash?"

"You keep the jackass, Donnelley," Lash retorted. "I want to know what your man finds, that's all. Fingerprints on the bridle, if there are any. Let him look around the ground. I want to know who has been using the jackass the last couple of days, and by who I don't just want a description of the man. I've got that. I want identification. Understand?"

"Yes, of course. This is going to cost you extra."

"All right, I'll pay it. Anything on the other matter?"

"Yes, but it'll take a few more minutes to make sure. One of the boys just called

271

in, said he's located the woman at the El Mirage Hotel — "

"El Mirage?" Lash exclaimed softly.

"Yeah, a cheap dump on Ivar Street. She's registered as Anne Lupton. He's trying to verify the identification. He'll call in again in a few minutes. Where'll I reach you?"

"I'll call back in ten minutes." Lash hung up and shaking his head, whistled. "Anne Evanston's registered right here at this hotel."

Eddie winced. "Oh-oh!"

Lash went back to the telescope and adjusted it once more for the fourth floor. He turned it slowly in a horizontal direction, from left to right. At the fifth office window he stopped.

"There he is, Eddie," he said. "A swell view. Now, just for practice, you call him while I watch."

"What'll I say to him?"

Lash grinned. "Tell him you've got a jackass which can bray, 'Oh Susanna.' Carry on from his lead, then."

Slocum shrugged and looked up Wade's number in the phone directory while Lash studied the Oddity Man through the telescope. Wade seemed to be engrossed in reading a pamphlet which could very easily have been a racing form.

Behind him Lash heard Slocum putting in the call. Then he saw Wade reach for the telephone.

"Listen, Mr. Wade," Slocum said. "I've got a jackass that can bray 'Oh Susanna.' . . ."

The telescope was so powerful that Lash could see every feature of the Oddity Man's face. He saw it wrinkle in disgust and it seemed to him that he could almost hear Wade's reply . . .

"This is a real good jackass," Slocum persisted. "And boy, how he can bray. You can almost hear the words, 'Oh Susanna, don't you cry for me. I'm goin' to California with a banjo on my knee . . .'"

The expression of disgust disappeared from Wade's face. It was replaced by one of interest.

"What does he say, Eddie?" Lash asked.

"He wants to know my name and where I am."

"Hang up!"

Lash heard the click of the receiver being placed on the hook, then watched Wade replace his own receiver and scowl at the instrument. After a moment he got up and went to a closet door which he pulled open. He started in, then looked over his shoulder and returned to the desk.

Evidently the phone had rung for Wade picked it up. He spoke briefly, then seated himself and began fumbling with his polka-dot bow tie. Apparently he was expecting a visitor, a feminine one.

Lash mumbled under his breath. It was less than ten minutes since Slocum had telephoned Betty Dunlap. It would take her another ten minutes to arrive, even driving at top speed and having no difficulty parking her car.

The door of Wade's office opened and a woman came in. It was Anne Evanston. Lash inhaled softly. He kept his eyes glued to the telescope. Anne Evanston was smiling her prettiest as she extended her hand to Harold Wade. The latter bowed gallantly and spoke animatedly. Men usually did to Anne Evanston.

Wade pulled up a chair close to his

desk and Anne Evanston seated herself. Wade also sat down and leaned toward Mrs. Evanston.

"Eddie," said Lash. "Call Harold Wade again. Mrs. Evanston just entered his office."

Eddie Slocum chuckled. "Shall I ask her to come over here?"

"Don't be obscene, Eddie. Just a minute. Say to him that I've been up at Donner Lake and found a treasure of fifty thousand dollars that was buried there by a member of the Donner Party, back in 1847. Ask him if he'd like to have me on his next program."

"Shall I give him my name?"

"Yes. But try to make your voice sound a little different than before."

Eddie Slocum put in the call and Lash watched Wade reach for the phone. There was an expression of annoyance on his face, but it quickly changed as Slocum told him the details of the call. Lash saw the excitement on Wade's face, saw him glance quickly at Anne Evanston, then speak into the mouthpiece.

"What does he say, Eddie?" Lash whispered.

"He wants me to call him later."

"No! Make him talk now . . . "

"I'm sorry, Mr. Wade," Eddie Slocum said into the telephone, "I'm leaving this very moment on an urgent errand for Mr. Lash. You'll have to give me your answer now. Yes . . . ?"

A block away, Harold Wade was now covering the mouthpiece of the telephone. He turned to speak to Anne Evanston and she sprang from her chair and leaned over Wade. She gestured violently and Wade uncovered the phone an instant and said something into the mouthpiece.

"Did he say to hold on a moment, Eddie?"

"Yes."

"A little more of this and I'll be able to read lips," Lash said. "Here he comes again."

"Yes, Mr. Wade," Slocum said. Then, covering the mouthpiece, "He wants to know if you can *prove* that you found the cache."

"I'll show him the money," Lash lied.

Slocum relayed the information, then asked Lash another question. "He wants to know if that's *all* you found there, just the money?"

"Tell him no."

Slocum replied to that question and Lash could see Wade cover the mouthpiece once more. Anne Evanston spoke, then Wade nodded and uncovered the mouthpiece.

"He wants to know what?"

"Tell him something that would be of interest only to relatives of the Eckerts."

Slocum complied with the statement and was asked another question. "Is it a will?"

Lash laughed. "Say you don't know but that I sounded awfully excited about something."

After a couple of minutes, during which time Wade alternately spoke to Slocum and Anne Evanston, Eddie Slocum said to Lash: "It's a deal, chief. He's even willing to give you an emol — an emolument."

"Fine," said Lash.

Slocum said good-by to Wade and the latter turned and got into an excited conversation with Anne Evanston. It lasted for five minutes, when Wade's telephone rang and he scooped it up. He winced when he spoke briefly into it.

That was the signal for Anne Evanston to leave. She took her departure in a surprising fashion. Surprising for a married woman. She kissed Wade. And it wasn't just a peck. An ardent embrace accompanied the osculation.

Wade again adjusted his necktie, then noticed the open closet door and closed it tightly. As he turned away, Betty and Jim Dunlap came into the office. Wade seemed about to embrace Betty, but a slight shake of her head deterred him. Wade shook hands with Betty's father, but the latter did not act too cordial.

The trio began an animated conversation, which was punctuated after a minute or two by Dunlap banging his fist on Wade's desk and then shaking an index finger at him. Wade disclaimed responsibility for something by shrugging and turning up the palms of his hands.

The conversation was interrupted by another phone call and a quick consultation. Then Sheridan Eckert entered the office. He bowed to Betty, but did not offer to shake hands with either Dunlap or Wade. Dunlap, in fact, scowled at Eckert. The latter smiled suavely.

The conference, which began on a note of coolness, gradually warmed up. Lash was so intent on it, that he was startled by a sudden hoarse whisper in his ear.

"Chief, someone's knocked on the door."

Lash grimaced and whirled toward the door, intending to go to it and turn the key. He was too late. The door was pushed inwards and Anne Evanston came into the room.

"Well, well, boys," she said. "A couple of Peeping Toms, eh?"

Lash grinned at her. "How'd you know?"

"You forgot to pull down your shade. Just as I was leaving across the way, the sun flashed on the glass . . . "

"Pull down the shade, Eddie," Lash ordered. "Cut a hole in it and we'll look through that. If they get a flash they won't be able to spot what it is. Thanks, Mrs. Evanston . . . "

"Very nice going, Simon," said Anne

Evanston, coolly. "Now, spill it. What's the game?"

"No game, Mrs. Evanston."

"Turn the record over, Mr. Lash. Why'd you call Wade?"

"Why'd you visit him?"

"Ah," said Anne Evanston. "You're going to hold out. Very well . . . " She turned toward the door, but Lash stepped quickly past her and closed it. He turned the key in the lock and drawing it out slipped it into his pocket.

"Open that door," Anne Evanston said. "Open it, or I'll scream!"

She opened her mouth and at that moment, Eddie Slocum, coming up behind her, reached forward and placed his hand over her mouth. Mrs. Evanston began to fight Slocum, and Lash dashed into the bathroom and caught up a towel.

He returned to the room and watching his opportunity jammed the towel over Mrs. Evanston's mouth. At that, she got out the first note of a scream.

Then, as both men held her, Lash spoke hotly: "You little fool, you've been playing with dynamite all week. Promise

280

to behave and I'll tell you something. Blink twice."

For a moment Anne Evanston's eyes blazed at Lash, then they closed tightly, opened and closed again. Lash whipped the towel from her mouth.

Anne Evanston promptly screamed.

Lash lunged for her. Mrs. Evanston kicked Eddie Slocum's shin with a high heel and evaded Lash's hands.

Someone banged thunderously upon the door and a voice roared: "Open up in there!"

It looked bad.

"Yell your head off," Lash snarled at Anne Evanston. "This is your chance."

Anne Evanston stepped close. "Give me the paper you found at Donner Lake and I'll square this," she whispered.

Lash laughed and unlocked the door.

22

SERGEANT COONS and another human buffalo plunged into the room.

"Simon Lash, by all that's holy!" Coons roared. "And what a charge!" His baleful eyes darted to Anne Evanston.

"My client," Lash said, making a forlorn attempt.

"Yeah?" sneered Coons. "She was yelling for help and the door was locked." He turned to Mrs. Evanston for verification. "How about it, Miss — "

Anne Evanston looked at Lash's bitter face. Then she gave the proper answer. She hung her head . . . in shame. She lifted it again when Lash tossed in the sponge of defeat.

"Mrs. Evanston *is* a client, Sergeant Coons. She came up to see something that I'd found for her." Lash reached into his coat pocket and took out the round parcel he had mailed to himself from Truckee.

Anne Evanston's eyes widened. She came forward and Lash held up the cylinder so she could see the postmark. His eyes held hers challengingly. She turned and beamed at Sergeant Coons.

"Naturally, we didn't want to be disturbed." She laughed. "And after all," smiling at Eddie Slocum, "we had a chaperon." She reached and took the cylinder from Lash's hand.

Disappointment came to Sergeant Coons' eyes, but was replaced by a gleam of determination. "There's the other business, Lash. That fellow, Lansford Hastings — "

"Oh," said Lash. "That!"

"That," Sergeant Coons said. "It's not really important. Just a murder, you know."

"And you don't know who did it?"

"I was thinking maybe you did it."

Lash laughed. "Because I went down to the morgue to identify the body? I did that for Mrs. Evanston. You see, her husband had disappeared and she thought . . . "

"That's right," said Anne Evanston.

Sergeant Coons looked sharply at Mrs.

Evanston. "Why didn't you report your husband's disappearance to the police?"

Mrs. Evanston dropped her eyes coyly. "Because he's disappeared before. There's — I don't want to say it, but there's a hussy . . . "

"Oh," said Sergeant Coons. He suddenly noticed the telescope. "Of all the cheap, low-down tricks. Spying on a . . . " He crossed the room and, stooping, put his eye to the instrument. Then he gasped. "Say, those people . . . " He straightened and whirled. "What's the game, Lash? This isn't any divorce evidence stuff. Those are the Dunlaps and Eckerts. I questioned them on the Hastings case."

Lash smiled wearily. "You see, Mrs. Evanston."

Mrs. Evanston shook her head. "I'm sorry, Mr. Lash. And now, if you'll excuse me . . . "

Sergeant Coons shot a quick glance at Lash. The latter spread out the fingers of both of his hands and looked down at them. Coons said, "Wait a minute, Mrs. Evanston."

His partner promptly stepped into the doorway, blocking Anne Evanston's exit.

She turned to Coons in annoyance. "I don't understand . . . "

"Where *is* your husband, Mrs. Evanston?" Lash asked, quietly.

"I don't know. I don't see what that has to do with . . . "

"With Lansford Hastings? Why, it was in your husband's place that Hastings was killed."

Coons stared at Lash.

Lash said: "The man with the singing owls . . . "

"Lupton! Luke Lupton . . . "

"His great-grandmother married a man named Lupton."

"Mr. Lash," said Anne Evanston coldly. "You're talking through your hat."

"Where's your husband?" Lash asked. "Produce him and we'll settle this business."

"I don't know where he is."

Lash stepped to the telephone. "Mind?" he asked Coons and without waiting for a reply picked up the receiver and gave the number of the Donnelley Detective Agency.

"Lash," he said when he got the agency

head. "Did you get it?"

"I did!" Donnelley exclaimed. "The jackass, Mr. and Mrs. Evanston . . . "

"All together?"

Donnelley snorted. "Still cracking. Mr. and Mrs. Evanston are both at the El Mirage, but they've got separate rooms. And they're using different names. He's registered as Ford and she as Lupton. He's in Room 420 and — "

"Swell," said Lash. "And the jackass?"

"He was braying his head off up the canyon. So far my man hasn't found anything incriminating but he's gone back to scour the ground some more. He did say that there were no fingerprints on the jackass' halter or bridle or whatever you call it. It was wiped clean with oil."

"Good work, Donnelley," Lash said.

"Damn right it's good work. Do you take back now what you said . . . ?"

"No," said Lash and hung up.

He clapped his hands together. "Sergeant Coons, how did you know where to find me?"

"Mr. Anonymous."

"Ah," said Lash, "I thought so." He looked at Mrs. Evanston. "Shall we pick

286

up your husband on the way?"

"I told you I didn't know where — "

"Then I've earned the fee you paid me. Mrs. Evanston, you hired me to find your husband for you. I have. He's registered right here at this hotel . . . "

"He isn't!"

" . . . Under the name of Ford," Lash concluded. "Your anonymous informant, Sergeant Coons. He spotted me, probably, coming in with the telescope."

He suddenly sprang for the doorway. Coons' assistant, caught by surprise, threw up his hands, but Lash ducked under them and plunged out into the corridor . . . just as Richard Evanston popped out of the adjoining room.

Evanston cried out in chagrin and turned to run in the other direction. He discovered that he was charging toward a dead wall and whirled back. By that time Sergeant Coons was out in the hall, his gun in his fist.

"Stop!" he thundered.

Evanston pulled up. He made a tremendous effort to compose himself and laughed suddenly.

"Some fun, eh?" Lash asked.

"Dick," said Anne Evanston suddenly. "Get rid of this." The paper cylinder flew over Lash's head. Dick Evanston caught it and sidestepped into his room.

Sergeant Coons howled and leaped past Lash. The door of Evanston's room slammed in his face and by the time Coons got hold of the doorknob, the key had been turned in the lock.

"Open up," Coons cried. "Open up or I'll break down the door."

"Go ahead, Sergeant," Lash urged. "The hotel won't sue you."

Coons threw his shoulder against the door. He was joined by his assistant and between them they splintered the door. As Coons reached in to turn the key, Evanston appeared coming from the bathroom.

"Nice try," Lash called.

"You . . . !" Evanston swore.

"What did you flush down?" Coons demanded.

"Nothing," Evanston snapped.

"He's telling the truth, Sergeant," Lash said. "He was going to get rid of a piece of paper but the package was empty."

"Lash," screamed Mrs. Evanston, "you tricked — "

"Uh-huh," said Lash. "Now if you'll all come over to the broadcasting studio, why I think I'll be able to wash up this whole business."

"You can put the finger on the murderer?" Coons demanded. "And prove it?"

"And prove it."

Coons gestured to Evanston. Lash shrugged. "Come along. Eddie, pick up that enameled box from the top drawer of the chiffonier."

Eddie Slocum trotted back into the room, reappearing in a moment with the Japanese magic box. Sergeant Coons promptly took it away from Eddie. He opened it and exclaimed. "It's empty."

"That's right," said Lash, grinning. "You can carry it, if you wish."

He rang for an elevator. As they got in, Coons was still examining the box. Lash noted that both Mr. and Mrs. Evanston were watching. The ghost of a smile played over the latter's face.

Outside, Sergeant Coons got on one side of the group and his assistant

289

automatically fell in on the other side. They walked to Sunset then over to Vine.

As they entered the radio building, the detectives fell to the rear. They all marched into the elevator.

23

THEY all got off at the fourth floor and walked down a wide corridor to a ground-glass door on which was stenciled:

THE ODDITY MAN
Harold Wade

"Say," said Sergeant Coons' partner, who had been mute up to now. "I listen to his program every week."

"Like it?" Lash asked.

"You bet!"

"Good. Then you can get Wade's autograph." He pushed open the door and entered a nicely furnished reception room.

"Mr. Wade," Lash said to a redheaded girl. "He's expecting us."

"Your name . . . ?"

Sergeant Coons waved impatiently and pushed open a low gate. He bore down upon an oak-paneled door on which was the word PRIVATE. He started to open it, then stepped aside and signaled to Lash.

Lash entered the room and said, easily: "Hello, Miss Dunlap. Mr. Eckert, Mr. Dunlap and . . ." he snapped his fingers. "Let's see, I remember your face, but I can't recall the name . . . "

Wade's olive-tinted face darkened. "What's the idea?"

"Hade, Shade, Wade . . . ah, yes, Wade, now I remember," Lash said. "Allow me. Mr. and Mrs. Evanston, Slocum and — a couple of cops."

"What's the meaning of this?" Jim Dunlap demanded angrily.

"The gathering of the clan," Lash said. "The Evanstons are your cousins, thrice removed. You've met them, haven't you, Mr. Eckert?"

Sheridan Eckert smiled as suavely as ever. "You shouldn't have quit the legal profession, Mr. Lash. You have a nice sense of melodrama that would have, ah, wowed juries. Proceed, Mr. Lash."

"Thank you, Mr. Eckert, I shall. Members of the Eckert family . . . " He turned and bowed to Sergeant

292

Coons and the other detective. "And gentlemen of the jury. I have just returned from Donner Lake, where I have discovered the long-lost Eckert treasure . . . "

"I don't believe it," Jim Dunlap cut in. "There never was any Eckert treasure . . . "

"Oh, didn't Cousin Isaac telephone you? I thought surely he would. Mmm, he may be angry with you, because of the Rube Goldberg treasure-finding machine you made for him . . . "

Dunlap snorted. "The old fool insisted I make him a machine, so I did."

Lash grinned. "Did you stop to think how mortified he would be when he learned how simple an electromagnetic machine really is."

Dunlap looked inquiringly at Lash. "You know about that?"

"I do, now. I didn't before. But Eddie Slocum did. He saw some boys from the water department locate water pipes." He shook his head. "I borrowed one of the gadgets up in Reno, within sight of Isaac Eckert's place."

"And you found a water pipe?"

"No, I found the cache."

Exclamations went up in the room. Lash shrugged. "Well, I didn't exactly find the gold cache, but — "

"But you'll get it the next time out," Sheridan Eckert said, smoothly.

"That's what all the treasure hunters say. Only this time it's true. But I'll leave the finding of it up to you folks. I'll merely tell you where to look. It's in a keg, fifty feet under the water of Donner Lake. I should say, fifty feet of water, ice and snow. I'll give you exact directions later. The gold's not so important . . . Did you say something, Mr. Evanston?"

"No," said Evanston, thickly.

"Then, let me tell you the history of the Eckert family . . . "

"Please," said Betty Dunlap. "We — we all know it."

"I'm afraid you don't."

"We do," said Sheridan Eckert, "but go ahead. There's no stopping a lawyer once he gets going."

"You should know, Counsellor. I'll start with the Eckert family as of the winter of 1846 — leaving out certain details. There was Isaac Eckert, his wife Ellen, and their three children, Isaac Junior, Fremont and Elizabeth. There was also Ellen Eckert's daughter Ellen, by her first husband. History has almost lost sight of her because she was not a member of the Donner-Eckert Party, being already married. She remained in Ohio, with her young husband, taking care of the old farm while the rest of the family went out to California.

"All of you know what happened in California. Isaac Eckert and his wife both perished. Which brings us down to a fine legal point, which you, Mr. Eckert, will appreciate."

Sheridan Eckert spread out his hands. "Your point is that Ellen Eckert survived her husband?"

"Yes. The law is that when a wife and her husband die at approximately the same time, no evidence to the contrary, the husband is presumed to have survived his wife. In this instance, however, there is evidence that the wife outlived the husband. Ellen Eckert kept a diary, which Mr. Richard Evanston appropriated, I am sorry to say . . . "

"Prove it," Richard Evanston said, coldly.

"I can't. But *I* know there's a diary and *you* know it. Miss Dunlap, it was in the buffalo box . . . "

"But the box was empty!" Betty Dunlap cried.

"Yes and no," said Lash. "Sergeant Coons, the box."

Sergeant Coons looked suspiciously at Lash, but handed over the enameled magic box. "Where do you get the buffaloes?"

"Oh, that's another box. If any of you people had read closely the accounts of the Donner Party you might have tumbled. I imagine most of you skimmed too quickly over the early adventures of the party, before they reached Donner Lake. If you had showed more than passing interest in the everyday doings of the party on the trip across the plains you would have come across a little phrase, which referred to the evening entertainment after a hard day's traveling. The phrase goes something like this: ' . . . And Isaac Eckert entertained with feats of magic.' That's the clue.

296

Isaac Eckert was an amateur magician. They had them in those days, just as they have them today — thousands of 'em."

Lash tapped the Japanese box. "This is a modern counterpart of the buffalo box that Isaac Eckert carved." Lash cleared his throat and assumed the stance of a magician, shoulders thrown back, arms held out from his sides. "Observe, ladies and gentlemen — an empty box!"

He unlocked the box, showed the empty interior and locked the box. "Now, the magic word, *abracadabra!*" He unlocked the box, raised the lid . . . and revealed Ellen Eckert's will!

"Jeez!" exclaimed Sergeant Coons, voicing the surprise of most of the others in the room. "I'd like to buy a box like that."

"I'll sell you this one," said Lash.

"How does it work?"

"If I tell you," grinned Lash, "one hundred and eighty-four magicians will bawl the hell out of Frank Gruber for exposing magician's tricks." He cleared his throat.

"This is the last will and testament of

Ellen Eckert. Let me read some extracts: *... Children, your father passed away on February 15 and I fear I have no more than a day or two myself ... My children, Isaac, George, Elizabeth and Ellen, I want you all to share equally in everything I leave.*"

Lash lowered the will. "There's more, but at the moment that's all that's important. It established the prior death of Ellen Eckert's husband and it indicates the disposition of her estate. That is the most important point of all. Ellen Eckert left her estate equally to *all four* of her children. We don't know but that Isaac wouldn't have remembered his stepdaughter had he been the survivor, but since he passed away first and his wife clearly provides for her eldest daughter, the half sister of — "

"All right," Jim Dunlap cut in harshly. "You've made your point. The gold is split four ways ... if we find it."

"Mr. Evanston thanks you for that," said Lash, "since he is the direct descendant of Ellen Eckert's daughter by her first husband. But Mr. Evanston may not thank you for the rest of it. The will reads: 'Share equally in *everything* I leave.' That doesn't mean just what was left there by Donner Lake, the property Ellen Eckert inherited from her husband. It means also her own property, the farm she left back in Ohio . . . "

Richard Evanston cried out in consternation.

"Oh, but I'm afraid it is, Mr. Evanston. And real estate doesn't come under the Treasure Trove law. Heirs to the umpteenth generation retain their rights. I'm afraid you'll have to split that old farm you inherited."

"Mr. Lash is right," said Sheridan Eckert. "But how big is the farm?"

"I don't know," Lash replied truthfully. "Probably a quarter section."

Sheridan Eckert pursed up his lips. "In Ohio? A hundred dollars an acre perhaps . . . "

"Perhaps," said Lash. "And perhaps a little more. Will you tell them, or shall I, Mr. Evanston?"

A fine film of perspiration covered Richard Evanston's face. He shook his head. His wife laughed. "S'tough, Dickie. Well, Cousins and Uncles, the old homestead ain't what she used to be. They spoiled it by cutting it up into streets and lots and building great big buildings all over the barnyard. Dick's grandpappy started it, his pop carried it on and Dickie built the last little subdivision himself."

"Columbus, Ohio," Lash amplified. "The farm became a large part of the city . . . "

The Eckerts expressed their astonishment and Dick Evanston groaned.

"Damn Fremont Eckert!"

"Lansford Hastings," Lash said to Sergeant Coons. "The corpse out on Longridge Avenue . . . " Sergeant Coons' eyes gleamed. "Go ahead."

Lash winked at Harold Wade. "Good for your program?"

"It would be better for the Lost Heirs Program," Wade replied.

"But you find it interesting? You should, since you started the trouble by having Lansford Hastings on your program. The desert rat. Now, for the sixty-four-dollar question. Mr. Wade, just why did you have Lansford Hastings on your program?"

"I told you that once or twice already. One of the acts failed to show up and — "

"Wait a minute. The act that failed to show up was a man with singing owls. A Mr. Luke Lupton. Mr. Wade, meet Mr. Lupton, rather Mr. Evanston."

Wade's eyes widened in astonishment. "Of course! I thought his face was familiar . . . "

"You have such a poor memory for faces and names, Mr. Wade. Tsk. Tsk. Anyway, you put Mr. Hastings on the air and precipitated his murder. Someone stole the buffalo box from your fiancée's house . . . " Wade stiffened and Lash looked quickly at Betty Dunlap. Her lips were taut. "My error," he murmured. "Anyway, the box disappeared and was then returned; coincident with the arrival of Old Cousin Isaac, pappy of Fremont. So Fremont was killed. Why . . . ?"

Lash reached into his vest pocket and took out a folded newspaper clipping. "Before I can tell you why I've got to correct the genealogy of the Eckert family. As stated previously, three Eckert children survived; Isaac Junior, Fremont and Elizabeth. Elizabeth married a man named Dunlap, the father of Mr. Dunlap, present. Fremont produced two children, Cousin Isaac now eighty years of age and his brother, Fremont, who died in infancy. That leaves Isaac II. The family history records that he was killed in a mining camp in his early manhood. I hate to uncover old wounds, but I must. Isaac was killed all right, away back in 1856. The method of his death is undoubtedly the reason the family have always passed over Isaac quickly. He was, alas, the black sheep of the family and he was killed in a manner suggested by the name of place where the demise occurred. A mining town called Hangtown . . . "

Jim Dunlap cleared his throat. "You don't have to go into it, Lash."

"But I must. Let me read you a clipping from the Placerville newspaper — Placerville is the modern name of Hangtown." He unfolded the clipping, read the first paragraph, then skipped down to: "Leona pleaded for his life, but the mob was angry and somewhat inclined to hang her along with her spouse. Only her condition saved her." He paused. "I repeat the delicate phrase, 'her condition.' Mrs. Isaac Eckert bore an heir, an heir with, shall we say, an olive skin?"

Betty Dunlap's eyes were the first to go to Harold Wade. The Oddity Man's nostrils flared. "Well?" he snapped.

"Your grandmother, or grandfather, Mr. Wade?" Lash asked. "I haven't had the time to check up but I can easily enough."

"You don't have to. It was my grandmother. She married a man named Wade."

"Another cousin," said Sheridan Eckert drily. "How do you do, Cousin Harold."

"Another slice off the old homestead," said Anne Evanston brightly.

Lash nodded. "Unfortunately, Mr. Wade wanted several slices. He thought to marry one and acquire the others by murder . . . "

"What?" cried Wade.

"Why, you killed Fremont Eckert, didn't you?"

Wade flinched as if struck, then took

a step toward Lash. "Take that back, you . . ."

Sergeant Coons stepped in between Lash and Wade. "Hold it, Wade. And you, Lash, you've pulled some rabbits out of the hat, but this time you've come up with an elephant. And I don't think the hat's big enough to hold an elephant . . . "

Lash regarded Wade thoughtfully. "Do you want to tell it, Wade?"

"I've got nothing to tell, you half-wit. I don't know what you're talking about."

Lash sighed. "You're being most non-co-operative. After all, I didn't see you do the things so I have to guess at a few of the details. I may be slightly wrong . . . but not in the major points. You might correct me, as I go along."

"I'll sue you for slander," Wade gritted. "And beat your brains out in addition."

"You'll get a chance to do both — if I'm wrong. But I don't think I am. Perhaps none of this would have happened if Richard Evanston had remained back there in Ohio with his subdivisions. But no, Richard had piled up a lot of money and as he sat there counting it, day after day — "

"You're wasting your talents as a detective," Evanston said, bitterly. "You could clean up as a medium or fortuneteller."

"I'll think about it. As I was saying, Evanston was sitting there counting his money and one day he came across the buffalo box and accidentally discovered its secret — "

"Wrong, Mr. Lash," said Anne Evanston. "*I* discovered the false bottom. But that's all there was."

"Ah, Pandora. Anyway, you showed it to your husband and he immediately broke out in a rash. He didn't particularly care about searching for the buried treasure because he had one right in his own lap. A treasure so big that he hated the thought of losing three-fourths of it. 'Share equally' Ellen Eckert had said. Evanston knew the family story pretty well. He pored over all existing accounts and he came across one item that staggered him, a line which told

305

of Elizabeth Eckert, the child, carrying with her upon her rescue a hand-carved box. Evanston had such a box and, while it was empty, was it possible that Isaac Eckert had secreted something in the second box? Was it possible that he had a reason for making a second box, when he knew that he was about to die? Richard Evanston got to thinking about that. The secret of his own box had remained undiscovered for almost a hundred years. Perhaps the second box was no longer in existence, perhaps its secret had been discovered years ago, but if it had, the Evanston family had not been told about it. Nor had any of the historians of the Donner-Eckert Party. While I personally think Mr. Evanston would have been a great deal better off if he'd just let things alone, Mr. Evanston decided otherwise. He came out to California with his own little box. He located the Dunlaps and surviving Eckerts. He probably made discreet inquiries . . . ”

"Not so discreet," Jim Dunlap offered. "Private detectives were falling all over themselves for a while, a few weeks back. They asked all sorts of personal questions. We didn't know what it was all about ... "

"But you began to wonder. Evanston carried out his inquiries in Reno and got Old Isaac and Fremont all hot and bothered. Isaac came to visit the Dunlaps and Betty's box disappeared. Fremont brought it to my place — wearing his desert rat disguise. Mmm, at this point I have to make a rather difficult guess. I hope someone will correct me. Perhaps you, Mr. Evanston. Why did you persuade Fremont to go on Harold Wade's radio program?"

Evanston chewed his lower lip a moment. "Well, I don't think it's particularly important ... now. I'd traced Harold Wade's ancestry and I was curious to know if Wade himself knew. I thought a mere hint, the mention of the Donner name ... "

"And you unleashed the holocaust!"

"Lash!" snarled Wade.

"Later, Wade. Anyway, Fremont returned the box to the Dunlaps ... "

"Wrong," said Evanston. "That was

my box. Fremont stole it."

"Oh! Then Wade — never mind. Anyway, Fremont was eliminated. He'd played his part and he was no longer required. But murder excites people. Everyone else got interested now. Betty Dunlap came to me. *Her* box had been stolen."

Jim Dunlap sighed. "Isaac insisted on searching for it. The box never left our hands. When I heard that Betty had employed you, I gave the box back to her . . . "

"And tried to call me off. Unfortunately, murder had been committed and I was as good a suspect as the police had. So even if you people wanted to quit I couldn't. I had to find the murderer of Fremont Eckert and I did."

"Who?" asked Sergeant Coons, his lip curling. "You've done a lot of talking but you haven't kicked in with a single tangible piece of evidence."

"Evidence? Oh, evidence! Of course . . . "

Lash suddenly turned and strode to the closet. As he pulled open the door there was a sudden scuffle behind him. But Lash didn't look until he had reached into the closet and brought out a pair of dusty, rundown-at-the-heels boots, a pair of flannel trousers, a plaid shirt and a battered hat.

By that time handcuffs had been placed on Harold Wade's wrists.

Lash said: "I saw it with my little telescope."

Sergeant Coons swore roundly. "Damn you, Lash, this is the outfit that Lansford Hastings wore. I thought you told us that that was the guy you called Fremont Eckert."

"It was, the first time. But Harold Wade liked it so well he duplicated the disguise. Somehow he got it out of Fremont that the latter had come to me with his screwy story about being Lansford Hastings. The idea appealed to Wade, particularly as he figured he could confuse things quite a bit. Lansford Hastings had ridden down Hollywood Boulevard on a jackass. Lansford Hastings was dead, but Lansford Hastings continued to ride down Hollywood Boulevard once a day. Mix up a lot of people that way. And all that Wade needed to look like a stock desert rat was a set of false whiskers, this outfit and a jackass!"

★ ★ ★

Lash went to sleep in his own bed at five-thirty in the afternoon. He slept until ten the next morning and would have slept even longer except that Eddie Slocum woke him up and dropped a small flat package on the bedclothes.

Lash yawned, then saw the package and tore it open. He took out the cracked, aged diary of Ellen Eckert.

"The fee," he said.

"Now, we're going in for original manuscripts," Eddie said, bitterly. "The question is, how much will Eisenschiml lend us on it?"

"Nothing," said Lash. "Because I'm not going to sell it to him."

Slocum walked to the bookshelves and scanned the titles. He took down a volume and reached for a second.

"What are you doing, Eddie?" Lash snapped.

"Books," Slocum replied. "You won't sell the manuscript so I'll have to take down some of the books and hock them . . . "

"Put them back, Eddie. I said I wouldn't sell this to Eisenschiml and I mean it. He couldn't pay me enough for it. I didn't say I wouldn't sell it to a library. As a matter of fact, I've already arranged with the Hargraves Library." He cleared his throat. "Libraries *love* manuscripts. And they pay big money for them. I'm getting $3500 for this little diary. Not bad, eh?"

THEY'RE LISTENING!

They don't wear uniforms. They don't carry placards. Their names aren't Fritz or Giuseppi. They look like you and me and they're at all the places where we go. They're at the theater and the ball game, the club and the tavern. They talk as patriotic as anyone else and they usually don't have accents.

They're nice, friendly fellows because that's part of their business. They talk quietly and make awfully good listeners because they know that they can hear a lot of things that way. They want to know what you know so that they can pass it on to their employers.

They're spies!

Frank Gruber

TO FIGHT THE WILD
Rod Ansell and Rachel Percy

Lost in uncharted Australian bush, Rod Ansell survived by hunting and trapping wild animals, improvising shelter and using all the bushman's skills he knew.

COROMANDEL
Pat Barr

India in the 1830s is a hot, uncomfortable place, where the East India Company still rules. Amelia and her new husband find themselves caught up in the animosities which seethe between the old order and the new.

THE SMALL PARTY
Lillian Beckwith

A frightening journey to safety begins for Ruth and her small party as their island is caught up in the dangers of armed insurrection.